Academic Couples

Academic Couples

· · · · · · · · · ·

Problems and Promises

Edited by

Marianne A. Ferber

and

Jane W. Loeb

University of Illinois Press

Urbana and Chicago

© 1997 by the Board of Trustees of the University of Illinois
Manufactured in the United States of America
1   2   3   4   5   C   P   5   4   3   2   1
This book is printed on acid-free paper.
Library of Congress Cataloging-in-Publication Data
Academic couples : problems and promises /
edited by Marianne A. Ferber and Jane W. Loeb.
p.   cm.
Includes bibliographical references and index.
ISBN 0-252-02316-1 (acid-free paper). —
ISBN 0-252-06619-7 (pbk. : acid-free paper)
1. Academic couples—United States. 2. College teachers—
Employment—United States.
I. Ferber, Marianne A., 1923– . II. Loeb, Jane W.
LB1778.45.A33   1997
378.1'2—dc20
96-35658
CIP

To Joan Huber,

half of an academic couple, and all of a scholar, colleague,

and friend

Contents

. . . .

Introduction

Marianne A. Ferber and Jane W. Loeb

"Attention Academic Couples" is the heading of an ad in the October 14, 1994, *Chronicle of Higher Education.* "Three liberal arts colleges in southern Maine—Bates College, Bowdoin College, and Colby College— are conducting searches for appointments beginning in the Fall of 1995. Our experience has been that the following information may be useful for dual-career academic couples. Bates, Bowdoin, and Colby are within one hour of each other, and two to three hours from Boston. This joint announcement is meant to encourage applications from couples, and from all qualified candidates." This advertisement makes clear the major impact that dual-career couples are having on the academic labor market. The prevalence of couples is a relatively new phenomenon and follows upon the major influx of women into the labor market.

The percentage of women in the labor force increased from about 34 percent in 1950 to 58 percent in 1993, and it was substantially greater for highly educated women—75 percent for those with four or more years of college. More recently, the labor force participation of married women with children has sharply increased. During 1993, fully 60 percent of those with children under six were employed, while for those with children aged six to seventeen the figure was 75 percent, compared with 44 percent in 1966 (U.S. Dept. of Labor 1994). As a result of these changes, the number of dual-earner couples has increased, as has the number of dual-career couples, in which both partners are committed to a profession.

Not surprisingly, therefore, there has been a substantial number of studies of dual-career couples, some concerned with the experiences and adjustments of the partners and the family, and others focused on adjustments made by the institutions employing these individuals. It is clear that virtually all types of employers have been affected by the increase in dual-career couples. For example, spouses' employment plans and options have influenced military reenlistment (Lakhani and Gade 1992), the willingness of corporate employees to accept transfers (Brett, Stroh, and Reilly 1993), and faculty recruitment and retention in higher education (Burke 1988; Matier 1990). Much remains to be learned, however, about the advantages and disadvantages of the growing proportion of two-earner and two-career couples, both for the couples themselves and for their employers.

The higher education sector of the United States economy will be especially affected by the rise in the number of dual-career couples that is expected to continue in the near future. The recent increase in the number of academic couples has been fueled not only by the overall increase in women's labor market participation but also by the greatly increased number of women in doctoral programs. Combined with a tendency of young people to defer marriage into the years when most aspiring academics are graduate students, these trends would predictably produce a growing number of academic couples. However, whether aspiring academic couples will find employment as professors depends on conditions in the academic labor market in addition to factors that are more controllable by the individuals involved, such as their willingness to entertain a wide variety of job options, including the possibility of a commuting relationship.

Much has been written on the near-term future of the academic labor market. Several factors argue for an increase in the number of jobs available relative to the number of jobs sought. Many faculty members who were hired in preparation for the enrollment of the baby boomers are expected to retire in the next ten to twenty years.[1] In their analysis of results of the 1988 national survey of postsecondary faculty, Russell, Fairweather, Hendrickson, and Zimbler (1991) found that 30 percent of the full-time regular faculty members employed in the fall of 1987 will have reached age sixty-five by the year 2000, and 51 percent expected to stop teaching at the postsecondary level by then. At the same time, the supply of new graduates from Ph.D. programs, especially U.S. citizens and permanent resident aliens, has declined in many liberal arts fields (e.g., see Lomperis 1990 and Carter and Wilson 1993). As a result, it was widely believed in the early 1990s that the academic market would boom at the end of the 1990s. For example, Hensel (1991) pointed out that the large number of expected vacancies would provide institutions with an incentive to adopt innovative policies that would lead to unprecedented diversification and to the hiring of more of the new female Ph.D.'s, as well as members of minority groups, than they have tended to do in the past. At the same time, Schuster (1990) warned that the quality of our higher education institutions was in jeopardy given the projected imbalance between supply of and demand for new faculty.

More recently it has seemed that countervailing factors may be slowing the rate of retirement and reducing the rate at which institutions may replace recently retired faculty members. One recent study (Massy and Goldman 1995) even maintains that we are producing too many graduates of doctoral programs in the sciences and engineering; others who have studied this question in detail, however, have criticized these findings for failure to deal adequately with the many nonacademic employment opportunities in these fields (Kuh 1995) and have recommended not a reduction in size but a restructuring of Ph.D. programs in these fields to better prepare students for a variety of career options outside as well as inside academe (National Academy of Sciences 1995; Griffiths 1995).

One major factor that could slow the hiring of new faculty is the "uncapping" of retirement. When first introduced as a legislative possibility, the January 1, 1994, end of mandatory retirement based on age was expected by many to cause grave problems in higher educational institutions that provide tenure to their faculties. Recent studies of the issue (e.g., Rees and Smith 1991), however, suggest that the effects of uncapping will be small for most institutions, and administrators at the overwhelming majority of colleges and universities no longer expect this change to cause problems (El-Khawas 1994; Bader 1995). Nonetheless, whatever small delays occur in faculty retirements will work, at least temporarily, to reduce the number of faculty positions expected to result from the aging of the professoriate. In addition, the financial stringency facing higher educational institutions in the 1990s, brought about by such factors as recession in the first years of the decade and reduced federal and state support since then, has constrained replacement of those faculty who leave. Often, budget pressures have been addressed by increasing class sizes, especially at the undergraduate level, and greater reliance on part-time, visiting, or other temporary faculty. Some of these practices may have been adopted as short-term strategies to get past temporary problems. For example, a visiting faculty member can cover a department's otherwise unmet teaching obligations until a hiring freeze on permanent positions is lifted. Nonetheless, knowledgeable observers expect that obtaining adequate funding will be the most important challenge facing higher education for the rest of the 1990s (Peltason 1995).

Regardless of the state of funding for higher education, the retirement rate will almost inevitably increase in the next ten to twenty years. Even though retiring faculty will probably not be replaced one-for-one (Brodie 1995), there will be vacancies in many fields and it seems safe to expect institutions to continue to feel pressure to accommodate partners of academics they are anxious to recruit. Under these circumstances it is particularly important that we gain a better understanding of the problems and promises of dual-career couples in academe: their numbers, their productivity levels, and the ways in which institutions can recruit, retain, and assist these individuals in developing highly productive work lives.[2]

A Brief History of Academic Couples

For a long time academic couples were rare in this country. In addition to the generally low participation of women in the labor force, a number of other factors contributed to this. Foremost among these was that few women earned higher degrees. During 1899–1900, women received only 6 percent of the doctoral degrees awarded. This figure gradually rose to 15 percent by 1929–30 but declined to less than 10 percent during 1949–50 when many men finished their advanced education on the GI Bill. It was not until the 1970s that women once again reached and then surpassed their earlier peak percentage of doctoral degrees earned. Similarly, women earned 19 percent of the master's degrees awarded during 1899–1900 and 40 percent in 1929–30, but only 29 percent during 1949–50; again, the previous high was not reached again until the early 1970s. No data are available for first professional degrees for the earlier years, but we know that women earned only 5 percent of them during 1969–70; this figure, however, climbed rapidly to 25 percent ten years later (U.S. Dept. of Education 1994).

According to data presented by Stephan and Kassis (this volume), be-

tween 1899–1900 and 1929–30 the percentage of women on college faculties slowly rose from 20 percent to 27 percent, only to decline to a low of
22 percent as recently as 1959–60. It was not until the 1960s that it began
a steady, albeit at first very slow, rise to reach 32 percent in 1991 (U.S. Dept.
of Education 1994). Thus the representation of women on college and
university faculties in the early decades of the century was about as large
as could be expected, given the small proportion of advanced degrees they
earned. This is true even when we take into account that in those days
candidates with master's degrees were generally hired by even the most
prestigious colleges and universities in virtually all fields. At the same time,
although women's numerical representation was about what might be
expected given the number with advanced degrees, there can be little
doubt that discrimination impeded their career progress.

The extent to which unequal treatment was present and even taken for
granted is illustrated by two statements found in Caplow and McGee
(1958): "Women tend to be discriminated against in the academic profession, not because they have low prestige but because they are outside the
prestige system entirely and for this reason are of no use to a department
in future recruitment" (111). "Women scholars are not taken seriously and
cannot look forward to a normal professional career. This bias is part of
the much larger pattern which determines the utilization of women in our
economy. It is not peculiar to the academic world, but it does blight the
prospects of female scholars" (226). It should also be noted that women
were not the only group to suffer from such treatment. As Caplow and
McGee point out, African Americans—both men and women— were
almost entirely excluded from white academia.

The very small percentage of wives who were employed was relatively unimportant during this time because of the very large percentage of
women with advanced degrees who were single. For instance, only 41
percent of women who received Ph.D.'s in 1950 and 1960 were married,
compared with 88 percent of men during the same years (Centra 1974).
It is worth noting, however, that as late as the 1970s, highly educated
women who were married were not likely to be employed, particularly
if their husbands were employed by a college or university located in a
small community with few opportunities for professional jobs (Ferber
1973; Martin 1975). Antinepotism rules, which often forbade the hiring
of spouses by the same institution, even if they were in different departments, were partially responsible for this phenomenon (Martin 1975;
Sigworth 1974).

The initially slow increase in the representation of women on faculties in the 1960s began to accelerate in the 1970s, mainly as a result of the rapid changes in women's roles in the economy and in society, including the rapid increase in women's participation in the labor force and the dramatic rise in the percentage of advanced degrees earned by women, both noted before. By 1991, women earned 37 percent of doctoral degrees, 54 percent of master's degrees, and 39 percent of first professional degrees (U.S. Department of Education 1994). In recent years, a contributing factor to this marked increase was the decline in the percentage of male college graduates who pursued doctoral degrees (Lomperis 1990).[3] Although it is doubtful that discrimination is entirely behind us, women have clearly become a far more integral part of academia, and with their improved status has come an increase in the number of academic couples.

The number of academic couples has also increased because the percentage of academic women who are married has risen appreciably, although it continues to remain lower than for men. By 1989–90 as many as 62 percent of full-time faculty women were married, compared with 82 percent of men. Another 17 percent of women and 8 percent of men had been married at an earlier time (Astin and Milem, this volume). An additional 4 percent of women and 2 percent of men reported that they were single with a partner. While low, the number of cohabiting couples has probably increased during recent years, given the somewhat more tolerant attitudes that have developed since the 1950s toward cohabitation of partners of the opposite sex, and to a lesser degree toward partners of the same sex. Further, men appear to be increasingly influenced by concern for their partners' careers so that "compromise over geographic relocation for job advancement is probably a more salient issue among dual-earner couples today than it was in the 1970s" (Bielby and Bielby 1992:1262).[4] Finally, antinepotism rules have virtually disappeared, and an increasing number of institutions are even adopting practices intended to facilitate the hiring of partners.

As a result of all these developments, by the beginning of the 1990s between one-fourth and one-third of all full-time faculty members had spouses or partners who were also academics (Astin and Milem, this volume). In view of these large numbers, the issue of what accommodations should be made for academic couples is becoming ever more important for colleges and universities (Burke 1988);[5] it always has been important for the individuals concerned.

The Current Status of Women and Couples in Academe

In the spring of 1993, Marianne Ferber and Marcia Bellas conducted a survey of faculty members at colleges and universities in Illinois. They obtained data on their professional and personal histories to investigate the influence of personal factors and living arrangements on the performance and careers of academic couples. The results of the survey are discussed at some length in chapters 6 and 7, but a brief description of the sample and the information obtained is given here so that we can provide a broad picture of academic couples today.

Two thousand questionnaires were sent in equal numbers to male and female faculty members from twenty-two colleges and universities in Illinois. Both private and public institutions, from research universities to two-year colleges, were selected.[6] With a response rate of 43 percent, the information obtained from this survey is broadly representative of the population of academics in the state,[7] except that the ratio of women to men is larger in the sample than it is among all faculty members.

To determine the percentage of female faculty members, Ferber and Bellas obtained official data on the total number of women and men at two of the campuses and counted male and female faculty members listed in directories from the twenty remaining institutions, using first names as indicators of their sex.[8] As seen in table I-1, women constitute 28 percent of the faculty as a whole, but the ratio varies substantially between, and to some extent within, categories of schools. It ranges from about one-fifth at Institutions B and D[9] to slightly over half at the two-year colleges.[10]

Some of the information obtained from this survey simply confirms the findings of earlier studies, as well as Astin and Milem's recent findings (this volume), with respect to gender differences. First, as the data in table I-2 show, there continue to be substantial differences in the distribution of women and men by field. Only 1 percent of women are in engineering and 6 percent in the physical sciences and mathematics, compared with 3 percent and 14 percent, respectively, of men. On the other hand, a larger percentage of women than men are found in education and home economics, 20 percent of women as compared with 14 percent of men, and particularly in the health sciences, with 16 percent of women compared with only 6 percent of men. Second, as many as 71 percent of men but only 54 percent of women have doctoral degrees.[11]

Third, as seen in table I-3, women have, on average, published less than men over their lifetime in all but two categories (co-authored texts and co-authored other books), and in five of the six categories for sole authorship the differences are large enough to be statistically significant.[12] That as many as 79 percent of women, compared with only 58 percent of men, obtained their terminal degree in 1974 or later in part

TABLE I-1. Women Faculty Members at Twenty-Two
Illinois Institutions

	Number	Percentage
Research Universities I		
Institution A (public)	1,649	24.6
Institution B (public)	2,268	19.6
Institution C (private)	3,377	24.4
Institution D (private)	1,802	20.9
Research Universities II		
Institution E (public)	2,468	24.1
Doctoral Granting University I		
Institution F (public)	1,043	30.4
Institution G (private)	654	36.1
Doctoral Granting University II		
Institution H (public)	981	33.8
Comprehensive University I		
Institution I (public)	760	40.7
Institution J (public)	367	37.9
Institution K (private)	321	28.7
Institution L (private)	279	41.2
Comprehensive University II		
Institution M (private)	190	43.2
Institution N (private)	201	41.8
Liberal Arts Colleges I		
Institution O (private)	110	28.2
Institution P (private)	47	36.1
Liberal Arts Colleges II		
Institution Q (private)	99	44.4
Institution R (private)	69	29.0
Community Colleges		
Institution S (public)	226	50.4
Institution T (public)	206	51.0
Institution U (public)	249	51.8
Institution V (private)	50	36.0
Total	17,416	27.7

explains the differences, since women also have substantially less professional experience. While 49 percent of women have been employed ten years or less, this is true of only 31 percent of men, suggesting that on an annual basis, these differences in publication rates would be a good deal smaller.[13] It should also be noted that other researchers, such as Bentley and Blackburn (1992), who investigated the number of publications in two-year periods found that gender differences had narrowed considerably since 1969. In addition, the distribution of men and women by field may also help explain the gender differences in publication rates because the average number of publications varies considerably by discipline and so do the types of publications that are most common. Finally, some scholars have concluded that women continue to be constrained by the male culture of academia and by the scarcity of mentors, especially for young faculty women (Fox 1995).

The preponderance of recent hires among faculty women also has other implications. The proportion of women on faculties has been increasing in recent decades and is likely to continue to do so because a considerably larger proportion of men than women will reach retirement age over the next few decades. As a result, we can expect the substantial remaining gender differential in rank to decline further. At present, women constitute 15 percent of full professors, but about half of instructors and lecturers (Fox 1995).

Similarly, as can be seen in table I-4, the Illinois survey confirms that women continue, on average, to receive lower salaries than men. The

TABLE I-2. Percentage of Men and Women in Academic Fields

Field	Men	Women
Behavioral and social sciences	16.0	11.4
Biological sciences	7.9	5.4
Business and professions	18.1	15.3
Education and home economics	13.6	19.7
Engineering	3.1	1.3
Fine arts	5.2	7.3
Health sciences	5.5	16.2
Humanities	16.2	17.3
Physical sciences and mathematics	14.4	6.0
Total	100.0	99.9

most striking difference is that more than half of the women, but fewer than one-third of the men, earn less than $40,000.[14] Because salary tends to increase with years on the job, the fact that a much larger percentage of women has been hired recently obviously helps to explain these lower earnings as well and suggests that the differential may be expected to

TABLE I-3. Mean Number of Publications by Men and Women

	Men	Women
Refereed articles		
sole author**	6.35	2.65
co-authored	3.65	2.76
Chapters in books		
sole author**	1.00	0.56
co-authored	0.74	0.42
Textbooks		
sole author*	0.27	0.05
co-authored	0.09	0.34
Edited books		
sole author	0.40	0.15
co-authored	0.62	0.10
Other books		
sole author**	0.29	0.11
co-authored	0.08	0.11
Other publications		
sole author**	4.90	2.33
co-authored	1.55	1.09

* $p < .05$.
** $p < .01$.

TABLE I-4. Salary Distribution of Men and Women Employed Full-Time (percent)

	Men	Women
Less than $20,000	1.2	1.4
$20,000–$39,000	29.7	51.5
$40,000–$59,000	49.9	35.1
$60,000–$79,000	13.3	7.3
$80,000–$99,000	4.0	3.3
$100,000 and over	1.9	1.4

decline. Whether it explains all of the difference in salary remains to be investigated in a later chapter (Ferber and Hoffman, this volume).

In addition to the data shown above, Ferber and Bellas collected information about present and past living arrangements of the respondents, as well as the level of education and the employment status of their partners, defining "partner" as any person with whom the respondent had a relationship for at least three years. The results were consistent with the usual evidence that more faculty women than men are single; 15 percent of women and 8 percent of men in this sample have never had a partner. These figures are very similar to those reported by Astin and Milem (this volume). Of the remainder, 72 percent of women and 79 percent of men have had only one partner, while among both men and women, 13 percent have had multiple partners. Only seven women and seven men reported that they had same-sex partners, figures that appear excessively low and probably biased by unwillingness to reveal this information. Similarly, Miller and Skeen (this volume) had a very low response rate to their request for information from unmarried couples, whether same-sex or opposite-sex, most likely because contemporary attitudes toward such couples are still rather adverse, especially toward same-sex couples. Hence, until they experience much greater acceptance, it will most likely continue to be very difficult to develop reasonably large, representative samples of such couples. A final point revealed by the survey is that a somewhat larger proportion of men than women, 77 percent and 69 percent, respectively, reported that at some time they had children living in their household.

As would be expected, the level of education of the partners of faculty members is very high. Fully 40 percent of women's first partners had a doctoral degree and an additional 27 percent had a master's degree. Fewer of the men's first partners had doctoral degrees, at 15 percent, but more of them had master's degrees, at 47 percent.[15] These data suggest that in a very substantial percentage of cases both members of the couples in this sample were formally qualified to be in academia. In fact, 18 percent of men's first partners, and 35 percent of those who were employed, also were employed by an academic institution when the relationship began; the comparable figures for women were even higher, 24 percent and 39 percent, respectively. As many as 38 percent of men's first partners and 50 percent of women's first partners were employed at the same institutions at some time. Clearly, academic institutions employ large numbers of couples.

Interestingly, although only 4 percent of partners of male respondents with master's degrees had doctorates, it is not unusual for women in this sample to be more highly educated than their partners, many of whom are probably not in academia. As many as 23 percent of partners of female respondents with doctoral degrees have only master's degrees, and 19 percent have only baccalaureate degrees. It was undoubtedly far less common in earlier days for a woman to be married to a man with less education, although no data are available to confirm this.

In short, current evidence suggests that women and couples will continue to increase in numbers on college and university faculties. Their recruitment and retention will continue to be important to institutions, which will probably need to become more proactive in meeting their needs.

Issues in the Employment of Couples

Employing couples has potential disadvantages for institutions, as Hornig (this volume) notes. It may be difficult to find appropriate openings for two people, so one partner may have to be hired for a position that has a relatively low priority in the eyes of the department or the campus. Highly valued scholars with bargaining power may use their influence to have their less-qualified partners hired, retained, and perhaps given other advantages. In the worst case, if a couple breaks up, the more highly qualified partner is more likely to find an attractive position elsewhere, leaving the employer with a bad bargain indeed. Beyond these concerns, colleagues are often apprehensive about partners forming political alliances, particularly when both are members of the same small unit. Last, but not least, as Shoben (this volume) discusses, special programs to accommodate couples are sometimes viewed as conflicting with affirmative action policies and procedures.

At the same time, such concerns are easily exaggerated. For one, some of the problems mentioned arise with respect to friends as well as partners, and faculty members may be rather less restrained about gaining advantages for, or forming alliances with, favorite colleagues. There is also evidence that when two partners are offered jobs, it is not unusual for the employer to offer both less favorable terms, and they are, apparently, often willing to accept them, presumably for lack of better alternatives (Barbee and Cunningham 1990). In any case refusing to hire couples frequently serves to deprive institutions of the talents of highly qualified individuals, especially in geographic areas with few alternative employment opportunities for highly educated people.

Similarly, academic couples also encounter difficulties and enjoy advantages. Although few people today would be expected to agree with the once prevalent view that dual-career marriages tend to be mutually destructive because neither partner provides the other the kind of support received from spouses with no career aspirations of their own, it is generally recognized that members of professional couples are likely to experience stress from the competing demands of job and family.[16] This may be particularly true for academic couples, because the years when the pressures for achieving tenure and establishing a scholarly reputation tend to be greatest coincide with the child rearing years. It has been suggested that these pressures account for the smaller percentage of women in academia being married, and a larger percentage being divorced, than among other women with comparable training (Simeone 1987).

As noted above, it is often difficult for academic couples to find two jobs within commuting distance, especially when one is employed by, or receives an offer from, an institution in a relatively remote location without other colleges or universities nearby. Hence, couples may have to accept lower level positions and smaller salaries in order to be employed at the same institution or accept lower raises and slower promotions after they have been hired. Adding insult to injury, they may encounter resentment from some colleagues who perceive them to be "double-dipping" because they receive two salaries.

On the other hand, faculty members generally have relatively flexible schedules compared with those of many other professionals. Like others, however, they usually receive incomes that enable them to purchase many labor saving goods and services, so that it is considerably easier for them than for dual-earner couples with lower incomes to manage their homemaking responsibilities. Also, as academics, they often benefit from exchanging ideas with each other and adding to each other's professional networks, all the more so if they are in the same or in closely related fields, as is often the case.[17] Hence it is not surprising that research provides evidence that many such couples "obviously enjoyed the challenge of their lifestyle; it might have left them exhausted but it also brought them a sense of elation at having successfully overcome a series of dilemmas and crises. Women, particularly, felt self-esteem, and this theme was dominant in all . . . interviews" (St. John-Parsons 1978:41).

Except for the work by Astin and various co-authors (Astin 1978; Astin and Bayer 1979; Astin and Davis 1985; Davis and Astin 1987; Astin and Milem, this volume),[18] there have been few systematic studies of the careers of academic couples. Hence, relatively little is known about the careers of members of academic couples as compared to other faculty members, whether there are differences between members of such couples in performance, or whether men and women partners are rewarded differently. Both the institutions and the individuals involved need a better understanding of the realities confronting them if institutions are to make rational decisions about hiring, retention, and salaries and men and women are to make rational decisions about their careers.

Current Issues Concerning Academic Couples

The authors who have contributed to this book come from a variety of disciplines and write from a variety of perspectives. About half of the chapters, those by Miller-Loessi and Henderson, Astin and Milem, Bellas, Ferber and Hoffman, Loeb, and Raabe are written by social scientists. Most of these use regression analysis or other statistical techniques to analyze their data. On the other hand, Stephan and Kassis as well as Perkins have unearthed considerable information using historic records, while Shoben makes use of legal precedents. Still others, particularly Miller and Skeen as well as Hornig, deal with subjects for which no extensive data or historic records are available. To provide information on their important topics they have had to rely on anecdotal evidence as well as their own firsthand knowledge and expertise. Together the chapters provide an overview of much of the available information about academic couples and add considerable new information to that body of knowledge.

Chapter 1 places the increasing number of academic couples in the context of larger societal changes and especially emphasizes the situation of women. Miller-Loessi and Henderson point out that the status of women has improved, especially in recent decades, but they also emphasize that considerable inequality remains, both in the labor market and in the family. In addition they show that similar problems affect academic women as well, although academic work does offer advantages, such as a good deal of flexibility and relatively high incomes.

Chapter 2 focuses specifically on the history of women and couples in academe. Stephan and Kassis begin by reviewing the position of women faculty from the earliest years of academic institutions. Next they examine how the gender composition of doctoral recipients has changed since the 1920s. They then discuss the role of marriage in the lives of women faculty members during the first sixty years of the twentieth century. Finally, the authors present in-depth case studies of five traditionally white institutions of higher education in the United States, ranging from a small southern women's college to one of the Ivy League universities, and examine the gender composition of their faculty since the founding of each. These case studies provide a useful reminder that what is true in the aggregate need not be true of individual institutions. They reveal that although some faculty couples were employed at private institutions as early as the nineteenth century, they were virtually nonexistent at public institutions and single-sex private schools even during the first half of the twentieth century and that only since then did the hiring of academic couples achieve more general acceptance at these institutions.

Chapters 3 and 4 offer an in-depth look at the specific situation of minority couples and unmarried couples. In chapter 3, Perkins recounts the history of African-American professional couples with special emphasis on those in academe, focusing on the important role played by husband and wife teams in the early days of historically black institutions where African-American administrators appeared to act on the conviction that they could not afford to waste the considerable talents and knowledge of well-educated African-American women. There is much to be learned from the experience of these institutions, which managed to accommodate couples successfully at a time when other institutions of higher learning, if they hired women at all, routinely insisted that women had to resign if they married another faculty member.

In chapter 4, Miller and Skeen use anecdotal evidence to sketch the special problems of unmarried couples, especially those who are gay or lesbian. While no systematic sample was available to them, their review serves to highlight the problems of stigma and invisibility with which members of these couples contend. The authors also focus on the extent to which institutions of higher education offer the same benefits to these couples as to married partners, an issue that arises whenever special programs for couples are considered.

In chapter 5 Astin and Milem investigate the characteristics, educational preparation, employment status, and performance of faculty with academic partners and compare them to those of faculty with nonacademic partners. Their analyses are based on a national sample of 51,574 academics who responded to a survey conducted during the 1989–90 academic year. The results indicate that women with academic partners tended to do better than those whose partners were not in academia, but that the reverse was true for men. The authors suggest the explanation may be both that women who do not have careers often tend to help their husbands in a variety of ways, frequently providing them with social, clerical, and even research support, and that men with partners who themselves have academic careers tend to be more involved in homemaking responsibilities. The authors note that their evidence is consistent with the view that dual-career partners with relatively equal academic qualifications are also likely to have relatively egalitarian arrangements not only in the workplace but at home as well.

Chapter 6 focuses directly on the question of whether faculty who have had an academic partner differ from other faculty in their publication patterns. As previously noted, Bellas used data from a random sample of faculty from twenty-two Illinois institutions. Her findings indicate that, after controlling for the effects of other individual characteristics, their productivity did not differ on a composite measure that combined articles, books, and chapters. Nor did it differ in terms of specific productivity measures on sole-authored publications. On the other hand, faculty with academic partners had more "other" professional achievements produced with partners, did publish more book chapters and journal articles with partners, and also men (but not women) published more journal articles with persons other than partners. However, for all but the first of these, their higher productivity could be explained by other characteristics associated with productivity.

Chapter 7 examines how faculty members with academic partners at the same institution fare in terms of the quality of institutions where they work, the rank they attain, and the salary they receive compared with other faculty members. Using the Illinois sample described earlier, Ferber and Hoffman find that there is little evidence that the careers of faculty members, and especially women, are influenced by household-related variables, including their partners' level of education and employment status as well as the presence of children. These results suggest that respondents with partners on the same faculty are about equally likely to be hired by research universities, are promoted to full professor at about the same rate, and are paid about the same as other faculty with comparable qualifications. Similarly, there is little evidence of any direct effect of sex on an individual's professional career.

In chapter 8, Raabe describes the current and planned responses of academic institutions to the needs of academic couples. A 1991 survey of academic institutions reveals considerable variation among universities and colleges in their policies supportive of faculty who combine family responsibilities with a challenging career. However, in comparison with other employers, they do relatively well in offering flexible and reduced work schedules and in providing child-care services. In recent years they have also provided greater opportunities for extending the time to achieve tenure and even make it possible for some part-time faculty members to achieve tenure. It remains to be seen whether further progress will be made.

In chapter 9 Shoben examines the legal questions that arise when institutions give preference in hiring to partners of promising candidates they want to recruit or faculty members they wish to retain. Although the legality of such programs under employment discrimination law has not been tested so far, Shoben explores related case law on nepotism and antinepotism to predict the likely outcome of any possible challenge. She concludes that partner preference programs can probably be defended, but that it would be wise for institutions to take steps to monitor and document existing practices in anticipation of possible litigation.

Chapters 10 and 11 report on the implementation of programs to help accommodate academic couples and the extent to which some of these have been successful. In chapter 10, Hornig draws on her own extensive experience with a host of academic administrators and institutions to emphasize the point of view of administrators, who bear responsibility for the long-term health of the institution as well as the current interests of the faculty. She discusses in detail the risks and advantages generally involved in dual-academic hiring, but also points out the many factors that conspire to make almost each case unique. In chapter 11, Loeb describes one active program providing employment assistance for academic spouses, shows data on the types of accommodations made, and explores the extent to which the arrangements have been successful. She concludes that there is little evidence to support the major qualms expressed about such programs, at least as implemented at this one large institution.

In "Findings and Conclusions", we summarize these authors' findings, pointing out both the consistent themes that emerge from these investigations and the gaps in the picture that might usefully be filled in by further research.

Notes

1. The large enrollment declines widely expected to follow the baby boomers' completion of college failed to materialize. A larger proportion of the college-age cohort has been attending college, and this trend is predicted to continue since labor market trends favor college graduates (Harrington and Sum 1988).

2. It is very surprising, for instance, that a book published in the 1990s (Caplan 1993) with a multitude of useful suggestions for women who want to enter academia does not even mention the issues that arise when a candidate has an academic partner.

3. To the extent this is the case, it is consistent with the theory proposed by Reskin and Roos (1990) and Strober (1984): women tend to gain access to occupations they previously found difficult to enter when men begin to find them less attractive.

4. However, as recently as 1980 Bryson and Bryson (1980) reported that both husband and wife considered her career to be secondary.

5. Hence it is not surprising that we are seeing such articles as "Colleges Discover That Winning a Top Faculty Recruit Sometimes Depends on Finding Work for a Spouse" (Mangan 1989) and "Married—with Tenure" (1992).

6. They include institutions from all nine categories in the Carnegie classification, described in Carnegie Foundation for the Advancement of Teaching (1987): research universities I and II; doctorate-granting colleges and universities I and II; comprehensive colleges and universities I and II; liberal arts colleges I and II; and two-year community, junior, and technical colleges. The sampling method is described in some detail in Bellas (this volume).

7. Telephone calls to a sample of nonrespondents revealed no nonresponse bias.

8. Persons with names commonly used for both men and women, such as Pat, Chris, or Robin, were omitted, as were unfamiliar, typically non-Western names. Very few exclusions were necessary, however.

9. Because the data were provided by institution B, they may not be entirely comparable to the broad definition of "faculty" we used in our own counts from directories.

10. These data do not provide an adequate basis for estimating the percentage of women among the total population of faculty members in the state because the unweighted numbers are not representative of faculty members at all institutions of higher learning in Illinois. Nonetheless, the overall estimate of 28 percent is comparable with the figures for women as a percentage of full-time faculty for the country as a whole published by the National Center for Education Statistics (1994). The center reports that women constitute 28 percent of the faculty at comprehensive universities, 29 percent at liberal arts colleges, and 38 percent at two-year colleges.

11. These percentages are somewhat higher than those reported by Astin and Milem (this volume) but the ratio of men to women with doctoral degrees appears to be very similar.

12. This self-reported information is not likely to be entirely accurate. This is suggested by the clustering of reported numbers around multiples of five.

13. It is also interesting to note that the differences for co-authored publications, unlike those for single-author publications, are not significant. This is surprising, since in predominantly male fields women are at a disadvantage in finding collaborators (McDowell and Smith 1992). The fact that women are nonetheless relatively more likely to collaborate than men suggests that they may be particularly successful in working with colleagues when they do have the opportunity.

14. Rather surprisingly, the percentage of men and women who earn $80,000 or more—6 and 5, respectively—is not very different.

15. Thus, as many as 67 percent of first partners of female faculty members and 62 percent of partners of male faculty members had advanced degrees. The data for present partners were virtually the same in both cases: 68 percent for partners of females and 61 percent for partners of males. While we do not have strictly comparable data for earlier years, Feldman (1975) reports that in 1969 only 24 percent of spouses of male graduate students and 55 percent of spouses of female graduate students were attending graduate school at the same time. Even taking into account that one of the spouses is likely to have attended graduate school earlier or later, these figures suggest that the average level of education of partners of faculty members, and particularly of partners of male faculty members, was probably considerably lower than it is today.

16. There is evidence that in earlier days, when few women had careers, men received a great deal of such support. Simeone (1987), for instance, reports that in 1947 as many as 72 percent of male psychologists saw marriage as a professional asset and only 5 percent thought it was a hindrance. For female psychologists, on the other hand, the corresponding figures were 28 percent and 34 percent, respectively.

17. It is not as clear whether professional collaboration and coauthorships are beneficial for both partners; it has not been uncommon for the husband to receive most of the credit for research grants received and for items published (Reskin 1978).

18. Beyond that, there are some largely descriptive reports, chiefly providing accounts of problems and achievements of particular couples, often selected from one discipline. The main sources of information are studies concerned with the status and progress of academic women, which are only incidentally concerned with issues related to partners. Some work has also been done on dual-career couples, but only a few of these investigations have focused on academia.

Bibliography

Astin, Helen S. 1978. "Factors Affecting Women's Scholarly Productivity." In *The Higher Education of Women: Essays in Honor of Rosemary Park,* ed. Helen S. Astin and W. Z. Hirsch, 133–57. New York: Praeger.

———. 1992. "Academic Women, 1989–90." Paper presented at the conference "Sustaining Faculty Diversity in the Research University," University of Arizona, Tucson, Feb.

Astin, Helen S., and Alan Bayer. 1979. "Pervasive Sex Differences in the Academic Reward System: Scholarship, Marriage, and What Else?" In *Academic Rewards in Higher Education,* ed. Darrell R. Lewis and William E. Becker Jr., 211–29. Cambridge, Mass.: Ballinger Publishing.

Astin, Helen S., and Dianne E. Davis. 1985. "Research Productivity across the Life and Career Cycles: Facilitators and Barriers for Women." In *Scholarly Writing and Publishing: Issues, Problems, and Solutions,* ed. Mary F. Fox, 147–60. Boulder: Westview Press.

Bader, Jeanne E. 1995. "The Effects of 'Uncapping' a Summary of Research." *Academe* 81 (Jan.–Feb.): 36–37.

Barbee, Anita P., and Michael R. Cunningham. 1990. "Departmental Issues in Dual-Academic Marriages." Paper presented at the annual meeting of the American Psychological Association, Boston, Aug.

Becker, Gary S. 1991. *A Treatise on the Family.* Boston: Harvard University Press.

Bentley, Richard J., and Robert T. Blackburn. 1992. "Two Decades of Gains for Female Faculty?" *Teachers College Record* 93 (Summer): 697–709.

Bielby, William T., and Denise D. Bielby. 1992. "I Will Follow Him: Family Ties, Gender-Role Beliefs, and Reluctance to Relocate for a Better Job." *American Journal of Sociology* 97 (Mar.): 1241–67.

Brett, Jeanne M., Linda K. Stroh, and Anne H. Reilly. 1993. "Pulling up Roots in the 1990s: Who's Willing to Relocate?" *Journal of Organizational Behavior* 14 (Jan.): 49–60.

Brodie, James M. 1995. "Whatever Happened to the Job Boom?" *Academe* 81 (Jan.–Feb.): 12–15.

Bryson, Jeff B., and Rebecca B. Bryson. 1980. "Salary and Job Performance Differences." In *Dual-Career Couples,* ed. Fran Pepitone-Rockwell, 241–59. Beverly Hills: Sage Publications.

Burke, Dolores L. 1988. *A New Academic Marketplace.* Contributions to the Study of Education no. 30. Westport, Conn.: Greenwood Press.

Caplan, Paula J. 1993. *Lifting a Ton of Feathers: A Woman's Guide for Surviving in the Academic World.* Toronto: University of Toronto Press.

Caplow, Theodore, and Reece J. McGee. 1958. *The Academic Market Place.* Garden City, N.Y.: Doubleday.

Carnegie Foundation for the Advancement of Teaching. 1987. *A Classification of Institutions of Higher Education.* Princeton: Carnegie Foundation for the Advancement of Teaching.

Carter, Deborah J., and Reginald Wilson. 1993. *Minorities in Higher Education.* Washington, D.C.: American Council on Education.

Centra, John A. 1974. *Women, Men, and the Doctorate.* Princeton: Educational Testing Service.

Chamberlain, Mariam K., ed. 1988. *Women in Academe.* New York: Russell Sage Foundation.

Davis, Diane E., and Helen S. Astin. 1987. "Reputational Standing in Academe." *Journal of Higher Education* 58 (3): 261–75.

El-Khawas, Elaine. 1994. *Campus Trends, 1994.* Washington, D.C.: American Council on Education.

Feldmann, Saul D. 1975. "External Constraints: Marital Status and Graduate Education." In *Teachers and Students,* ed. Martin Trow, 249–64. New York: McGraw-Hill.

Ferber, Marianne A. 1973. "Educational and Employment Survey of University Faculty Wives: A Case Study." *Sociological Focus* 6 (Spring): 95–106.

Fox, Mary F. 1995. "Women in Higher Education: Gender Differences in the Status of Students and Scholars." In *Women: A Feminist Perspective,* ed. Jo Freeman, 220–37. Mountain View, Calif.: May Field Publishing.

Griffiths, Phillip A. 1995. "No PhD Glut in Science and Engineering." *Washington Post,* letter to the editor (July 19): A12.

Harrington, Paul E., and Andrew M. Sum. 1988. "Whatever Happened to the College Enrollment Crisis?" *Academe* 74 (Sept.–Oct.): 17–22.

Hensel, Nancy. 1991. *Realizing Gender Equality in Higher Education: The Need to Integrate Work/Family Issues.* ASHE-ERIC Higher Education Report no. 2. Washington, D.C.: George Washington University.

Kuh, Charlotte. 1995. "Comments on the Usefulness of the Massy/Goldman Study in the Formulation of National Policy Concerning the Graduate Education of Scientists and Engineers." Mimeographed.

Lakhani, Hyder, and Paul A. Gade. 1992. "Career Decisions of Dual Military Career Couples: A Multidisciplinary Analysis of the U.S. Army." *Journal of Economic Psychology* 13 (Mar.): 153–66.

Lomperis, Ana Maria Turner. 1990. "Are Women Changing the Nature of the Academic Profession?" *Journal of Higher Education* 61 (Nov.–Dec.): 643–77.

Mangan, K. S. 1989. "Colleges Discover That Winning a Top Faculty Recruit Sometimes Depends on Finding Work for a Spouse." 1989. *Chronicle of Higher Education,* Sept. 20:A13–14.

"Married—with Tenure." 1992. *Northwestern Perspective* (Chicago Historical Society) 5.

Martin, Donna. 1975. "The Wives of Academe." In *Women on Campus: The*

Unfinished Liberation, ed. Editors of *Change* Magazine, 35–43. New Rochelle, N.Y.: Change Magazine Press.

Massy, William F., and Charles A. Goldman. 1995. *The Production and Utilization of Science and Engineering Doctorates in the United States.* Stanford: Stanford Institute for Higher Education Research.

Matier, Michael W. 1990. "Retaining Faculty: A Tale of Two Campuses." *Research in Higher Education* 31 (Feb.): 39–60.

McDowell, John M., and Janet K. Smith. 1992. "The Effect of Gender Sorting on Propensity to Coauthor: Implications for Academic Promotion." *Economic Inquiry* 30 (Jan.): 68–82.

National Academy of Sciences, National Academy of Engineering, and Institute of Medicine Committee on Science, Engineering, and Public Policy. 1995. *Reshaping the Graduate Education of Scientists and Engineers.* Washington, D.C.: National Academy Press.

National Research Council Commission on Human Resources. 1979. *Climbing the Academic Ladder: Doctoral Women Scientists in Academe.* Washington, D.C.: National Academy Press.

Peltason, Jack W. 1995. "Reactionary Thoughts of a Revolutionary." Seventeenth David Dodds Henry Lecture, University of Illinois at Urbana-Champaign, Oct. 18.

Rees, Albert, and Sharon P. Smith. 1991. *Faculty Retirement in the Arts and Sciences.* Princeton: Princeton University Press.

Reskin, Barbara F. 1978. "Sex Differentiation and the Social Organization of Science." *Sociological Inquiry* 48 (Winter): 6–37.

Reskin, Barbara F., and Patricia A. Roos. 1990. *Job Queues, Gender Queues: Explaining Women's Inroads into Male Occupations.* Philadelphia: Temple University Press.

Russell, Susan H., James S. Fairweather, Robert M. Hendrickson, and Linda J. Zimbler. 1991. *Profiles of Faculty in Higher Education Institutions, 1988.* NCES 91–389. Washington, D.C.: U.S. Department of Education Office of Educational Research and Improvement, National Center for Education Statistics.

Schuster, Jack H. 1990. "Faculty Issues in the 1990s: New Realities, New Opportunities." In *An Agenda for the New Decade,* ed. Larry W. Jones and Franz A. Novotny, 33–41. San Francisco: Jossey-Bass.

Sigworth, Heather. 1974. "Issues in Nepotism Rules." In *Women in Higher Education,* ed. W. Todd Furniss and Patricia Graham, 110–20. Washington, D.C.: American Council of Education.

Simeone, Angela. 1987. *Academic Women Working toward Equality.* South Hadley, Mass.: Bergin and Garvey.

St. John-Parsons, Donald. 1978. "Continuous Dual-Career Families: A Case Study." *Psychology of Women Quarterly* 3 (Fall): 30–42.

Strober, Myra H. 1984. "Toward a General Theory of Occupational Sex Segregation." In *Sex Segregation in the Workplace: Trends, Explanations, Remedies,* ed. Barbara F. Reskin, 144–56. Washington, D.C.: National Academy Press.

U.S. Department of Education, National Center for Education Statistics. 1994. *Digest of Education Statistics.* Washington, D.C.: GPO.

U.S. Department of Labor, Bureau of Labor Statistics. 1994. *Monthly Labor Review* 117 (Jan.).

Vetter, Betty M., and Eleanor L. Babco. 1987. *Professional Women and Minorities: A Manpower Data Resource Service.* 7th ed. Washington, D.C.: Commission on Professionals in Science and Technology.

1

. . . .

Changes in American Society:
The Context for Academic Couples

Karen Miller-Loessi and Deborah Henderson

THE INCREASING INCIDENCE of academic couples can be understood in the context of larger societal changes. As noted in the introduction, with the exception of African-American couples at historically black colleges (see Perkins, this volume) there were few couples in academia until relatively recently; most academics were men, and most of the few women with academic careers were unmarried. But changes in the economy and society during recent decades have radically altered the professoriate in a number of way, including dramatically increasing the number of couples.[1] Most important among these changes are that more women have attained high levels of education, more women work outside the home than ever before, and more women combine paid employment with marriage and/or parenthood. Although academic couples have unique problems and receive unique rewards, it is useful to view their situation in the context of the larger phenomenon of dual-career couples and of working couples, in general, in the current economy.

Because the altered lifestyles of women have caused the rapid increase in couples seeking academic positions, we begin this chapter by briefly chronicling the historical and economic factors affecting women's entry into the workplace. Second, we analyze the extent to which that movement can be considered an "unfinished revolution." Third, we offer a feminist framework for understanding the current situation of women and men in the workplace. Finally, we examine the extent to which academic couples share the widespread problems we have identified, discuss other issues more specific to academic couples, and suggest an agenda for further research.

Historical and Economic Contexts

The accelerating entry of women into the labor market since the late 1950s is a dramatic movement that has been called "the basic social revolution of our time" (Hochschild 1989:239). This revolution follows the change in the United States in the nineteenth century from an agricultural to an industrial economy. Although the United States began as an agricultural society in which both women's and men's work centered in and around the home, with the family as the economic unit (Matthaei 1982), industrialization resulted in work moving into the factory and the office. This was true at first mainly for men, while most women remained in the home. For example, it is generally estimated that in 1860 only 15 percent of women were employed, mostly as domestic servants (Hochschild 1989). However, women's overall labor force participation steadily increased from the early 1800s through World War II, when many women replaced men who enlisted or were drafted (Goldin 1990). Just after World War II women's overall labor force participation briefly decreased as men returned from the front and women returned, willingly or not, to the home. But, this brief decline was reversed by the early 1950s, and soon after that the pace of women's entry into the labor market dramatically picked up. The rise was especially marked for married women with young children; between 1960 and 1987, the labor force participation rate of married women with children under three years of age increased from 15 percent to 54 percent.

Looking at the history of the last two centuries, then, women's economic contribution has been substantial and their overall labor force participation has risen virtually throughout, with only a brief reversal after World War II. As argued cogently by Ferber (1992:205): the so-called traditional family, "with a husband who goes out into the world to earn a living and to manage the affairs of state, while the wife and mother takes care of the children and tends to hearth and home, making sure it is an attractive, comfortable place for the head of the family to retreat to from his toil and struggles, developed late in human history, was never universal, and proved to be rather short-lived." It has also been generally limited in U.S. society to the white middle class. Thus the still-dom-

inant image of the employed husband/at-home wife has never corre-
sponded well to social reality. In this perspective, the increasingly commonplace phenomenon of both husband and wife working should not
be viewed as a deviation from an established norm, but as a continua-
tion of a long-term trend, albeit one that accelerated after the middle
1950s. It is useful to examine some of the major factors motivating this
trend.

First, there is no question that economic need is and always has been
a major explanation for the employment of women, particularly for
poor women. It must, for instance, be recognized that throughout history women of color have been much more likely than white women to
work outside the home (Goldin 1990:18); for most of them, staying at
home was an unaffordable luxury, while others worked because they
were determined to use their talents and their education to further the
progress of their race (see Perkins, this volume).

There are other reasons why in recent years more women in the
United States have needed to earn their own income. One is that a growing proportion of women are single mothers. In many cases they are
virtually the sole economic support of themselves and their children
(England and Browne 1992). Furthermore, the high divorce rate, and the
generally disadvantageous outcomes of divorce for women (Holden and
Smock 1991), may make many married women want to invest in job
experience as insurance against the risk of divorce (Burkhauser and
Duncan 1989).[2] Married women might also want to invest in job experience to protect their families in the event of their husband's layoff—
this reason became particularly important with the sizable increase in
the number of layoffs in the 1980s (Hodson and Sullivan 1990). Finally,
in times of falling real wages for most men, when prices increased more
than their money wages, women have gone to work to avoid a decline
in the family's standard of living (Ferber and O'Farrell 1991; England and
Browne 1992). A decline in men's wages may *necessitate* women's entry
into the labor force only for poorer families, but even for most affluent
families a decline in the standard of living is experienced as a difficulty.

More positive reasons have motivated women's labor force entry as
well. For many women, particularly those with high levels of education,
employment opportunities have become increasingly attractive in the
last few decades. Since the late 1970s, women's real wages have continued to grow, while men's have declined slightly (England and Browne
1992). Job opportunities for women have increased because occupations

traditionally held by women, particularly in the service sector, have grown even though many traditionally male occupations, such as in manufacturing, have declined. In addition, the demands of the home have declined with lower fertility;[3] women live longer and thus have more years not devoted to child care; and there is a proliferation of consumer items such as labor-saving devices and fast foods that can substitute for work at home. Partly as a result of these changes, the social acceptability and prestige of women's careers have increased, while the availability of intrinsically and extrinsically rewarding jobs for women has also increased, especially for women with higher education (Reich 1991; England and Browne 1992).[4]

The rapid increase in the number of academic couples is one result of the revolution in women's career opportunities. Locating academic couples in the general economic picture today, it is clear that they are part of a select group—two-income professional couples—that enjoy a substantial economic advantage over most of the population. Assuming that academic couples, on average, earned about double the 1993–94 mean academic year salary of $47,780 (American Association of University Professors 1994:table 4, p. 17), they were at approximately the ninety-second percentile of households in the United States in terms of income.[5] Thus, academic couples are typically affluent. There are, of course, many exceptions, such as an assistant professor in a relatively poorly paid field at a college where salaries are low with a spouse who is a part-time instructor. But for most academic couples, financial resources make possible options not available to many in American society.

The Unfinished Revolution

Looked at through rosy lenses, both partners in such couples benefit personally and professionally because each has a prestigious, challenging, well-paid job, a committed relationship, and, often, a family. Until recently, only men—and generally only white men with privileged backgrounds—could aspire to this fortunate set of circumstances. Only a very few women could hope for a fulfilling and well-paid career, many women could expect a committed relationship and a family, but almost no women—of any race or class—could have it all. Slater and Glazer (1987:123), commenting on the life of a married woman physician practicing early in the twentieth century, noted that "very few of her contemporaries, even among the superperformers, attempted to 'have it all.'

Such expectations are much more common on the part of educated women today."

Such an optimistic view of contemporary women's success in entering the workplace and combining family with career does not tell the whole story, however. The revolution that brought women into the work force has not eradicated all inequities either in the workplace or at home. Bianchi and Spain (1986:241–42), in their analysis of what 1980 census data show about women's situation, speak of a "cultural lag" between the realities of women's current lives and institutional benefits. They note that the three main indicators of such a lag are the gender gap in pay; the lack of affordable, quality child care (although this is a far more serious problem for lower-income families than for others [Ferber and O'Farrell 1991:74–84]); and the disproportionate share of the housework shouldered by women. In a similar vein, Hochschild (1989:12) refers to a "stalled revolution": "The exodus of women into the economy has not been accompanied by a cultural understanding of marriage and work that would make this transition smooth. The workforce has changed. Women have changed. But most workplaces have remained inflexible in the face of the family demands of their workers and at home, most men have yet to really adapt to the changes in women. This strain between the change in women and the absence of change in much else leads me to speak of a 'stalled revolution.'"

Workplace Inequities

In general, women still earn less than men although, as noted above, their wages have been increasing relative to those of men since the late 1970s. Among all full-time wage and salary workers in 1992, the median weekly earnings of women were 75 percent of those of men, up from 62 percent in 1975 (U.S. Department of Commerce 1993:table 671; U.S. Department of Labor 1977). It should be noted, however, that the narrowing gap is partly due to the slight net decline in men's real wages since 1973 and not solely due to real progress for women (England and Browne 1992). Further, as Miller-Loessi (1992) noted, there are still many barriers to full gender equity: persistent occupational segregation by gender (Reskin and Roos 1990) and devaluation of social and nurturant skills (Steinberg 1990) being paramount among them. In addition, Reskin (1988) argues that a fundamental reason for pay inequity is that men, like any dominant group, tend to act in ways that preserve their advantaged position. Federal legislation mandating equity and affirmative action is based on the principle that such behavior needs to be counteracted, but the extent to which sanctions against unequal access are enforced is crucial for the effectiveness of the laws.

Another barrier to women's progress in the workplace is the presupposition that people work full-time continuously from the moment they leave school and enter the work force until they retire (Bem 1993). Women's disproportionate responsibility for family caregiving makes this difficult, so that women frequently are unable to compete on equal terms with men. These disproportionate home responsibilities are especially costly for career women who are expected to establish their reputation precisely during the years when they are most likely to have young children to care for and even more so for those in academia, where the all-important tenure decision also tends to be made at that time.

Still, as already noted, these problems of highly educated women must be placed in the context of an increasingly class-polarized labor force (Harrison and Bluestone 1988; Reich 1991; Chafe 1991; Acker 1992). Well-educated women, in favorable circumstances, can now achieve entree to far better career opportunities than in earlier days; but the majority of women in the labor force have not been so fortunate. Women workers' median money income in 1991 was only about $10,500 a year (U.S. Bureau of the Census 1993:table 729), somewhat below the poverty line for a family of three. Indeed, poverty has increasingly become "feminized," to use Pearce's term (1978); almost two-thirds of poor adults are women, and one out of every three families headed by a woman is poor (England and Browne 1992). Further, the risk of poverty is much higher for women of color than for white women. Clearly, the gains achieved in recent decades have not been equally distributed among women of all races and social classes; professional women are a relatively privileged group, in spite of the problems they face.

Child-Care and Housework Issues

The continued gender difference in the allocation of family care and housework is one of the reasons for women's intermittent or part-time participation in the labor force. Similarly, women's unequal status in the labor market inhibits greater equality in the division of labor in the household. However, it is not clear to what extent even the attainment of equal status in the labor market among heterosexual couples is likely to lead to an egalitarian division of labor and authority within the family. Hertz (1986) found that among dual-career couples in which both husband and wife had high-powered corporate positions, economic equality did tend to contribute to greater equality among spouses, but mainly because the couples hired others to do a great deal of the necessary household work, not because husbands took on a greater share of household responsibilities. Thus, women in these couples gained more time for their careers, while men did not sacrifice much of their time to family work.

This solution is not, however, available to less affluent couples, including the growing number of young, untenured, relatively egalitarian couples in academia. There is evidence that the amount of time women spend on housework has declined since the 1970s, while the amount of time men spend has increased slightly (United Nations 1991), and it may well be that the change has been greater among academics. However, even in academic couples, women and some men, like the majority of working mothers in the general population, have to add their unpaid work to paid jobs. According to Hochschild (1989), for women in general this amounts to a "second shift" of a month of twenty-four-hour days every year.

Government policies in the United States have done less than those in many other nations to alleviate the difficulties of combining paid work and family. For example, as of 1991, "of the 118 countries covered in a survey by the International Labour Organization (1985), only the United States lacked any national legislation regarding maternity rights and benefits" (Ferber and O'Farrell 1991:161), and many countries mandate leave for fathers as well as mothers. In 1993, the United States passed the Family and Medical Leave Act, requiring employers with fifty or more workers to grant up to twelve weeks of unpaid leave to employees, male and female, for care of their infants, sick family members, or because of their own serious medical conditions. Many workers are not, however, in a position to take advantage of unpaid leave because they cannot manage without the income.

The lack of government-sponsored child care also distinguishes the United States from other industrialized nations of the world (Kahn and Kamerman 1987; Zigler 1990; Benin and Chong 1993). For example, a number of European countries offer publicly funded child care for preschoolers over the age of three (Ferber and O'Farrell 1991). In the United States, child care is left to individual parents to work out as best they can, either on their own or, in some instances, with the assistance of their employers (see, for example, Raabe, this volume). Two-earner couples in the United States use a variety of means to care for their children:

family members, nonrelative caretakers, and commercial and nonprofit child-care centers. The quality of care, as well as the cost, in each of these settings is extremely variable (Benin and Chong 1993). Poor-quality, costly, and undependable child care has many deleterious consequences for all parties concerned: the parents, the employers, and, of course, the children.[6] Mothers are considered primarily responsible for solving these problems: it is they who generally make the arrangements, make the adjustments, and, frequently, fill in the gaps (Hochschild 1989).

Reframing the Issues

Despite considerable progress, there remain substantial problems and inequities in the labor market and in the family that are detrimental to women. Many couples continue to operate in less than equal partnerships in academia as well as elsewhere.

Part of the problem is that issues of work-family disjuncture and strain are still often viewed as largely "women's problems" or "women's issues," and women are expected to adjust to institutions that seem unaware of such concerns. For example, as just noted, women are still expected to solve child-care problems. Miller (1986:128) argues that we should reframe the issue by asking: "If we as a human community want children, how does the total society propose to provide for them?" Similarly, we should not ask how women can fit into, and advance in, the institutions as organized for men, but how these institutions can be reorganized to support the family responsibilities of their workers, including care for impaired or elderly family members and children. Unfortunately, if such care-giving needs are not sufficiently met, women's entry into the workplace is often blamed.

The larger issue, as identified by many feminist scholars, is that the lives and concerns of men, who were assumed to have wives who took care of their families, have stood as the cultural standard by which all others have been evaluated, and the lives of women and men with family responsibilities have been subordinated to this standard (Bem 1993). Thus, the workplace, the family, and society as a whole are not only androcentric—centered around men—but also centered around men in so-called traditional families. The corollary to this has been that women who wish to or, for economic reasons, are forced to try to succeed in the workplace must struggle to catch up within this rigidly constraining structure. As Astin and Milem (this volume) suggest, husbands in relatively egalitarian couples also face these problems to some extent.

Acker (1990) develops the idea that workplace organizations quite universally continue to be "gendered." She argues that this is true even though on paper the concepts "job" and "hierarchy" are purportedly based on disembodied abstractions independent of gender. The use of disembodied abstractions is part of the legitimating ideology of bureaucracies—they are intended to be universalistic. Acker, however, argues that even though jobs are defined on paper in these terms, "an abstract job can exist, be transformed into a concrete instance, only if there is a worker. In organizational logic, filling an abstract job is a worker who exists only for the work. Such a hypothetical worker cannot have other imperatives . . . that impinge upon the job" (149). Moreover, the higher one goes in the hierarchy, the more important this undivided commitment to the job becomes—thus making women (and perhaps men with family responsibilities) suspect, if not obviously unsuitable, as incumbents for those positions. Having children, caring about and for others, and openly expressing emotion are considered by the dominant logic of organizational control to be detrimental to the organization. To succeed within the organization, everyone has to align their priorities accordingly.

Thus, as Slater and Glazer (1987) point out, "traditional" models of both work and family create serious difficulties for professional women. "The standards of performance and the expectation of accomplishment for women in their public lives are now, as in the past, modeled on male patterns of commitment, attendance, and single-minded devotion to duty. Similarly, women's responsibilities as mothers are modeled on older styles of engagement from an era when mothering was considered a full-time 'profession'" (124). Thus, women professionals with families, in general, exhaust themselves trying to manage two professions instead of one—an extraordinary feat at best—and to the extent that husbands in egalitarian relationships take on family obligations they encounter similar difficulties.

The Situation for Academic Couples

Turning the focus to academia, we now ask to what extent college and university campuses might be a less gendered environment than most work organizations—one in which institutional supports make it easier for employees to work out equitable, nondiscriminatory arrangements for their personal and family lives. We might expect that among work environments the academic workplace, presumably the product of one of society's more progressive institutions, on the cutting edge of social change, would come closest to meeting this ideal. Returning to the three most widespread problems confronting women that were identified by Bianchi and Spain (1986)—workplace inequities, lack of child care, and housework inequities—let us consider how well academia does on these fronts. We will then suggest several additional problems more specifically relevant to academic couples.

With respect to workplace inequities, although women have made progress toward full participation in academia, as chronicled in the next chapter, there still exists considerable disparity between men and women faculty. In 1993–94, 58 percent of all full-time lecturers and instructors were women, compared with 43 percent of all assistant professors, 30 percent of all associate professors, and only 15 percent of all full professors (calculated from American Association of University Professors 1994:table 14, p. 25). These data are explained, in part, by the substantially larger proportion of women who have been hired more recently, though some studies continue to find discrimination in promotions as well. Also, within *every* rank, including instructors and lecturers, women on average earn lower salaries than men (American Association of University Professors 1994:table 5, last panel, p. 18), in part because they are heavily concentrated in lower-paying fields (Astin and Milem, this volume)[7] or, as Bellas (1994) argues, when the proportion of women in a field rises, pay declines. In short, gender inequity still remains in academia. That, in itself, is an important issue far beyond the specific concerns of academic couples. However, the extent to which such inequity also exists *within* academic couples is an interesting question. If one partner's career is more financially rewarding, that partner's interests will not only tend to take precedence when career moves are considered but may also affect, at least somewhat, the way priorities and duties are allocated within the marriage (Maret and Finlay 1984; Spitze 1986).

With respect to child care, academia offers both plusses and minuses compared with other work situations. On the plus side, academic work has certain characteristics, particularly flexible work schedules and the option of doing some of the work at home, that make it easier for couples to meet their child-care needs. In addition, some academic institutions have adopted innovative policies to help faculty members with family obligations, in particular reduced work schedules, expanded time for achieving tenure, and tenure for part-time faculty (Raabe, this volume, gives detailed data). Furthermore, many campuses, for years, have had on-site child care centers, mainly as laboratories to help train university students for teaching careers or for research on child development ("Campus Child Care" 1992). Recently, these centers on some campuses have been moving away from a predominantly academic mission and toward a greater emphasis on service, with increased flexibility of hours and ages of children served (Herr and Zimmerman 1989). According to the *National Report on Work and Family* ("Campus Child Care" 1992), child-care centers can be and are increasingly being used as recruiting tools by colleges and universities just as they are by corporations. Child-care centers are viewed as an attractive benefit by many potential new faculty and staff members and students.

On-site child care is much more prevalent in academic institutions compared with other workplaces (Raabe, this volume, provides detailed data on their incidence in both settings).[8] However, colleges and universities are *less* likely than other types of workplaces to provide financial assistance for child care, and colleges and universities are *less* likely than large corporations to have job-sharing or elder-care programs in place (Raabe, this volume). Thus, with respect to family care academia offers both advantages and disadvantages for academic couples compared with the situation confronted by other two-career couples.

We know considerably less about how household responsibilities are shared by academic couples. Over the years, a large number of studies have investigated the amount of time women and men spend on housework and child care. In addition to the data collected by the United Nations (1991), these include Walker and Woods (1976), Robinson (1977), Coverman (1983), Coverman and Sheley (1986), Spitze (1986), Blair and Lichter (1991), and Juster and Stafford (1991). They all document that the unequal division of labor in the household has been slow to change among couples in general, although there is some evidence that the division is more equal among dual-earner than among single-earner couples (Blau and Ferber 1992:50–52), and more highly educated men appear to have more egalitarian attitudes than others (Goode 1982; Huber and Spitze 1983). Male-female cohabiting couples in general have a slightly more equitable distribution of household labor than married couples, but women in such couples still do the majority of the housework (Denmark, Shaw, and Ciali 1985; Blair 1994). Among the same-sex couples in their study, Blumstein and Schwartz (1983) found that gay men and lesbians did more housework if they were not fully employed, and that gay men, like heterosexual men, felt that a successful partner should not have to do much housework. On the issue of housework equity specifically within academic couples, however, we know of no precise information indicating how household labor is divided between partners, though Astin and Milem's data (this volume) suggest that academic couples are somewhat more egalitarian than others and that male members of more egalitarian couples tend to pay a career penalty for taking on a larger share of family responsibilities. We still do not know whether, in general, it is the women in academic couples, like the women in Hochschild's (1989) study, who are doing a "second shift" of chores at home after a long day of teaching, grading papers and exams, committee work, and maybe a fragment of research (on a good day). To the extent that this is the case, there may be adverse impacts on their careers, their health and well-being, and their family life (Hochschild 1989). These questions need further research; they are quite difficult to study empirically, but are increasingly seen as "central to [women's] low status in industrialized societies" (Spitze 1986:689) and there is every reason to believe that they would also affect women's status in academia.

In sum, the research agenda for academic couples overlaps a great deal with the agenda that is critical for women's status in society in general, as identified by Bianchi and Spain (1986). Gender equity in rank and pay; workable, high-quality child-care options; and shared responsibility for housework are issues for academics as well as for everyone else in society. In addition to these broad problems, there are several other concerns that are important for academic couples and on which research is needed.

One subject of considerable interest that has received relatively little attention is the effect of mobility on the careers of academicians. Geographic mobility is generally necessary for maximizing a career in academia (Brooker-Gross and Maraffa 1989), just as it frequently is for some other careers such as marketing and sales (Brett, Stroh, and Reilly 1993). In traditional marriages, moves to maximize the husband's career have been the norm (Bielby and Bielby 1992; Ferber and Kordick 1978; Shaklee 1989). In a study of academic couples at one university (Weishaar, Chiaravalli, and Jones 1984), only 3 percent of the men but 43 percent of the women had moved exclusively for their spouse's career. In another study of faculty members in criminology, only 5 percent of the men as opposed to 21 percent of the women had left an academic position for family reasons, the most common being spouse's employment (McElrath 1992). However, the primacy of the husband's career may be changing as women increasingly make strong career commitments (Bird and Bird 1985). Brett, Stroh, and Reilly (1993) found that in Fortune 500 companies, women were as likely as men to be willing to relocate, although women were less likely than men to be offered the opportunity (Hendershott 1995). Furthermore, Bielby and Bielby (1992) found that those couples with "co-provider" or other nontraditional gender-role ideologies were not likely to give precedence automatically to the husband's career. Bielby and Bielby suggest that more research is needed on the processes of making migration decisions and the personal and family factors that are taken into consideration in making these decisions. But in terms of institutional responses to these dilemmas, it is now clear that "reaching beyond the ever-smaller pool of white males with traditional marriages to staff organizations in the 1990s is going to require catering to the needs of spouse and family" (Brett, Stroh, and Reilly 1993:59). Raabe's data in this volume give us some idea of the extent to which academic institutions are already responding to this problem.

The costs of a career relocation can be severe. Traditionally these costs have been borne by the wife, but it is our impression that increasingly husbands move because of their wives' careers and become "trailing spouses" looking for jobs in the new setting. For academic women, moves that favored their husband's careers have certainly disadvantaged their own (Ferber and Huber 1979; Marwell, Rosenfeld, and Spilerman 1979). McElrath (1992) found that for untenured women who left jobs, the length of time before obtaining tenure increased and the probability of becoming tenured decreased. Brooker-Gross and Maraffa (1989) found that many academic women who moved for their husbands' jobs were unable to find academic employment, and many found themselves either unemployed or underemployed. It should also be kept in mind that some costs, both financial and emotional, may be incurred by the family as a whole in any relocation (Shaklee 1989; Bielby and Bielby 1992; Hendershott 1995). And the cost-benefit ratio may vary by race or ethnicity: for example, Fields and Erkut noted that African-American dual-career couples contemplating a relocation considered the possibility of social and cultural isolation and the concern that the job offer might be "just so much affirmative action window dressing" rather than a career move with solid potential (1983:8). Finally, geographic moves may be even more difficult for same-sex and male-female cohabiting couples because they have even less legal or socially sanctioned claim to support services from the organization than do married couples. The whole issue of academic relocations is one in need of further research, in particular with respect to men moving as "trailing spouses" to accommodate their wives' careers, the factors considered by different racial and ethnic groups in considering such a move, and the problems of same-sex and cohabiting couples.

One solution chosen by dual-career couples who face job offers in different locations is long-distance commuting. It is likely that academics comprise a substantial proportion of such couples (Gerstel and Gross 1984; Johnson 1987); in a tight academic market, it may be the best or only way for each member of the couple to have an academic career. Some of the stresses, dilemmas, and advantages of this lifestyle have been enumerated (Gerstel and Gross 1984; Johnson 1987; Winfield 1985; Hendershott 1995), and there is evidence (Bellas, this volume) suggesting that commuting may help women's careers but hinder men's. However, additional research is needed on the career impacts of and institutional responses to commuter marriage among academics in order to enlarge our understanding of this group of academic couples.

From this chapter's brief review, several research questions emerge. As family configurations and institutional demands change, what is the current situation and what are the prospects for the future with respect to more equitable work and family arrangements? Do women in academic couples experience the same inequities as academic women in general? Are disproportionate housework and child-care burdens a factor in academic wives' career advancement? To the extent that academic couples strive for greater equality, what are the costs to men in those relationships? For example, what proportion of men give precedence to their wives' careers when deciding whether to move and what are the institutional responses to this "trailing spouse" phenomenon? How does commuter marriage impact on academic couples and on institutions? We need research—including research with respect to couples of different racial and ethnic groups and with respect to same-sex and unmarried heterosexual couples—on all these questions.

We are not suggesting the problems we raise in this chapter are easy to solve. Profound transformations of both society and academia may be needed. And many of the political and financial pressures facing academia today work against positive solutions. Yet, academia is also an arena for fresh thinking on old problems. As scholarly research on gender and work proliferates, we hope to find new insights that will help the unfinished social and economic revolution for women move toward the fulfillment of its promise. We hope that the workplace can be made more equitable and more humane and the disjuncture between work and family less wrenching. Perhaps academia as an institution can help lead the way.

Notes

1. In this chapter we focus mainly on heterosexual married couples, although we also discuss some issues important for cohabiting heterosexual and same-sex couples. See also Miller and Skeen, this volume.

2. It should be noted that women's increased labor force participation may be a cause, as well as a result, of the higher divorce rate, although the empirical evidence for this is mixed (England and Farkas 1986:64–65; Blau and Ferber 1992:264–67).

3. Lower fertility may, of course, be a response to the perceived need for women to add to the family income or to their improved labor market opportunities.

4. Rubin (1976) noted that even low-paying unskilled jobs outside the home were often considered by working-class women to be rewarding compared with an unbroken home routine.

5. To arrive at this estimate we converted the 1993–94 salary into 1989 dollars and used the household income distribution for 1989 obtained from 1990 census data (U.S. Bureau of the Census 1991). The assumption that couples would earn double the mean salary might lead to a high estimate, since women academics earn less on average than men academics. On the other hand, the income estimate we used did not take into account earnings other than base salary, which in 1987 averaged an additional 23 percent (National Center for Education Statistics 1991).

6. We note here that child-care workers, mostly women, are among the lowest paid workers in our economy and that they, too, suffer from our current system (Wrigley 1995).

7. Astin and Milem (this volume) also found that women's representation tends to be smaller at more highly ranked institutions.

8. We still lack complete information on availability and cost of these on-site services. It is our general impression that there are often long waiting lists and that the fees may be quite high.

References

Acker, Joan. 1990. "Hierarchies, Jobs, Bodies: A Theory of Gendered Organizations." *Gender and Society* 4 (June): 139–58.

———. 1992. "The Future of Women and Work: Ending the Twentieth Century." *Sociological Perspectives* 35 (Spring): 53–68.

American Association of University Professors. 1994. "The Annual Report on the Economic Status of the Profession, 1993–94." *Academe* 80 (Mar.–Apr.): 5–89.

Bellas, Marcia. 1994. "Comparable Worth in Academia: The Effects on Faculty Salaries of the Sex Composition and Labor Market Conditions of Academic Disciplines." *American Sociological Review* 59 (Dec.): 807–21.

Bem, Sandra Lipsitz. 1993. *The Lenses of Gender: Transforming the Debate on Sexual Inequality.* New Haven: Yale University Press.

Benin, Mary, and Yinong Chong. 1993. "Child Care Concerns of Employed Mothers." In *The Employed Mother and the Family Context,* ed. Judith Frankel, 229–44. New York: Springer.

Bianchi, Suzanne M., and Daphne Spain. 1986. *American Women in Transition.* New York: Russell Sage Foundation.

Bielby, Denise D., and William T. Bielby. 1992. "I Will Follow Him: Family Ties, Gender-Role Beliefs, and Reluctance to Relocate for a Better Job." *American Journal of Sociology* 97 (Mar.): 1241–67.

Bird, Gerald A., and Gloria W. Bird. 1985. "Determinants of Mobility in Two-Earner Families: Does the Wife's Income Count?" *Journal of Marriage and the Family* 47 (Aug.): 753–58.

Blair, Sampson Lee. 1994. "Marriage and Cohabitation: Distinctions and Similarities across the Division of Household Labor." *Family Perspective* 28 (1): 31–52.

Blair, Sampson Lee, and Daniel T. Lichter. 1991. "Measuring the Division of Household Labor: Gender Segregation of Housework among American Couples." *Journal of Family Issues* 12 (Mar.): 91–113.

Blau, Francine D., and Marianne A. Ferber. 1992. *The Economics of Women, Men, and Work.* 2d ed. Englewood Cliffs, N.J.: Prentice Hall.

Blumstein, Philip, and Pepper Schwartz. 1983. *American Couples: Money, Work, Sex.* New York: William Morrow.

Brett, Jeanne M., Linda K. Stroh, and Anne H. Reilly. 1993. "Pulling Up Roots in the 1990s: Who's Willing to Relocate?" *Journal of Organizational Behavior* 14 (Jan.): 49–60.

Brooker-Gross, Susan R., and Thomas A. Maraffa. 1989. "Faculty Spouses: Their Post-Migration Searches." *Initiatives* 52 (2): 37–43.

Burkhauser, Richard V., and Greg J. Duncan. 1989. "Economic Risks of Gender Roles: Income Loss and Life Events over the Life Course." *Social Science Quarterly* 70 (Mar.): 3–23.

"Campus Child Care Shedding Academic Focus; Service Orientation Helps Recruitment, Retention." 1992. *National Report on Work and Family* 5 (4): 1–3.

Chafe, William H. 1991. *The Paradox of Change: American Women in the Twentieth Century.* New York: Oxford University Press.

Coverman, Shelley. 1983. "Gender, Domestic Labor Time, and Wage Inequality." *American Sociological Review* 48 (Oct.): 623–37.

Coverman, Shelley, and Joseph F. Sheley. 1986. "Men's Housework and Childcare Time, 1965–1975." *Journal of Marriage and the Family* 48 (May): 413–22.

Denmark, F. L., J. S. Shaw, and S. D. Ciali. 1985. "The Relationship among Sex Roles, Living Arrangements, and the Division of Household Responsibilities." *Sex Roles* 12 (5–6): 617–25.

England, Paula, and Irene Browne. 1992. "Trends in Women's Economic Status." *Sociological Perspectives* 35 (Spring): 17–52.

England, Paula, and George Farkas. 1986. *Households, Employment, and Gender: A Social, Economic, and Demographic View.* New York: Aldine.

Ferber, Marianne A. 1992. "Women and the American Economy." In *Challenging Times: The Women's Movement in Canada and the United States,* ed. Constance Backhouse and David H. Flaherty, 205–14. Montreal: McGill-Queen's University Press.

Ferber, Marianne A., and Joan Huber. 1979. "Husbands, Wives, and Careers." *Journal of Marriage and the Family* 41 (May): 315–25.

Ferber, Marianne A., and Betty Kordick. 1978. "Sex Differentials in the Earnings of Ph.D's." *Industrial and Labor Relations Review* 31 (Jan.): 227–38.

Ferber, Marianne A., and Brigid O'Farrell, with La Rue Allen, eds. 1991. *Work and Family: Policies for a Changing Work Force.* Washington, D.C.: National Academy Press.

Fields, Jacqueline P., and Sumru Erkut. 1983. "Relocation as Nemesis: A Study of Black and White Dual Career Couples." Wellesley College Center for Research on Women Working Paper no. 100.

Gerstel, Naomi, and Harriet Gross. 1984. *Commuter Marriage: A Study of Work and Family.* New York: Guilford Press.

Goldin, Claudia. 1990. *Understanding the Gender Gap: An Economic History of American Women.* New York: Oxford University Press.

Goode, William J. 1982. "Why Men Resist." In *Rethinking the Family,* ed. Barrie Thorne and Marilyn Yalom, 131–47. New York: Longman.

Harrison, Bennett, and Barry Bluestone. 1988. *The Great U-Turn: Corporate Restructuring and the Polarizing of America.* New York: Basic Books.

Hendershott, Anne B. 1995. *Moving for Work: The Sociology of Relocating in the 1990s.* Lanham, Md.: University Press of America.

Herr, Judy, and Karen Zimmerman. 1989. *Results of the 1989 National Campus Child Care Study.* Cascade, Wisc.: National Coalition for Campus Child Care, Inc.

Hertz, Rosanna. 1986. *More Equal than Others: Women and Men in Dual-Career Marriages.* Berkeley: University of California Press.

Hochschild, Arlie, with Anne Machung. 1989. *The Second Shift.* New York: Avon Books.

Hodson, Randy, and Teresa Sullivan. 1990. *The Social Organization of Work.* Belmont, Calif.: Wadsworth.

Holden, Karen C., and Pamela J. Smock. 1991. "The Economic Costs of Marital Dissolution." *Annual Review of Sociology* 17:51–78.

Huber, Joan, and Glenna Spitze. 1983. *Sex Stratification: Children, Housework, and Jobs.* New York: Academic Press.

International Labour Organization. 1985. *Maternity Benefits in the 80's: An ILO Survey (1964–84).* Geneva: ILO.

Johnson, Sharon Ervin. 1987. "Weaving the Threads: Equalizing Professional and Personal Demands Faced by Commuting Career Couples." *Journal of NAWDAC* 50 (Winter): 3–10.

Juster, F. Thomas, and Frank P. Stafford. 1991. "The Allocation of Time: Findings, Behavioral Models, and Problems of Measurement." *Journal of Economic Literature* 29 (June): 471–522.

Kahn, Alfred J., and Sheila Kamerman. 1987. *Child Care: Facing the Hard Choices.* Dover, Mass.: Auburn House.

Maret, Elizabeth, and Barbara Finlay. 1984. "The Distribution of Household Labor among Women in Dual-Earner Families." *Journal of Marriage and the Family* 46 (May): 357–64.

Marwell, Gerald, Rachel Rosenfeld, and Seymour Spilerman. 1979. "Geographic Constraints on Women's Careers in Academia." *Science* 205 (Sept. 21): 1225–31.

Matthaei, Julie A. 1982. *An Economic History of Women in America: Women's Work, the Sexual Division of Labor, and the Development of Capitalism.* New York: Schocken Books.

McElrath, Karen. 1992. "Gender, Career Disruption, and Academic Rewards." *Journal of Higher Education* 63 (May–June): 269–81.

Miller, Jean Baker. 1986. *Toward a New Psychology of Women.* 2d ed. Boston: Beacon Press.

Miller-Loessi, Karen. 1992. "Toward Gender Integration in the Workplace: Issues at Multiple Levels." *Sociological Perspectives* 35 (Spring): 1–15.

Pearce, Diana. 1978. "The Feminization of Poverty: Women, Work, and Welfare." *Urban and Social Change Review* 11 (1–2): 28–36.

Reich, Robert. 1991. *The Work of Nations: Preparing Ourselves for Twenty-First Century Capitalism.* New York: Alfred A. Knopf.

Reskin, Barbara F. 1988. "Bringing the Men Back In: Sex Differentiation and the Devaluation of Women's Work." *Gender and Society* 2 (Mar.): 58–81.

Reskin, Barbara F., and Patricia A. Roos. 1990. *Job Queues, Gender Queues: Explaining Women's Inroads into Male Occupations.* Philadelphia: Temple University Press.

Robinson, John P. 1977. *Changes in America's Use of Time.* Cleveland: Communications Research Center, Cleveland State University.

Rubin, Lillian Breslow. 1976. *Worlds of Pain: Life in the Working Class Family.* New York: Basic Books.

Russell, Susan H., James S. Fairweather, Robert M. Hendrickson, and Linda J. Zimbler. 1991. *Profiles of Faculty in Higher Education Institutions, 1988.* NCES 91–389. Washington, D.C.: U.S. Department of Education Office of Educational Research and Improvement, National Center for Education Statistics.

Shaklee, Harriet. 1989. "Geographic Mobility and the Two-Earner Couple: Expected Costs of a Family Move." *Journal of Applied Social Psychology* 19 (June, pt. 2): 728–43.

Slater, Miriam, and Penina Migdal Glazer. 1987. "Prescriptions for Professional Survival." *Daedalus* 116 (Fall): 119–35.

Spitze, Glenna. 1986. "The Division of Task Responsibility in U.S. Households: Longitudinal Adjustments to Change." *Social Forces* 64 (Mar.): 689–701.

Steinberg, Ronnie. 1990. "Social Construction of Skill: Gender, Power, and Comparable Worth." *Work and Occupations* 17 (Nov.): 449–82.

United Nations. 1991. *The World's Women, 1970–90: Trends and Statistics.* New York: United Nations.

U.S. Bureau of the Census. 1991. Census of Population and Housing, 1990: Summary Tape File 3C Extract on CD-ROM (machine-readable data files). Washington, D.C.: Bureau of the Census (producer and distributor).

———. 1993. *Statistical Abstract of the United States.* 113th ed. Washington, D.C.: GPO.

U.S. Department of Labor. 1977. *Earnings and Employment.* Washington, D.C.: GPO.

Walker, Kathryn E., and Margaret E. Woods. 1976. *Time Use: A Measure of Household Production of Family Goods and Services.* Washington, D.C.: American Home Economics Association.

Weishaar, Marjorie, Kathy Chiaravalli, and Ferdinand Jones. 1984. "Dual-Career Couples in Higher Education." *Journal of NAWDAC* 47 (Summer): 16–20.

Winfield, Fairlee E. 1985. *Commuter Marriage: Living Together, Apart.* New York: Columbia University Press.

Wrigley, Julia. 1995. *Other People's Children.* New York: Basic Books.

Zigler, E. 1990. "Shaping Child Care Policies and Programs in America." *American Journal of Community Psychology* 18 (Apr.): 183–215.

2

. . . .

The History of Women and Couples in Academe

Paula E. Stephan and Mary Mathewes Kassis

IN 1948 LOUISE RUSSERT LEFT graduate school at the University of Michigan with all but her dissertation completed to take a position at the University of Arkansas in the department of zoology. Nineteen years later, in 1967, she signed a contract for an identical job and began (again) a career that had been on hold during much of the intervening period. Her story is not atypical of women in academe during this time. When two years after arriving at the University of Arkansas she married Bill Kraemer, a fellow faculty member, antinepotism rules forced her to resign from her tenure-track position, while her husband remained on the faculty and was promoted through the ranks to professor. During all those years she was frequently on the payroll as a part-time faculty member, filling in when various departments needed instructional assistance, but never holding a tenure-track position.[1] Her story is instructive for two other reasons. First, almost from its inception, the University of Arkansas had women on the faculty, although the number of women hired appears at times to have been intentionally limited. Louise Russert's 1948 job offer came precisely because the one woman in the department was retiring that year. Second, the university had an apparent preference for single women. When Louise resigned because of the antinepotism rules, the department hired a single woman who remained at the university (and single) until her retirement in 1988.[2]

By all accounts there were many Louise Russerts in 1948 and they were preceded by earlier generations of Russerts who had attempted to create a place for themselves in the academic world. The goal of this chapter is to provide the reader with a sense of what their careers were like and how the opportunities facing generations of Russerts changed over time. Whenever possible, we examine the ways in which marriage affected their careers; this is a challenging task because no historic faculty database exists that records marital status, let alone occupational status of a spouse.

Our approach is four-pronged. First, we review the history of women in academe. Given the large amount of work that exists on the topic, our discussion is brief; it is included to provide a context for other information presented in this chapter and elsewhere in this book. Second, we use the rich data provided by the Doctorate Records File to examine how the gender composition of Ph.D. recipients has changed since the 1920s. Third, we piece together several studies to make inferences about the role of marriage in the lives of women faculty during the first sixty years of the twentieth century. Fourth, we present case studies for five institutions of higher education in the United States, examining the gender composition of their faculty in ten-year intervals since the founding of each institution. Whenever possible, we present evidence regarding the prevalence of couples on their faculties. The five institutions are Agnes Scott College, the University of Arkansas, Grinnell College, the University of Illinois, and Yale University. Agnes Scott permits us to examine the fate of women faculty at a women's college; Grinnell enables us to look at a liberal arts college; Yale affords the opportunity to study an elite private institution that was, for many years, exclusively for men. The University of Illinois and the University of Arkansas provide case studies of land-grant institutions, one situated in the North, the other in the South.

The History of Women Faculty

The historian George Paul Schmidt (1953:19) describes the years from 1770 to 1870 as the "era of the college, the time when this unique American institution dominated the field [of higher education] without serious challenge." According to Schmidt, by 1860 somewhere between 150 and 200 colleges and universities had survived and were dispensing their version of a liberal education to approximately twenty thousand men and a handful of women. Some of the largest, such as Yale, the University of North Carolina, and the University of Virginia, had approximately five hundred undergraduates each, but the majority had a hundred or fewer students. Expansion had been slow; between 1840 and 1860 college enrollment in the Northeast did not even keep pace with population growth. Faculties ranged in size from twenty-four at Harvard in 1860 to a president and a couple of tutors at some of the newly founded colleges, where "thirty or forty students, one small building, a shelf of Latin and Greek classics, and a few biological specimens constituted the enterprise" (Schmidt 1953:20).

The first women's colleges were founded in the late 1800s. Some, like Radcliffe, were established as extensions of a men's institution. Others, such as Bryn Mawr, were modeled on male institutions such as Johns Hopkins.[3] Most initially had male presidents, though some were quick to gain female heads. Alice Freeman, for example, became president of Wellesley College in 1881 when she was twenty-six years old and the college was six (Bordin 1993).

The data in Table 2-1 give a historical summary of U.S. faculty in higher education from 1869–70 to 1983–84. Faculty are defined to include part-time as well as full-time employees (Vetter and Babco 1987:133). The reliability of the earliest data may be questioned because the number of institutions reported for 1869–70 is more than twice the number reported by Schmidt. The sharp increase followed by a decrease in the percentage of women faculty members reported from 1869–70 to 1889–90 also suggests that these early entries may be unreliable. After that, however, the data appear to be more consistent. To allow a comparison of women's employment on faculties with overall labor force participation, data for the percentage of the labor force that was female are also provided in table 2-1. To easily compare the position of women in academe with the overall position of women in the labor force, the ratio of the percentage of women on the faculty to the percentage of women in the labor force is also reported.

The data in the table suggest that during the late 1800s women constituted a fairly sizeable proportion of the faculty at institutions of higher education, given the context of the time, when 17 percent of the labor force was female.[4] The early 1900s was a period of rapid growth of faculty and expansion of the burgeoning land-grant colleges. With their strong programs in the "home arts," land-grant institutions looked to women to play increasingly important roles in certain departments. While the percentage of women faculty members did not change much

TABLE 2-1. U.S. Faculty in Higher Education by Sex, 1869–70 through 1983–84

Years	Total Number of Institutions	Total Number of Faculty[a]	Number of Male Faculty	Number of Female Faculty	Percentage of Female Faculty	Percentage of Labor Force That Was Female	Ratio[b]
1869–70	563	5,553	4,887	666	12.0	—	
1879–80	811	11,522	7,328	4,194	36.4	—	
1889–90	998	15,809	12,704	3,105	19.6	17.0	1.15
1899–1900	977	23,868	19,151	4,717	19.8	18.1	1.09
1909–10	951	36,480	29,132	7,348	20.1	—	
1919–20	1,041	48,615	35,807	12,808	26.3	20.4	1.29
1929–30	1,409	82,386	60,017	22,369	27.2	21.9	1.24
1939–40	1,708	146,929	106,328	40,601	27.6	25.2	1.09
1949–50	1,851	246,722	186,189	60,533	24.5	28.8	0.851
1959–60	2,008	380,554	296,773	83,781	22.0	32.3	0.680
1969–70	2,525	450,000	346,000	104,000	23.1	37.1	0.620
1979–80	3,152	675,000	486,000	189,000	28.0	41.9	0.668
1981–82	3,253	696,000	496,000	200,000	28.7	42.7	0.672
1983–84	3,284	723,000	511,000	212,000	29.3	43.2	0.678

a. Includes part-time faculty. For 1969 forward only faculty with the rank of instructor or above are included.

b. Ratio = percent female faculty divided by percent women in the labor force.

Sources: Vetter and Babco 1987:133, table 5-17. Labor force data prior to 1959–60 are data for the first year in the decade from U.S. Bureau of the Census 1975:Series D 29–41, p. 131. Data from 1959–60 forward are from CITIBASE 1978. These data are averages calculated from September to August.

during the first ten years of the twentieth century, by 1920 it had risen to 26 percent. This share remained fairly constant during the 1930s and early 1940s, but then began a decline that lasted until the 1960s. Indeed, a college student was less likely to have been taught by a woman faculty member during the academic year 1959–60 than in any of the previous forty years. Moreover, while before World War II the percentage of faculty members that was female was consistently larger than the percentage of the labor force that was female, the relationship was reversed by 1950. Furthermore, as women increasingly found employment in traditional female occupations in the 1950s and 1960s, the divergence grew. It was not until 1979–80 that the gap between the percentage of women that were on faculties and the percentage of women in the labor force began again to narrow.

Jessie Bernard, in her 1964 book on women in academe, attributes much of the decline in the percentage of women on faculties that began in the 1940s to a shortage of women available for faculty jobs. This judgment is questionable for two reasons. First, as we will see in the next section, the percentage of doctoral degrees earned by women did not decline dramatically until the 1950s and the *actual* number of women receiving the degree never declined. Second, a doctoral degree was not a requirement for faculty status. Using the Doctorate Records File, we estimate that there were at most 50,000 individuals with doctoral degrees in the United States in 1940 compared to a total faculty of 146,929 (Survey of Earned Doctorates:unpublished tables).

It seems much more likely that the decline in the percentage of women on faculties was a result of attitudes that began to take root during the depression years when jobs became increasingly scarce. Not only were antinepotism rules instituted in some colleges and universities during the depression but a movement to hire men for positions that had typically been held by women arose. This eventually included the attempt by schools of social work in the 1950s to gain in prestige by hiring men as deans as well as the later move to recruit men to positions of leadership in the field of home economics (Riesman 1964:xvii). Status seeking may also explain the shift in gender composition that began to occur in the faculty of women's colleges during the 1940s. Table 2-2 shows the percentage of women on the faculties in selected women's colleges for 1940–60. Among four of the five colleges for which data are available for both 1940 and 1956, the percentage of women faculty declined sharply. In most instances, the percentage continued to decline during the rest of the 1950s.

TABLE 2-2. Percentage of Female Faculty at
Women's Colleges, 1940–41 through 1960–61

	1940–41	1956	1960–61
Agnes Scott	—	67.0	—
Barnard	—	59.0	—
Bryn Mawr	51.8	50.0	34.4
Connecticut College	61.8	—	57.4
Douglass	—	13.0	—
Goucher	72.1	60.0	47.8
Hunter	—	59.0	—
Mills	51.5	—	51.3
Mount Holyoke	—	64.0	—
Newcomb	—	50.0	—
Smith	58.3	37.0	43.5
Sweet Briar	68.4	—	66.2
Trinity	—	82.0	—
Vassar	70.0	62.0	53.0
Wellesley	90.1	67.0	62.8

Source: Bernard 1964:55, table 314.

An increase in the percentage of women on faculties of higher education as a whole was reported in 1969–70 (table 2-1). This gain, though extremely modest, undoubtedly reflected the seller's market for Ph.D.'s during a time of rapid expansion in graduate education. Market conditions quickly deteriorated, however, and by the early 1970s it became questionable whether women could sustain these gains. For example, Astin's (1973) analysis of the employment plans of new Ph.D.'s in 1969–70 suggests that the poor market conditions were more likely to be felt by women than by men (158–59).

During the early 1970s, frustration over the slow progress being made by women in academe and fear of increased discrimination as the academic marketplace became more competitive led women to pressure the government to enforce Executive Order 11246 against colleges and universities and to pass laws designed to equalize opportunities for women in higher education. Although there were other factors involved as well, including an increase in the proportion of the Ph.D. pool that was female, the data in table 2-1 suggest that these laws were helpful in broadening the opportunities for women at a time when market conditions were not favorable to academic job seekers. The percentage of women faculty increased from 23 in 1969–70 to 29 in 1983–84.

TABLE 2-3. U.S. Full-Time Faculty in Higher Education,
1974–75 through Fall 1991

Rank and Sex	1974–75		1977–78		1980–81	
	N	%	N	%	N	%
Total faculty	364,097		389,033		395,992	
Men	277,787	76.3	290,289	74.6	291,329	73.6
Women	86,310	23.7	98,769	25.4	104,663	26.4
Professors	83,619		93,042		104,857	
Men	75,462	90.2	84,247	90.5	94,174	89.8
Women	8,157	9.8	8,795	9.5	10,682	10.2
Associate professors	83,302		94,286		97,195	
Men	69,412	83.3	77,161	81.8	77,395	79.6
Women	13,890	16.7	17,125	18.2	19,800	20.4
Assistant professors	105,229		103,122		96,868	
Men	76,725	72.9	70,497	68.4	63,171	65.2
Women	28,504	27.1	32,625	31.6	33,697	34.8
Instructors	67,666		34,700		30,754	
Men	40,289	59.5	17,143	49.4	14,857	48.3
Women	27,377	40.5	17,557	50.6	15,897	51.7
Lecturers	4,861		5,655		6,257	
Men	2,932	60.3	3,199	56.6	3,360	53.7
Women	1,929	39.7	2,456	43.4	2,897	46.3
Other faculty	19,420		58,228		60,061	
Men	12,967	66.8	38,017	65.3	38,371	63.9
Women	6,453	33.2	20,211	34.7	21,690	36.1
Total labor force	94,913		102,797		109,808	
Men	57,770	60.9	60,769	59.1	63,384	57.7
Women	37,143	39.1	42,028	40.9	46,461	42.3
Ratio[a]		0.606		0.621		0.625

a. Ratio = percent female faculty divided by percent women in the labor force.
Sources: Faculty data are from National Center for Education Statistics 1975–93. The data

In recent years detailed data have been compiled concerning women on full-time instructional faculties. These data are summarized in table 2-3 and provide, in addition to information on the number and percentage of faculty members that are women, comparable information by academic rank. We see from the table that the percentage of full-time faculty positions held by women grew from 24 percent in 1974–75 to 32

Fall 1983		Fall 1985		Fall 1991	
N	%	N	%	N	%
457,823		464,072		520,327	
330,930	72.3	336,009	72.4	355,111	68.2
126,893	27.7	128,063	27.6	165,216	31.8
117,450		129,269		144,336	
103,380	88.0	114,258	88.4	123,173	85.3
14,070	12.0	15,011	11.6	21,163	14.7
108,300		111,092		116,639	
83,589	77.2	85,156	76.7	84,311	72.3
24,711	22.8	25,936	23.3	32,328	27.7
112,974		111,308		126,244	
73,810	65.3	71,463	64.2	76,129	60.3
39,164	34.7	39,854	35.8	50,125	39.7
81,421		75,411		78,082	
46,468	57.1	43,251	57.4	41,124	52.7
34,953	42.9	32,160	42.6	36,958	47.3
9,005		9,766		11,275	
4,744	52.7	5,098	52.2	5,362	47.6
4,261	47.3	4,668	47.8	5,913	52.4
28,673		27,226		43,651	
18,939	66.1	16,783	61.6	25,012	57.3
9,734	33.9	10,443	38.4	18,639	42.7
113,993		117,637		127,231	
64,862	56.9	66,178	56.3	70,071	55.1
49,131	43.1	51,459	43.7	57,160	44.9
	0.643		0.631		0.707

are reported by academic year from 1974 to 1982 and as of fall from 1983 forward. Labor force data are in thousands of persons and are from CITIBASE 1978.

percent in the fall of 1991 and that there was an increase within each academic rank as well.[5] We also see that the percentage of full professors who were women did not begin to increase until the early 1980s, while the percentage of associate and assistant professors that were women began to increase earlier. These differences reflect in part the time required for newly hired assistant professors to progress through the ranks to full professor. The data also indicate that throughout the entire period the non-tenure-track positions of instructor, lecturer, and "other faculty" have been far more likely than the tenure-track positions to be held by women.

The ratios of the percentage of faculty members that were women to the percentage of the labor force that were women are also included in table 2-3. Because the latter includes people working part-time, the ratio is biased downward. Comparisons over time are, nonetheless, instructive. While the ratio is less than one throughout the period, indicating that women are represented to a greater extent in the labor force than on full-time faculties of colleges and universities, it has increased gradually over time, especially between the fall of 1985 and the fall of 1991.[6]

Because men and women with Ph.D.'s are distributed differently among academic disciplines, it is important to examine employment trends by field as well. Table 2-4 displays the percentage of women on faculties in the broad fields of engineering, mathematics, science, and social and behavioral science, the fields for which such information is readily available. The data indicate that the representation of women in these fields has increased, but remains low, particularly among engineers, physical scientists, and environmental scientists.

TABLE 2-4. Percentage of Women Scientists and Engineers Employed Full-Time in Colleges and Universities, 1974–85

Profession	1974	1978	1980	1982	1984	1985
Engineer	1.5	2.4	2.7	3.1	3.8	4.2
Environmental scientist	5.0	7.0	7.9	9.4	9.4	9.9
Life scientist	20.3	20.4	22.3	24.9	27.7	28.4
Math/computer scientist	13.1	14.3	15.7	17.2	18.7	19.3
Physical scientist	7.2	8.8	8.9	9.4	9.9	10.1
Psychologist	21.3	24.8	25.8	26.5	26.3	28.1
Social scientist	15.8	18.1	19.0	19.5	19.1	19.9
Total	14.7	16.1	17.3	18.9	20.4	21.1

Source: Vetter and Babco 1987:125, table 5-9.

Women Doctorates: Their Prevalence and Incidence

According to M. Carey Thomas, the first dean of Bryn Mawr, there were only four women with Ph.D.'s in the world when Bryn Mawr was founded in 1883. Two of the degrees were in math. Given the decision of the college to hire only candidates with Ph.D.'s, Thomas reports that "we could appoint only three [women] including myself as professor of English and the rest of our faculty had to be men" (Bernard 1964:56).[7] Although Thomas undoubtedly undercounted, the data on Ph.D. production for the years from 1870 on are consistent with her observation of the minute numbers of women with doctorates. The U.S. Census (1975:386) reports that in 1870 no woman received a Ph.D. in the United States, while in 1880 3 of the 54 Ph.D. recipients (6 percent) were women. In 1890 only 2 of the 149 recipients were women (1 percent), but by 1900 6 percent of the 382 degrees awarded were earned by women, and ten years later the figure was approximately 10 percent.[8]

While having a Ph.D. was not a necessary condition for holding a faculty position in the late nineteenth century, it certainly helped, particularly at established institutions. The twenty-eight Yale faculty members with Ph.D.'s in 1883 constituted 35 percent of the faculty; the three with Ph.D.'s that the University of Illinois employed on the faculty in 1888 represented a sixth of that university's total faculty. Given the low percentage of Ph.D.'s held by women, it is, therefore, not surprising that so few faculty members were women during these years.

From 1920 on, reliable annual statistics are available on doctoral production, so that a more detailed picture emerges of the composition of degree recipients by gender. The data are drawn exclusively from the Doctorate Records File, which since 1958 has been compiled from the Survey of Earned Doctorates rather than from university records, the source of the file's earlier information.[9] The file is not a sample but instead reports numbers for the population. In addition to those with Ph.D.'s, recipients of other types of doctoral degrees, such as the Ed.D., are included. We use these data to take a more in-depth look at the gender composition of doctoral degrees conferred since the 1920s.

Table 2-5 gives the percentage of doctorates awarded to women for seven decades, both overall and by seven broad disciplinary groupings. We see that in the 1920s over 15 percent of all doctoral degrees awarded were earned by women, a figure 50 percent larger than the 1910 percentage reported above. After that, however, the percentage of doctorates bestowed on women began a steady decline that did not turn around until the 1960s. When the analysis is broken down by year instead of by decade, we find that the percentage of doctorates conferred on women was greatest between 1925 and 1932,[10] when approximately one in six such

TABLE 2-5. Percentage of Doctorates Awarded to Women, 1920s–1980s

Field	1920s	1930s	1940s	1950s	1960s	1970s	1980s
Education	18.1	19.6	22.8	18.2	19.5	30.0	51.4
Engineering	0.9	0.7	0.5	0.4	0.4	1.4	5.9
Humanities	23.7	22.9	20.5	14.5	18.4	31.0	43.5
Life sciences	15.9	15.0	12.7	9.1	11.6	18.7	32.2
Physical sciences	7.5	6.6	5.0	3.7	4.6	8.1	15.2
Professional/other	10.1	12.4	19.1	12.5	14.5	16.9	31.5
Social sciences	17.1	15.8	14.5	11.1	14.4	24.5	40.5
Total	15.3	14.7	13.5	10.0	11.7	20.7	33.9

Source: Survey of Earned Doctorates, Doctorate Records File.

degrees were earned by women. Not until 1972 was the percentage to return to this level.

Both economic and social factors help to explain the steady decline that began in the 1930s. Decreased economic opportunities for women, especially married women, and reduced economic circumstances of parents, for whom providing educational support for a daughter was often of secondary concern, undoubtedly were factors in the decline. World War II did not reverse the decline in the percentage of degrees received by women, although anecdotal evidence suggests that certain departments that had rarely admitted women made exceptions during the war, only to return to their previous practices when the war ended.

Changing social values also had a great deal to do with the sharp decline in the 1950s. It is no accident that during this period of record-breaking birthrates, when *Ozzie and Harriet* and *Leave It to Beaver* reigned on television, the percentage of women receiving doctorates sank to its lowest level since the turn of the century. The decline cannot all be explained by a change in social values, however. The GI Bill was a major factor as well, since under its auspices men went to graduate school in heretofore unheard-of numbers.[11] During the same period the actual number of doctorates granted to women also rose, but at a lower rate so that women constituted a steadily declining percentage of the total. Just when the GI Bill benefits for World War II veterans were about to run out, Korean veterans returned and their GI benefits provided support for another cohort of male graduate students.

When the turnaround occurred in the share of doctoral degrees earned by women, it happened fairly rapidly. Between 1965 and 1970, the percentage went from 11 to 14, an increase of one-fourth. By 1975 women were receiving over 20 percent of all doctorates and by the early 1980s the figure had gone above 30 percent. The increase can be partially attributed to an increase in the number of doctoral degrees being awarded in education (2,736 in 1965; 7,586 in 1980),[12] a field in which women received a disproportionally large share of the doctoral degrees awarded.

It was not only the field of education that attracted an increasing percentage of women. A growing share of the Ph.D.'s awarded in the social sciences and the humanities went to women. The increase in the physical and life sciences was considerably more modest. Indeed, as women began to receive a larger percentage of doctoral degrees, the gender discrepancy among fields initially widened. Thus, while in the 1920s and 1930s the share of degrees earned by women was slightly more than twice as high in the social sciences as in the physical sciences, by 1970 it was three times greater. The life sciences, which had initially tracked the social sciences fairly closely, also fell behind during this period in terms of the percentage of degrees going to women.

Engineering shows a somewhat different pattern. In the 1920s, 1930s, and 1940s one could literally count on the fingers of two hands the number of women who received doctorates in that field. Although the number rose after that, women continued to receive only a minute share of engineering Ph.D.'s. Similarly, the percentage of doctoral degrees awarded to women in the professional/other category, which includes fields as diverse as architecture, home economics, law, library science, social work, and theology, remained quite low prior to the 1980s, in part because few degrees were awarded in the traditional female fields in this category.

Several factors explain the turnaround that occurred in the late 1960s and early 1970s. First, much of it, as we have already noted, can be attributed to the increase in the number of women receiving advanced degrees in areas traditionally thought of as "women's fields," such as education and social work. Second, the upturn in women's share of doctorates gained momentum when the market for doctoral degrees began to collapse in a number of fields, so that many men (but far fewer women) opted for degrees in law and business instead, and the number of men receiving Ph.D.'s actually declined.[13] Laws that improved women's access to graduate education, as well as changing attitudes among faculty and women themselves, also contributed to the upturn.

Some of these trends can be more easily understood by examining table 2-6, which focuses on doctorate production for women from the

TABLE 2-6. Distribution of Doctorates Awarded to Women by Field,
1920s–1980s

Field	1920s	1930s	1940s	1950s	1960s	1970s	1980s
Education	11.4	16.2	26.4	30.9	28.3	32.1	32.6
Engineering	0.1	0.2	0.2	0.3	0.4	0.6	1.8
Humanities	34.5	34.8	29.4	22.5	23.9	22.1	14.3
Life sciences	20.7	20.2	17.9	16.5	16.3	14.2	17.2
Physical sciences	13.3	11.6	9.9	8.5	8.3	6.0	6.5
Professional/other	1.9	2.1	2.1	2.5	3.7	3.9	5.6
Social sciences	17.8	14.8	14.1	18.9	19.1	21.1	22.0
Total number	1,827	3,780	4,123	8,271	18,966	66,394	108,417
Percentage of U.S. female population 25–34	0.02	0.04	0.04	0.07	0.16	0.42	0.54

Sources: Doctorate degree information is from the Survey of Earned Doctorates, Doctorate Records File. The population information for 1920–70 is from U.S. Bureau of the Census 1975:Series A119–134, p. 15. The population information for 1980–90 is from U.S. Bureau of the Census 1993:15, table 14.

1920s to the 1980s, giving both the total and the distribution of degrees awarded by field. The data demonstrate that the number of degrees awarded to women rose each decade. To put these figures in some perspective, we have also calculated the total as a percentage of the number of women twenty-five to thirty-four years old during each decade. We see that the percentage of women receiving doctoral degrees grew from the 1920s to the 1930s, stayed essentially constant during the 1940s, grew somewhat in the 1950s, and then increased sharply in the 1960s and 1970s. This reaffirms the conclusion that while the *percentage* of doctoral degrees awarded to men rose between 1930 and the mid-1960s, there was never a period when either the absolute number of women or the percentage of young women who obtained doctoral degrees declined.

Table 2-6 also reveals changes over time in the distribution of women among the various disciplines. We see that as doctoral degrees in education gained in popularity in the 1930s and 1940s they constituted a sizeable percentage of advanced degrees received by women. The data also indicate that the *number* of women receiving advanced degrees in the humanities stayed fairly constant during the 1970s and 1980s. Thus it would be a mistake to infer from table 2-5 that women entered the humanities in unprecedented numbers during these years. Instead, the remarkable increase in the percentage of degrees in the humanities conferred on women was the result of a sizeable flight on the part of men from the field. Given the poor job prospects in the humanities during this period, it would appear that men were more likely than women to respond to market signals.

The Role of Marriage

In her paper "The Meaning of College in the Lives of American Women: The Past One-Hundred Years," Goldin (1992) argues that for the earliest cohort she studied, born around 1890, "college more often than not presented a clear set of alternatives between family and career. For most women in this group, it was one or the other, and when the selection was a career, it almost always involved teaching" (2). For the second group, born around 1930, college offered women the opportunity to have both family and paid employment. But the two "were serially scheduled. Family would come first, in terms of timing and priority, and only after would come employment" (2). Once again, the employment of choice for educated women was teaching, for teaching allowed such serial timing without a large earnings penalty. In the third group, born since 1960 and graduating after 1980, Goldin concludes that college appears to offer women the opportunity for "true equality with their male counterparts" (3). Even if one does not entirely agree with this conclusion, it is clear that this cohort is different. Women from this generation no longer focused on either career or family as the first cohort did, or on family followed by career as the second cohort did. Instead, for the most part, they combined career and family.[14]

Although Goldin studied all female college graduates, not just those who received advanced degrees, the picture she draws is nonetheless relevant to women faculty members. For the cohort born around 1890 her characterization is based on case studies and anecdotal evidence that consistently show that faculty women tended to be single. For women born in the 1850s and 1860s, however, the anecdotal evidence with regard to marriage is mixed. Alice Freeman, for example, upon falling in love with George Herbert Palmer, a widowed professor of philosophy at Harvard, stepped down as president of Wellesley in 1888 to accommodate her husband's wishes to live close to Harvard (Bordin 1993). Four years later, however, she accepted William Rainey Harper's invitation to help launch the University of Chicago. Her husband refused to join her in what one author describes as "the first big-time spousal package" in the history of academe, and Freeman commuted from Cambridge to Chicago, where she was dean of women (Woodford 1994).

It is difficult to ascertain with certainty whether women faculty members in the 1950s and 1960s serially scheduled family and career in the same manner that college-educated women did, but the evidence suggests that this was the case. Astin (1969:18), for example, finds that the median age of women who received Ph.D.'s in 1957–58 was 37. Men who completed degrees during approximately the same period were about 5 years younger (National Science Foundation 1993:151). This suggests that the cohort studied by Astin tended to have families before embarking on careers—if they had families at all. Indeed, Astin (1969:29) found that 28 percent of married women with doctorates in her sample, whose median age was 44 years at the time of the survey, had no children. Many of the women in her sample, however, did not marry. The marriage rate of the doctoral group was about half the rate reported by Goldin for her middle cohort of college graduates.[15]

A study of Radcliffe women with Ph.D.'s conducted in the early 1950s also illustrates how marital status of women faculty members differed by cohort (Radcliffe College Committee on Graduate Education for Women 1956). Of the forty-three women with Ph.D.'s who held the rank of professor, only four were married. None had children. This group, born around 1910, corresponds closely to the first cohort described by Goldin. Associate and assistant professors responding to the survey were slightly younger and more likely to have children. For example, approximately one-quarter of the thirty-five associate professors were married and several had children. Among the assistant professors, born around 1920, a third were married and a majority of these had children.

Two additional studies offer some insights into the role marriage played in the careers of highly educated women during the late 1960s and early 1970s. One is a study of ten departments at Yale University; a second is a study of faculty wives at the University of Illinois. Unlike the Astin study, however, neither focuses on a single cohort, hence their findings cannot easily be related to the framework proposed by Goldin.[16] On the other hand, they have the advantage of providing some information about what it was like to be part of an academic couple during the 1960s and early 1970s.

The study of ten departments at Yale University was conducted in the early 1970s (Weissman et al. 1973).[17] Questionnaires were sent to all wives of faculty men as well as to all women on the faculty in these departments. In all, 282 (69 percent) of the women responded. About 11 percent of the wives reported that their highest degree was a Ph.D. or an LL.B. An additional 26 percent reported having M.A. degrees, and another 21 percent reported "some graduate work." Twenty-three of the 34 faculty wives with Ph.D or LL.B. degrees had jobs in the academic sector (16 at Yale, 7 at other colleges and universities). Four of the 34 were working outside academe and 7 were not employed. None of the women employed in academe were professors, only 1 (4 percent) was an associate professor, 30 percent were assistant professors, and 48 percent held non-tenure-track faculty positions. The remainder were nonacademic employees, including 1 secretary. As many as one-third were working part-time.

There were also 13 faculty women with Ph.D.'s or LL.B.'s who were not married to faculty members. Of these, 85 percent held tenure-track positions, a significantly larger percentage than that of doctorate-holding faculty wives employed in higher education in the New Haven area.[18] The difference most likely relates in part to the lack of mobility of faculty wives holding advanced degrees.

Ferber's (1973) study of faculty wives at the University of Illinois is for approximately the same period of time and has approximately the same response rate. Unlike the Yale study, however, she investigated only women married to faculty men. Ferber found that approximately 45 percent (146) held a degree beyond the B.A. and that 25 percent (80) of the faculty wives were employed at the university, either part- or full-time, while 36 had applied for a job at the university but had not been hired and 22 reported not having applied, mainly because they assumed they had no chance of being hired. Regrettably, Ferber does not report the percentage of the wives working at the university who held faculty rank.

Although no other systematic study of faculty wives appears to have been published, it is reasonable to assume that the experiences of these women were not atypical. Louise Russert Kraemer, as we have already noted, was unable to get a full-time position at the University of Arkansas until the late 1960s, and a faculty spouse at the University of Wisconsin recounted in an interview with one of the authors that she was told by officials in 1974 that she would never be offered a position on the faculty while her husband was also on the faculty.

Case Studies of Five Institutions

To present a more complete picture of the history of women in academe we conducted five case studies of institutions of higher education. The five institutions were chosen to provide diversity on a number of dimensions. With but one exception the data for the studies come from catalogs. We recorded the name, department, rank, and degree of faculty members in all programs except medicine and law, in ten-year intervals, either from the founding of the school or at the beginning of each decade.[19] In one case, data were obtained from several sources. Gender was determined as far as possible, by examining first names, supplemented by use of interviews and reference books. Inevitably, we were not successful in all cases.

In an effort to identify academic couples for the years up to 1970, we paired individuals of the opposite sex and same last name and then made inquiries about their marital status. Although this method undercounts couples, the summary presented in table 2-7 provides some information about their incidence. Even such rough estimates, however,

TABLE 2-7. Faculty Couples

Year[a]	Agnes Scott	Arkansas	Grinnell	Illinois	Yale
1860			1		0
1870		0	1	0	0
1880		0	0	0	0
1890		0	1[b]	0	0
1900		0[b]	2	0	0
1910	0	1[b]	3	0[b]	0
1920	0	0[b]	4	0[b]	0
1930	0	0[b]	4	0[b]	1
1940	0	1[b]	3	0[b]	1[b]
1950	0	2[b]	4	—[c]	0[b]
1960	0	10[b]	5	—[c]	6[b]
1970	0	14[b]	11	—[c]	6[b]

Note: A blank cell signifies that the institution has yet to be founded.

a. Data for each institution are reported for the decade closest to the time of collection. Thus the 1933 Yale data are reported for 1930. Medical and law school faculty were not included in our case studies. This study ends in 1970 due to the emerging pattern of women retaining their maiden names after marriage.

b. Lower bound—additional possibilities may exist but could not be verified (see text).

c. The data are not available because not enough information exists in our files to draw an inference.

were not attempted for more recent years, because it became common for academic women to retain their maiden names after marriage. Before presenting the results of the case studies, we will briefly describe the five institutions, beginning with the oldest.

Yale was chartered in 1701 as a collegiate school in Killingworth, Connecticut; in 1716, after an intermediate move, it came to its permanent home in New Haven. Colleges were added during the 1800s and the institution was renamed Yale University in 1887. The first woman student enrolled at Yale in 1892 in the graduate school. Women were admitted to the undergraduate program for the first time in 1969. The institution is highly selective. The median combined SAT score for math and verbal is above 1300.

Grinnell College dates from 1846 when a group of transplanted New Englanders with strong Congregational and social-reformer backgrounds organized as the Trustees of Iowa College. The college eventually moved from Davenport, Iowa, to Grinnell, Iowa, and subsequently adopted the name of its benefactor, Josiah B. Grinnell. Women were first admitted for degree study in the 1860s. Today the college has approximately 1,200 students, a number that has been fairly stable during the past thirty-five years. Since 1910 the college has awarded only bachelor's degrees. It reports a median SAT score in the 1200s.

The University of Illinois at Urbana-Champaign is a land-grant institution that opened in 1868. A pioneer in vocational education, the university grew during the twentieth century to be one of the larger universities in the United States. Women have been enrolled there since 1870. In recent years the university has become fairly selective. The median ACT score of undergraduate students is 27, which the University equates to an SAT score in the low 1100s.

The University of Arkansas, also a land-grant institution, was established five years later than the University of Illinois, in the town of Fayetteville. It has enrolled women since its inception. The university currently has an enrollment of approximately 14,000 students with widely diverse backgrounds.

The final case study is of Agnes Scott College, a women's institution that was established by Presbyterians in Decatur, Georgia, in 1889 and became a college in 1906. Unlike many of its sister institutions, the college has remained single-sex and today has an enrollment of approximately 550 women. It attracts students primarily from the South and reports median SAT scores in the mid-1000s.

Data for each of the five institutions are presented in tables 2-8 through 2-12. For each institution we give the year, number of women, percentage of faculty that is female, number of women with a Ph.D. or equivalent, and percentage of faculty with a doctoral degree that is female. The percentage of faculty with the rank of assistant professor or higher that is female is also included. We interpret the latter figure as the percentage of tenure-track faculty members who are women.[20] Finally, the last column lists the fields, if any, in which one-quarter or more of the women faculty members were employed.

Yale University

Until the early 1800s Yale had but a handful of faculty members, most of whom held the rank of "tutor." Early in the 1800s the rank of "professor" came into use and by 1823 seven of the fifteen faculty members listed in the catalog held this rank; one faculty member had a Ph.D. The number with doctoral degrees grew slowly during most of the 1800s but increased dramatically during the last three decades of the century so that by 1903, 111 faculty members held doctorates, approximately 50 percent of the faculty. It was into such an environment that Margaretta Palmer, Ph.D., was hired in the early 1900s as an assistant in the observatory. It is fair to say that she did not start a major trend, although during the next two decades the number of women on the faculty inched upward so that by 1943, fifty years after the first woman was admitted to Yale, there were eighteen women on the faculty, or approximately one in twenty-five. Not surprisingly, women were less likely to hold Ph.D.'s than their male counterparts and slightly less likely to be in tenure-track positions.

During the 1940s, 1950s, and early 1960s the percentage of Yale faculty members who were women increased ever so slightly, even though this percentage declined nationally. On the other hand, and not unexpectedly given an undergraduate program that was exclusively male, the percentage of Yale faculty members who were women was, by national standards, minimal. This changed substantially during the late 1960s and early 1970s, no doubt in response to Yale's decision to admit undergraduate women. By 1973, almost 12 percent of the faculty was female. They were heavily concentrated in the humanities and social sciences, and they remained less likely than their male counterparts to hold doctorates or to be in tenure-track positions.

The definition of faculty included in the Yale catalog changed between

TABLE 2-8. Yale University Case Study

Year	Number of Female Faculty	Percentage of Faculty Who Were Women	Number of Faculty of Unknown Gender	Number of Women with Doctorates	Percentage of Doctorates Held by Women	Percentage Ranked Assistant Professor or Higher Who Were Women	Fields Where 25 Percent or More of Women Were Employed
1903	0	0.0	2	0	0.0	0.0	Physical sciences
1913	1	0.3	5	1	0.6	0.0	
1923	3	1.0	3	1	0.6	0.5	Education, humanities
1933	9	2.1	4	2	0.8	1.3	Education, humanities
1943	18	3.7	4	7	2.5	3.1	Education, social sciences
1953	32	4.3	21	16	3.3	2.9	Humanities, social sciences, life sciences
1963	50	5.0	39	20	2.8	2.3	Humanities
1973	127	11.9	28	56	7.0	7.4	Humanities, social sciences
1983	118	14.4	36	—[a]	—[a]	12.2	Humanities
1993	202	22.5	56	—[a]	—[a]	17.0	Humanities

Note: Data prior to 1903 are not presented because there is no evidence that women were on the faculty before this time.
a. There is no information on degrees for this year.

1973 and 1983 so that the numbers recorded for 1983 and 1993 are not strictly comparable with the earlier numbers.[21] For the data that are recorded, however, we see that the percentage of faculty that were women increased slightly during the 1970s and then grew dramatically, so that by 1993 approximately one in four were women. Faculty women, however, remained less likely than their male counterparts to be in tenure-track positions.

It is reasonably easy to study couples at Yale University in the first years that women were on the faculty because the catalog gives addresses. We are thus fairly certain that 1933 is the first time a faculty couple was employed at Yale during one of the years we examined. In that year, Walter R. Miles and Catharine C. Miles, living at the same address, were professor of psychology and clinical professor of psychology, respectively. Both had Ph.D.'s. They were still on the faculty in 1943 and Catharine Miles remained on the faculty in 1953 after her husband had retired and become a professor emeritus. Unfortunately, in the 1940s and 1950s addresses were no longer provided in the catalogs, and we were unsuccessful in locating anyone with memory of the period to assist us. There are, however, several instances of faculty members of opposite gender with the same, somewhat uncommon, name, leading us to suspect that additional couples were employed at Yale during those years.

For 1963 and 1973 we were assisted by an emeritus professor at Yale University. With his help, we were able to definitely identify six couples employed in 1963.[22] In four of the instances the husband was in a tenure-track position; the wife was not. In three of these instances the wife did not have a doctoral degree. In one instance both the husband and the wife were in non-tenure-track positions and both reported "B.A." as their highest degree.[23] Only in one instance did both partners hold tenure-track positions: he was the C. Seymour Professor of History and she was an associate professor of history.

We also identified six couples at Yale in 1973. In one instance both were assistant professors in the sciences and both eventually became full professors. In another instance the husband was a chaired professor, the wife a senior lecturer who subsequently received tenure. In two of the other four cases the husband held the title of professor and the wife had a non-tenure-track title, while in the remaining two instances neither spouse was in a tenure-track position, although in both instances the husband was listed as a "senior lecturer," the wife as a "lecturer."

Grinnell College

In the early years of Grinnell's history, the position of women paralleled fairly closely the national pattern shown in table 2-1. The college, which had only a handful of faculty members, employed several women, usually in the "Ladies' Department," the women's division of the college, which offered a slightly watered-down curriculum on the assumption that the classics and higher math were too difficult for women. None of the women held the rank of assistant professor or higher. The only woman on the faculty during the first forty years who had a Ph.D. was Martha Crow, who was head of the Ladies' Department and herself a classicist.

From 1890 until the 1930s, Grinnell employed a significantly larger proportion of women faculty members than the national average. During most of these years almost one in three Grinnell faculty members were women and, with the exception of 1910, approximately one in six of the faculty members who had Ph.D.'s were women. Many of these women taught in the humanities; several taught in education. Although the proportion of women gradually declined, Grinnell continued to employ a significant number of women faculty members in 1930, 1940, and 1950.

The national decline in the proportion of faculty who were women that occurred in midcentury was modest, as table 2-1 will attest. The decline at Grinnell that occurred during the 1950s was not modest, and by 1960 the college had cut almost in half the number of women on the faculty. This was, no doubt, partly the result of the decision to improve quality by hiring a larger number of persons with Ph.D.'s. In all likelihood the move also reflected the social values of the times. During the 1960s the college began to hire more women, but their proportion remained considerably below the national average. Furthermore, few of the women hired held Ph.D.'s, nor did they have tenure-track status. Many were part-time faculty members, teaching laboratory sections, music lessons, and modern languages. By 1980, however, the college had made a substantial change and had hired a large number of women with doctorates. By 1990 women not only constituted slightly more than one-third of the faculty but were also almost equally well-represented among faculty members with doctoral degrees and with tenure-track positions.

Almost from the beginning, Grinnell College had a history of employing faculty couples (see table 2-7). The first couple on the Grinnell fac-

TABLE 2-9. Grinnell College Case Study

Year	Number of Female Faculty	Percentage of Faculty Who Were Women	Number of Faculty of Unknown Gender	Number of Women with Doctorates	Percentage of Doctorates Held by Women	Percentage Ranked Assistant Professor or Higher Who Were Women	Fields Where 25 Percent or More of Women Were Employed
1849	0	0.0	0	—[a]	—[a]	0.0	Other
1860	1	20.0	0	0	[b]	0.0	Other
1870	2	14.3	0	0	0.0	0.0	Unknown
1880	5	27.8	0	0	0.0	0.0	Humanities
1890	7	25.0	0	1	20.0	0.0	Humanities
1900	11	32.4	0	1	14.3	5.9	Humanities, unknown
1910	17	29.8	0	1	7.7	7.4	Humanities
1920	25	32.9	0	4	17.4	14.3	Humanities
1930	20	31.3	0	3	16.7	17.8	Humanities
1940	20	28.2	0	2	9.5	17.5	Humanities, education
1950	29	27.9	0	3	9.4	18.8	Humanities, education
1960	15	15.5	0	3	5.3	8.9	Humanities, education
1970	22	17.3	0	5	7.4	9.8	Humanities
1980	43	29.9	0	25	24.5	24.3	Humanities
1990	69	36.1	0	49	33.3	31.9	Humanities

a. There is no information on degrees for this year.
b. No faculty at Grinnell College had a Ph.D. or its equivalent in 1860.

ulty was the Parkers, who were listed in the 1860 catalog and constituted, between them, 40 percent of the Grinnell faculty. He was a professor of ancient languages and she was head of the Ladies' Department; both were graduates of Oberlin College. Martha Crow, the first woman with a Ph.D. at Grinnell, succeeded Candace Parker as head of the Ladies' Department. Her husband was also on the faculty, albeit not in one of the years we examined. After his death, she left Grinnell in 1891 for a position at the University of Chicago (Nollen 1953). In addition to the Crows and the Parkers, several other couples were on the college faculty during these early years.

By 1910 the college was employing three couples; for the next fifty years it continued to have in its employ three to five couples at any given time. During most of these years couples constituted between an eighth and a tenth of the faculty. In most instances the wife did not have a Ph.D. or a tenure-track position; often she was part-time. Most presumably had accompanied their husbands to Grinnell. This pattern continued through 1970, the end point of our historical study of couples. Exceptions, however, existed. For example, Clara Millerd, Ph.D. and professor of the history of philosophy, originally came to the college in 1896. Some twenty years later she met and married her husband, Johan Smertenko, the director of publicity at Grinnell. He was briefly on the faculty, listed as an instructor in journalism. Eventually they took positions at the University of Chicago. Laetitia Moon Conrad is another exception. She received her Ph.D. from Chicago and was appointed to the Grinnell faculty in 1926. By 1930, she was married to a professor of botany who had been on the faculty since 1906. During the 1930s she ran for governor of the state of Iowa on the socialist ticket.

University of Illinois

Data for the University of Illinois were collected in a somewhat different manner than for the other case studies. For the early years, data were taken from a directory of all persons who had been on the faculty at the university from its founding until 1918 (Scott 1918). For 1928 and 1938, data were obtained from university directories, and for the later years we used data collected by the university.

Although the University of Illinois did not have a woman on the faculty at the time of its founding, within ten years one woman had been hired in the humanities. By 1898 5 of the 49 faculty members were women. None held a doctoral degree. The university grew significantly dur-

TABLE 2-10. University of Illinois Case Study

Year	Number of Female Faculty	Percentage of Faculty Who Were Women	Number of Faculty of Unknown Gender	Number of Women with Doctorates	Percentage of Doctorates Held by Women	Percentage Ranked Assistant Professor or Higher Who Were Women	Fields Where 25 Percent or More of Women Were Employed
1868	0	0.0	0	0	[a]	0.0	
1878	1	8.3	0	0	0.0	0.0	Humanities
1888	1	5.6	0	0	0.0	0.0	Humanities
1898	5	10.2	0	0	0.0	6.9	Humanities
1908	20	11.1	0	2	3.2	3.8	Humanities, agricultural sciences[b]
1918	29	10.0	7	3	3.6	0.9	Humanities, agricultural sciences[b]
1928	70	14.9	0	15	6.8	5.4	Humanities
1938	85	12.1	0	29	7.6	7.3	Humanities
1950[c]	177	15.8	0	—	—	9.0	Education
1975[c]	342	13.1	0	—	—	8.5	Humanities
1990[c]	765	24.6	0	—	—	14.2	Humanities

a. No faculty had a Ph.D. or its equivalent in 1868.

b. Agricultural sciences include home economics.

c. The data do not give accurate totals. In 1950 faculty members with appointments in more than one college were counted more than once. In 1975 and 1990 faculty members with appointments in more than one department were counted more than once and a broader definition of "faculty" was used than was used for the earlier data. Where possible we tried to eliminate any noninstructional faculty and any faculty who appeared to have been counted more than once. At best the data for these later years provide rough estimates, and the percentages may be biased downward. No degree information is available for any of the later years.

ing the first three decades of the twentieth century. During these years a substantial number of women were hired, so that by 1928, 70 of the 471 faculty members were women, 15 of them with Ph.D.'s or the equivalent. One was Louise Dunbar, who was hired by the history department in 1920 and remained on the faculty until she retired in 1962 as an assistant professor of history (Treichler 1985:20).

The expansion of the university continued during the depression years of the 1930s. During this period the percentage of women declined; since almost all the women hired had doctoral degrees, the number with such degrees almost doubled. The fact that a similar, although less pronounced, trend existed at Yale leads us to believe that the relatively large number of women who received Ph.D.'s in the 1920s and 1930s produced market conditions that made women attractive employees for these institutions.

The summary data available for the years 1950–90 unfortunately do not provide information regarding doctoral degrees, nor do they produce accurate total counts, because faculty members with joint appointments were counted more than once. Therefore, we have only rough estimates for that period. The percentages should, however, be reasonably accurate unless there is a systematic relationship between multiple appointments and gender.

The number of female faculty members rose steadily but modestly from 1950 into the 1970s. After that, the proportion of women increased more rapidly, so that by 1990 almost one in four faculty members at the University of Illinois was female. Women also began to be more evenly distributed among academic disciplines during this period and the number of women in tenure-track positions increased as well, even though the total number of such positions for the whole faculty decreased.

We cannot say anything about faculty couples at the University of Illinois for the period 1950 forward because the information provided to us by the university did not contain last names. The data for the period 1908–38 contain twenty-three instances of two faculty members of opposite gender and same last name. In almost all cases the names are too common to warrant the inference that they were married. In one instance, however, in 1938, the match appears plausible, suggesting that there was at least one faculty couple employed by the university at that time. There is no indication that the University of Illinois employed any faculty couples prior to 1908.

University of Arkansas

The early history of women at the University of Arkansas is difficult to study because during several periods only initials, rather than full first names, were recorded for many faculty members. We were, nonetheless, able to glean some information. First, we know that two of the original nine faculty members were women. Both were in the field of education. Second, we know that in its early years the university had no faculty member with a Ph.D., but by 1900 the university had hired six, constituting 14 percent of the faculty. None were women although women constituted over a third of the faculty. Most of the women taught in the humanities.

This proved to be the high-water mark for women at the university, at least in terms of proportions. From 1900 until 1940 each successive decade witnessed a decline in the percentage of women, so that by 1950 only one in eight faculty members were women. Thus, compared with the country as a whole, the University of Arkansas started out employing a disproportionately large number of women but by the 1920s was employing a lower proportion than the national average. This situation has persisted to the present. In the most recent period of observation, only 17 percent of the faculty were women compared with 29 percent nationally.[24]

Compared with other institutions, the University of Arkansas was slow to hire women with Ph.D.'s. The first, Margaret Rose Richter, an instructor in English, appears in the 1930 data, by which time 42 of the faculty men had Ph.D.'s. A decade later the number of men with Ph.D.'s had almost doubled; the number of women remained at 1. By 1950 5 of the women on the faculty had doctorates. One was in the social sciences, 1 in education, and 3 in home economics. The number doubled during the next ten years but remained small by most standards. Since then, the number of women with doctorates has continued to increase so that by 1990, 87 of the 135 women faculty members at Arkansas held doctoral degrees. Nearly a quarter of these were in the college of education, although women with doctorates were employed throughout the university, including departments in the physical sciences and in engineering.

We were able to identify four faculty couples at the University of Arkansas during the first half of the twentieth century, one each in 1910 and 1940, two in 1950.[25] None of the women held a tenure-track position, nor did any have a Ph.D. By 1960 there were at least ten couples. In two of these cases both partners were in tenure-track positions. In

TABLE 2-11. University of Arkansas Case Study

Year	Number of Female Faculty	Percentage of Faculty Who Were Women	Number of Faculty of Unknown Gender	Number of Women with Doctorates	Percentage of Doctorates Held by Women	Percentage Ranked Assistant Professor or Higher Who Were Women	Fields Where 25 Percent or More of Women Were Employed
1873	2	22.2	0	0	[a]	0.0	Education
1880	3	20.0	2[b]	0	[a]	0.0	Other, humanities
1890	1	5.3	7[b]	—	—	0.0	Humanities
1900	16	36.4	0	0	0.0	0.0	Humanities
1910	14	20.0	4[b]	0	0.0	0.0	Humanities
1920	16	18.2	3	0	0.0	5.4	Humanities, education, agricultural sciences[c]
1930	20	14.4	0	1	2.3	7.9	Humanities, education, agricultural sciences[c]
1940	20	11.9	0	1	1.3	7.5	Education, agricultural sciences[c]
1950	46	12.8	1	5	4.0	7.8	Education
1960	67	14.7	3	10	4.4	8.7	Education
1970	107	16.1	11	28	7.3	10.4	Humanities, education
1980	119	15.8	8	69	12.1	13.6	Education
1990	135	17.4	10	87	13.9	15.3	Education

a. No faculty had a Ph.D. or the equivalent in 1873 or 1880.
b. There were several cases for which only initials were reported and archival research could not determine gender.
c. Agricultural sciences include home economics.

another instance, the wife held a tenure-track position and the husband did not. By 1970, fourteen couples could definitely be identified, with seven of the women in tenure-track positions. In one of these instances, the wife was an assistant professor, the husband an instructor.

Agnes Scott

Women faculty have always been in the majority at Agnes Scott College, but the role that they have played has changed substantially over time. At the time Agnes Scott became a college, twelve faculty members were women, six were men. Only one of the women had a doctorate, while two of the men did. As the college expanded, it hired significantly more women, keeping the number of men fairly constant. Not surprisingly, a large number of the women were single and lived in housing provided by the college. Many of the women hired by Agnes Scott during this period also had Ph.D.'s, so that by 1930 twelve of the thirty-eight women on the faculty had doctorates.

In the 1950s Agnes Scott began to make significant changes in its hiring practices. Elite women's colleges had started to hire increasing numbers of men ten years earlier (see table 2-2), arguably as a status-seeking device, and Agnes Scott joined the trend. An attempt to hire a larger proportion of faculty with doctoral degrees may also have played a part in the college's hiring decisions, since the number of faculty with doctoral degrees increased dramatically during this period. The widespread availability of women with Ph.D.'s and the fact that Agnes Scott appears to have practically had a "quota" on the number of women on the faculty during this period, however, makes one question this explanation.

The decline in the percentage of faculty who were women continued throughout the 1960s and 1970s. By 1980 approximately the same number of women were on the faculty at Agnes Scott as in 1950, despite the fact that the size of the faculty had risen dramatically during the period. Then in the 1980s, in response to declining enrollments, the college decided to downsize. During this time the few faculty members hired were more likely to be female than male, with the result that by 1990 the percentage of women faculty members had begun to increase. Although the percentage of the faculty who were female remained lower than it had been at the time the college was founded, by 1990 women were as well represented among tenure-track faculty members and those with doctorates as they were on the faculty at large. The college's first woman president was appointed in 1982.

TABLE 2-12. Agnes Scott College

Year	Number of Female Faculty	Percentage of Faculty Who Were Women	Number of Faculty of Unknown Gender	Number of Women with Doctorates	Percentage of Doctorates Held by Women	Percentage Ranked Assistant Professor or Higher Who Were Women	Fields Where 25 Percent or More of Women Were Employed
1906	12	66.7	0	1	33.3	—[a]	Humanities
1910	17	77.3	0	1	33.3	64.3	Humanities
1920	31	77.5	0	4	66.7	73.1	Humanities
1930	38	80.9	0	12	70.6	77.8	Humanities
1940	38	76.0	0	15	71.4	71.4	Humanities
1950	47	77.0	0	18	66.7	69.8	Humanities
1960	47	65.3	0	26	63.4	61.9	Humanities
1970	49	58.3	1	34	59.6	57.9	Humanities
1980	45	52.3	1	28	46.7	47.7	Humanities
1990	38	55.1	0	32	53.3	53.1	Humanities

a. There is no information on rank in 1906.

The task of studying faculty couples at Agnes Scott is quite easy because an unwritten rule at the college effectively forbade the employment of spouses (at faculty rank or in any other position) until the early 1970s,[26] although in the mid-1960s when two long-time faculty members married the college did not require either to resign. Twenty-five years after the rule was discontinued, the college had yet to recruit a faculty couple. The two couples on the faculty in 1990 met and married while at Agnes Scott. All four people held tenure-track positions.

Summary

The case studies are a good reminder that what is true in the aggregate need not be true of an individual institution. Not one of the five institutions was typical as defined by national averages except Grinnell, and then for only a few years. During other periods the college employed either relatively more women than the national average or relatively fewer. The University of Arkansas had a large percentage of women in its early years, but by the 1920s was below the national norm, a situation that persists today. Illinois has always hired proportionately fewer women than the national average. So has Yale, although in this instance what is surprising is that the college employed as many women as it did when it did not admit women as undergraduates. The case study of Agnes Scott reminds us that it was at women's colleges that educated women were likely to make their mark. During several decades this small college in Decatur, Georgia, employed, in *absolute* terms, consistently more women with doctorates than did Yale, the University of Arkansas, and Grinnell College combined.

The studies also suggest that institutions have often hired men with Ph.D.'s ostensibly in an attempt to raise "quality." This appears to have been the case at Grinnell College in the 1950s and 1960s, as well as at Agnes Scott (and other women's colleges). This quality rationale may also explain the fate of women at the University of Arkansas, where they constituted a sizeable percentage of the faculty when the university had no faculty members with doctoral degrees, but a substantially smaller percentage when the institution joined the mainstream of higher education and began hiring people with Ph.D.'s in the early decades of the twentieth century. The quality argument should, of course, not be oversold, because institutions could have upgraded by hiring women with Ph.D.'s as well. Instead, this may have provided a convenient excuse for seeking the higher status often associated with men.

With regard to faculty couples, our research shows, first of all, that they are not an invention of the twentieth century. Couples were employed at Grinnell College in the nineteenth century and, anecdotal evidence suggests, at the University of Chicago. At Grinnell, the wives typically had less formal education than their husbands and were often in part-time positions. Exceptions existed, however, in which the wife either had the same or more education than her husband and held equal or higher rank. Most of the wives appear to have been hired after their husbands were established on the faculty, although in some instances, particularly when the woman had a Ph.D., the couples met and married after both had faculty status. In some other instances, however, such as at the University of Chicago, couples appear to have been actively recruited.

Second, the case studies suggest that during the first half of the twentieth century faculty couples were rarely employed at public or single-sex institutions of higher education in the United States. The low marriage rates of women with Ph.D.'s provides only part of the explanation; there were also conscious policies against hiring couples, and not merely at Agnes Scott. The case studies also suggest that around the middle of the century it became slightly more acceptable to employ faculty couples. Generally only one spouse was in a tenure-track position, and that was usually the man. Exceptions, however, did exist. Finally, the case studies show that by the 1970s faculty couples were becoming somewhat more common, as were instances in which both partners held tenure-track positions. This proved to be a prelude to the present situation, discussed at some length in later chapters in this volume.

Notes

Case studies such as these could never have been completed without the help of numerous persons. We wish to express our special thanks to Bertie Bond, Rosemary Thomas Cunningham, Victor Erlich, Deborah Gautier, Marianne Ferber, Claudia Goldin, Sona Hoisington, Wenbing Jü, Louise Russert Kraemer, Allison Levin, Mollie Merrick, Cynthia Richmond, Andrea Saposnik, Ethel Simpson, Margaret and Stephen Stephan, Joseph Wall, and Tony Wappel. Janet Keene coded over nine thousand records cheerfully and accurately. Marianne Ferber and Jane Loeb made useful comments on an earlier version of this chapter. Bill Amis, as usual, has made numerous helpful suggestions. Financial support for this research was provided by the Policy Research Center and the College of Business Administration, Georgia State University.

1. Information concerning the career of Louise Russert Kraemer was gathered through interviews and from catalogs of the University of Arkansas. Louise Russert Kraemer received her Ph.D. from the University of Michigan in 1966, eighteen years after coming to the University of Arkansas.

2. It is also true that during this period there were few married women with Ph.D.'s in the sciences.

3. John Hopkins did not permit women to earn degrees but in exceptional cases did allow women to read for courses.

4. Goldin (1990), however, argues that women's labor force participation was understated during the last part of the nineteenth century. Thus, the differences may be less pronounced than they appear in table 2-1.

5. The data in table 2-1 are not strictly comparable to those of table 2-3 since table 2-1 includes part-time faculty and table 2-3 does not. Also, for 1969–70 forward table 2-1 includes only faculty with the rank of instructor or above.

6. The ratios of table 2-3 are distinct from those of table 2-1 because of a different definition of "faculty."

7. M. Carey Thomas (the M. stood for Martha, informally Minnie, which she dropped as a student in favor of the gender-neutral Carey) was educated at Cornell as an undergraduate and received her doctorate at Zurich in 1882. She wanted very much to be president of Bryn Mawr when the college was founded but, although the trustees were reportedly sympathetic, her tender age of twenty-seven was an impediment as was the question of her loyalty to Quaker principles (Bernard 1964:19).

8. Ph.D. recipients were reported in the census annually for the period 1870–1910. The gender composition is given only at ten-year intervals and then only for that year's recipients.

9. The Survey of Earned Doctorates is administered by the National Research Council. Funding for the survey comes from five federal agencies. Data for the pre-1958 records were collected by the National Research Council from graduation records.

10. The percentages fluctuated somewhat from year to year but the three highest years during the first four decades were 1925 (17 percent), 1929 (17 percent), and 1932 (16 percent).

11. The number of doctorates awarded to men in the United States doubled between 1940 and 1950, then rose by another 50 percent in the next five years (Survey of Earned Doctorates:unpublished tables).

12. The number of doctoral degrees in education began to decline in the early 1980s, no doubt due to declining school enrollments (Survey of Earned Doctorates:unpublished tables).

13. Between 1973 and 1985 the number of doctoral degrees awarded annually to men decreased from 27,754 to 20,553. During the same period the number of degrees awarded to women increased from 5,287 to 10,744 (Survey of Earned Doctorates:unpublished tables).

14. Goldin's data suggest that the cohort that graduated from 1970 to 1980 tried the route of career first and then family.

15. Astin reports that 45 percent were married at the time of the interview; when she includes formerly married women the percentage increases to 55. It should also be noted that 8 percent of the 1957–58 women with Ph.D.'s were nuns. Goldin reports that 18 percent of the group of women that graduated from college between 1948 and 1957 never married.

16. Even the Astin and Goldin studies are not strictly comparable. The former defines a cohort in terms of date of receipt of the Ph.D., the latter in terms of date of birth.

17. The ten departments sampled were political science, psychology, history, English, chemistry, mathematics, music (school and department), the School of Art and Architecture, the Law School, and the Department of Surgery, School of Medicine.

18. The null hypothesis that the proportions are equal can be rejected at the 99 percent confidence level (Chi square= 8.28).

19. Unfortunately, the types of jobs classified as faculty positions vary over time and among institutions, especially during the earlier years. In general, the definition of "faculty" tended to become more restrictive over time. More detailed information on these issues may be obtained from the authors.

20. The table also reports the number of individuals whose gender is unknown. Overall, this rate was 1 percent. The discussion which follows, therefore, in all likelihood, slightly undercounts women.

21. Many non-tenure-track positions were either eliminated or not reported, since the number of positions classified as lecturer or instructor in the Yale catalog declined in 1983 by about 100. The number of assistant and associate professors, however, also declined.

22. Three of the six couples eventually divorced. Note that our findings are different from those reported in the study by Weissman et al. (1973) because we did not include either the law school or the medical school.

23. In this instance the husband was an instructor; the wife was a lecturer.

24. The nadir was reached, however, twenty years earlier at the University of Arkansas than for the nation, most likely because a relatively large number of women were hired there during the rapid expansion of the institution between 1940 and 1960.

25. Information for the period 1940–70 was obtained from a professor emeritus and his wife. Quite possibly, two or three additional couples were on the faculty prior to that period, but we do not have enough information to be certain.

26. In a letter, now in the archives of Agnes Scott College, Lee B. Copple stated that he had not really thought that Dr. Alston would consider employing two persons from the same family because this had previously been thought to be against the rules. As it turned out, however, he could find no such ruling in print and decided not to raise the question.

Bibliography

Astin, Helen S. 1969. *The Woman Doctorate in America.* New York: Russell Sage
Foundation.
————. 1973. "Career Profiles of Women Doctorates." In *Academic Women on
the Move,* ed. Alice S. Rossi and Ann Calderwood, 139–61. New York: Rus-
sell Sage Foundation.
Bernard, Jessie. 1964. *Academic Women.* University Park: Pennsylvania Univer-
sity Press.
Bordin, Ruth. 1993. *Alice Freeman Palmer: The Evolution of a New Woman.* Ann
Arbor: University of Michigan Press.
CITIBASE: Citibank Economic Database (machine-readable magnetic data
file), 1946–Present. 1978. New York: Citibank, N.A.
College Entrance Examination Board. 1993. *The College Handbook, 1994.* 31st ed.
New York: College Entrance Examination Board.
Ferber, Marianne A. 1973. "Educational and Employment Survey of University
Faculty Wives: A Case Study." *Sociological Focus* 6 (Spring): 95–106.
Goldin, Claudia. 1990. *Understanding the Gender Gap: An Economic History of
American Women.* New York: Oxford University Press.
————. 1992. "The Meaning of College in the Lives of American Women: The
Past One-Hundred Years." NBER Working Paper no. 4099.
National Science Foundation. 1993. *Science and Engineering Doctorates: 1960–
91.* NSF 93–301, Detailed Statistical Tables. Washington, D.C.
Nollen, John S. 1953. *Grinnell College.* Iowa City: State Historical Society of Iowa.
Radcliffe College Committee on Graduate Education for Women. 1956. *Grad-
uate Education for Women, the Radcliffe Ph.D.: A Report by a Faculty Trustee
Committee.* Cambridge: Harvard University Press.
Riesman, David. 1964. "Introduction." In *Academic Women,* by Jessie Bernard,
xv–xxv. University Park: Pennsylvania University Press.
Schmidt, George Paul. 1953. "Colleges in Ferment." *American Historical Review*
59 (1): 19–42.
Scott, Franklin W., ed. 1918. *The Alumni Record, University of Illinois.* Urbana:
University of Illinois.
Survey of Earned Doctorates, sponsored by National Science Foundation (NSF),
National Institutes of Health (NIH), U.S. Department of Education
(USED), National Endowment for the Humanities (NEH), and the U.S.
Department of Agriculture (USDA) and conducted by the National Re-
search Council (NRC). Doctorate Records File.
Treichler, Paula A. 1985. "Alma Mater's Sorority: Women and the University of
Illinois, 1890–1925." In *For Alma Mater: Theory and Practice in Feminist
Scholarship,* ed. Paula A. Treichler, Cheris Kramarae, and Beth Stafford, 5–
61. Urbana: University of Illinois Press.
U.S. Bureau of the Census. 1975. *Historical Statistics of the United States, Colo-*

nial Times to 1970, Bicentennial Edition, Part 1. Washington, D.C: GPO.

——. 1993. *Statistical Abstract of the United States.* 113th ed. Washington, D.C.: GPO.

U.S. Department of Education, National Center for Education Statistics. 1976–93. *Digest of Education Statistics.* Washington, D.C.: GPO.

Vetter Betty M., and Eleanor L. Babco. 1975. *Professional Women and Minorities: A Manpower Data Resource Service.* Washington, D.C.: Scientific Manpower Commission.

——. 1987. *Professional Women and Minorities: A Manpower Data Resource Service.* 7th ed. Washington, D.C.: Commission on Professionals in Science and Technology.

Weissman, Myrna M., Katherine Nelson, Judith Hackman, Cynthia Pincus, and Brigitte Prusoff. 1973. "The Faculty Wife: Her Academic Interests and Qualifications." In *Academic Women on the Move,* ed. Alice S. Rossi and Ann Calderwood, 187–95. New York: Russell Sage Foundation.

Woodford, John. 1994. "Alice Freeman Palmer, Class of 1876: A New Woman of the Nineteenth Century." *Michigan Today* 26 (2): 2–3.

3

For the Good of the Race: Married African-American Academics— A Historical Perspective

Linda M. Perkins

The personal and professional challenges of being a spouse in a dual-career marriage have become a recent concern in American society. Such marriages can alter and limit career choices and mobility and their very nature affects their quality. This issue has become particularly acute in academe. Increasingly, marriages among academics have resulted in challenges for many institutions of higher education in recruiting and retaining faculty members. One study has indicated that in more than half of all commuting marriages both partners are academics (Hileman 1990:120).

Although commuting marriages may appear to be a recent phenomenon, among African Americans they have a long history. That many African-American women had to work out of economic necessity is well known, but little has been written on the many highly educated African-American professional women whose motivation for higher education and employment was driven by a desire to make a contribution to their race. The notion of "race uplift" from the devastation of slavery and its aftermath fueled the professional ambitions of many African Americans, particularly women, throughout the nineteenth century and in the early twentieth century. These women worked in various areas of social and educational "uplift" in the nineteenth century and by the twentieth century were found on the growing faculties of many black colleges and universities.

This chapter will focus upon the historical differences in gender roles and expectations within the African-American community from those of the larger society and the impact these differences had upon African-American dual-career marriages within higher education. Although gender role expectations within the African-American community began to reflect those of the larger society during the twentieth century, African Americans recognized the need for and largely supported the employment of women. In this chapter, I will discuss the numerous examples of African-American academic couples who taught, published, and worked together for a lifetime. These visible couples on black college campuses throughout the South served as role models for thousands of African-American youths. This chapter will also discuss several African-American academic women who were married to professional men and the impact dual careers had upon their marriages.

Slavery and the Formation of a More Egalitarian Ethos on Gender

The institution of slavery dramatically diminished the prevalence of patriarchy within the slave quarter community. Researchers have frequently remarked upon the interdependence of its members.[1] This interdependence continued to be stressed after slavery. To advance from the economic and educational devastation of slavery and its aftermath, African Americans stressed that the talents of all of its members were needed for the advancement and "uplift" of the race. Thus, during a period when women of the larger society were socialized to be emotionally and financially dependent upon men and to focus their attention upon the home, African-American women were socialized to believe that the entire race was their family. Thus, they understood their role in society and within their home to be for the good of the race.

African Americans were generally not allowed to have the same gender roles and expectations that whites had. Slavery and the subsequent legalized segregation of education and employment after Emancipation often deprived African-American men of the opportunity to assume the role of sole financial providers or even to be considered heads of their families. In addition African-American women during the nineteenth century were not included in the notion of "true womanhood" that depicted women as fragile and helpless.[2] Far from being fragile and helpless, African-American women had worked side by side with their men in the fields and after slavery shouldered an important responsibility for the economic well-being of their families. As the society at large created separate "spheres" for men and women in the nineteenth century, gender roles among African Americans were often blurred.

By the midnineteenth century African-American women were motivated by the notion of "racial uplift" and continued to work. Thus, after the abolition of slavery and due to some gains following emancipation, a small but steady number of African-American women were able to obtain enough education to move into the professional class and become teachers and activists.

The First Generation of College-Educated Women

The first generation of educated white women were portrayed as virtual freaks of nature and unmarriageable. The notable Harvard Medical School emeritus professor Edward Clarke used "scientific" research in a seminal study in 1873 entitled *Sex in Education* to demonstrate the negative impact higher education would have upon women. Clarke claimed such education would destroy both the reproductive and nervous systems of women. This study was so widely read that it went through seventeen printings. "Scientific" studies were also undertaken by noted scholars to "prove" that all African Americans, like white women, were physiologically and intellectually inferior to white males (Clarke 1873).

In addition to believing that higher education was physically and psychologically damaging to women, most people accepted that there was no utility in a woman obtaining a college degree; after she married she would not use it. Many historians of women's higher education have responded to the question, "After college, what?" In an important article on this topic, Antler (1980) analyzes the lives of white women graduates of the late nineteenth century who attended Seven Sister Colleges. In reviewing the lives of the 142 members of the class of 1897 of Wellesley College, she noted that only 1 of these women, a physician, worked after marriage.[3] The prevailing view within white middle-class America was that a married woman did not work outside the home. Even for those college educated white women who were unmarried but middle class during the late nineteenth century, working was not encouraged in most instances except when financially necessary. Antler quotes a 1910 Bryn Mawr graduate who reveals that even into the twentieth century this view prevailed among many members of the middle class. After college, she noted, a young woman was expected "to stay at home, help one's mother entertain, perhaps take a course in domestic science—these things were taken for granted. Anything more adventurous would have seemed out of the question" (1980:170).

During this same period, African Americans were seeking to obtain educational opportunities and build educational institutions for the entire race. The African-American press urged the education of all members of the race, both male and female. Thus, as small numbers of African-American women matriculated and graduated from institutions of higher learning in the North from 1860 through the 1880s, the African-American press and communities celebrated and counted their successes as achievements for the race.

For example, when Fanny Jackson graduated from Oberlin College in 1865, she was welcomed with great enthusiasm by the Philadelphia African-American community. Jackson went to Philadelphia to head the Female Department of the prestigious African-American classical high school, the Institute for Colored Youth. Although founded by Quakers this institution always had a faculty of highly educated African Americans. By 1869, Jackson was principal of the entire school (Perkins 1987).

That Fanny Jackson was appointed to head this coeducational high school with prominent male faculty members was a significant achievement. The all-white male Quaker board of managers recognized her brilliance as a teacher and her effectiveness and dedication as a leader and appointed her to head the institute without regard to her gender. Whether this decision to appoint a woman was an act of enlightenment or simply another example of white men viewing African Americans in general as different from whites is unclear. The board itself remained all male throughout Fanny Jackson's tenure as principal.

In December 1881, Fanny Jackson married Levi Coppin, a minister of the African Methodist Episcopal church. Although they met in Philadelphia, he was transferred prior to their marriage to a church in Baltimore. The Quaker board clearly expected Fanny Jackson Coppin to resign her position and even prematurely announced her resignation in the newspaper. However, she remained principal until her retirement in 1903. Members of the board of managers apparently never demanded that she relinquish her position, probably because they were fully aware that the school was her life. In fact, in Philadelphia the institute was often referred to as "Mrs. Coppin's School" (Isaac 1976). No doubt the board members were also impressed with Coppin's gifts as an educator. Her dedication to the African-American community of Philadelphia and the nation was indisputable. Devoted to the mission and the belief in "race uplift," Coppin noted in her autobiography that the purpose of her education was to "help her people" (1913:17).

Coppin met her husband at an event she had sponsored in Philadelphia to keep an African-American newspaper from bankruptcy. By all accounts, the Coppins' marriage was a strong and committed one. The couple had a commuting marriage for nearly four years until Levi was assigned a church in Philadelphia. More than a century ago, the commuting marriage, now considered a new phenomenon, was accepted by them. Fanny dedicated her weekdays to the work of the institute and commuted to Baltimore on the weekends to participate in the activities of her husband's church. Although her husband rose through the ranks of the AME church to the position of bishop and was required to travel through his districts to visit churches all year, Coppin remained committed to the institute during the school year and spent summers traveling with her husband. Bishop Coppin fully supported his wife's efforts and was extremely proud of her accomplishments on behalf of the race.[4]

The Coppins' marriage was not unique. There were many other African-American couples active in civil rights, social uplift, and educational activities. Another Oberlin-educated African-American woman, Mary Church, married Harvard-educated Robert Terrell in 1891, the year the Coppins married. Mary Church Terrell was required to resign her teaching position in Washington, D.C., as was the law for married women in the district. Thereafter she concentrated her efforts on the civil rights of African Americans and women. She rose to prominence as the first president of the National Association of Colored Women (1896); was appointed to the board of education in the District of Columbia (1895), the first African-American woman in the nation to hold such a position; and was one of the founding members of the National Association for the Advancement of Colored People. She was an active and influential suffragist and was a popular and effective public speaker throughout the nation and the world (Terrell 1968). Phyllis, her daughter, recalled that her father was extremely proud of her mother and encouraged her activities. He believed that her privileged education demanded that she speak out on behalf of the race (Langston 1980). On this point Mary Church Terrell did not have to be convinced. She stated that the purpose of her education was to "promote the welfare of [her] race" (Terrell 1968:60).

Ida B. Wells, an anti-lynching crusader, a journalist, and a women's rights activist, and Ferdinand Barnett, an attorney and a founder and editor of the *Chicago Conservator,* married in 1895 and soon became another prominent African-American couple on the national scene. As was true of Fanny Jackson Coppin, matrimony did not disrupt Ida B. Wells's professional activities. Wells was such a highly sought after public speaker that she had to change her wedding date three times because of conflicts with her schedule and lectured up to a week before the event. The couple had a baby the first year after their marriage, and when the child was four months old Ida Wells Barnett went back on the road to fulfill her engagements. She took the baby on her trips, nursed him, and brought a nurse along to help care for him. When the child was six months old, Barnett was offered a position with the Illinois State Central Committee of the Republican party to lecture throughout the state on voting rights for women. She continued to nurse her son and take him along on her travels. The Illinois State Central Committee provided nurses for her baby in each city in which she spoke, as had been agreed when she accepted the position. Barnett recalled years later that she was perhaps the only woman in America who traveled with a nursing baby to give political speeches (Duster 1970).

Barnett had four children and managed to juggle all of her political and professional interests with obligations to her family. She noted that her suffragist friend Susan B. Anthony did not approve of her marriage. Anthony believed that marriage was fine for certain women but thought Barnett had a "special call for special work" and that marriage would disrupt her mission and result in a "divided duty" (Duster 1970).

Combined, Not Divided Duties

Combined rather than divided duties was how most African-American women viewed their work and marriage. Work and service were facts of life for most African-American women. For Coppin, Terrell, and Barnett, however, the primary reason for this view was not economic. Their commitment was to the advancement of their race as well as humanity in general. Not only were they important models to other African-American women but their husbands were models to other African-American men as well. All three men had expectations of women's roles that differed from the white norm. Levi Coppin, Robert Terrell, and Ferdinand Barnett did not equate their worth and status as men with having stay-at-home wives. Quite the contrary, they all felt enormous pride in their wives' contributions. In each couple, the wife was the leader and public figure and the husband, while successful, did not have the same public acclaim or recognition. Long before it became the vogue in the late twentieth century, these women were always known by their own first names and their family surnames, not merely by their husbands' names. They were always Fanny Jackson Coppin, Mary Church Terrell, and Ida B. Wells Barnett, not Mrs. Levi Coppin, Mrs. Robert Terrell, and Mrs. Ferdinand Barnett.

The Growth of Black Colleges and Black Faculties

Black colleges and universities were established prior to the Civil War and grew in number throughout the latter half of the nineteenth century and in the early twentieth century. These institutions were funded through a variety of sources: black religious denominations, white philanthropists, the Freedman's Bureau, and the second Morrill Act of 1890 in which the federal government provided land for each of the southern and border states to establish separate state colleges for African Americans. The appointment of African Americans—men or women—to the faculties of black colleges was directly related to whether or not these institutions were headed by African Americans.

In general, black colleges that were funded by white philanthropists were slow in hiring African-American faculty members, while those funded by black religious denominations and the African-American land-grant colleges always had African-American presidents who were committed to building their faculties with African-American men and women. For example, Lincoln University, a black male institution founded in 1854 in Pennsylvania by Presbyterians, had white presidents and an all-white faculty until the 1920s. In contrast, Wilberforce College, founded in 1863 in Ohio by the African Methodist Episcopal church and headed by black clergy, employed both African-American men and women on its faculty. Mary Church Terrell's first job after graduating was with Wilberforce College. In her autobiography, Terrell noted that she had received offers from other black colleges but decided on Wilberforce because she knew her father would disapprove of her living in the South (Terrell 1968:60).

As the number of marriages among African-American academics grew, so did the presence of academic couples on black college campuses. The positive attitude among many African Americans toward married women holding faculty positions stood in sharp contrast to the views of most of those in the white world. Even at white women's colleges, whose growth paralleled that of African-American colleges, married women were not hired. Numerous prominent women educational historians such as Patricia A. Graham, Patricia Palmieri, and Margaret Rossiter have chronicled the difficulties of white women in academe. In her study of women scientists, Rossiter notes that a married woman would not be considered for employment at women's colleges, even when she was clearly the best qualified, and when a single white woman faculty member got married, she was expected to resign immediately. Rossiter pointed out that when this practice was challenged by a Barnard faculty woman who was engaged to be married in 1906, she was told by a Barnard dean that the college's trustees expected a married woman to "'dignify' her home-making into a profession, and not assume that she can carry on two full professions at a time" (Rossiter 1982:16). Palmieri notes that all fifty-three women faculty members at all-female Wellesley from 1895 to 1920 were single (1983:197). In an important article entitled "Women in Academe," Graham, herself an academic spouse, discusses the plight of her mother, whose academic career was cut short by marriage and antinepotism rules (1970:1286).

In a study of white academic couples in diverse geographical and institutional settings in the first decade of the twentieth century, Stephan and Kassis found that Grinnell College in Iowa did employ spouses of male faculty members. However, they noted that these positions were often held by women who did not have doctorates and the appointments were usually part-time and non-tenure-track (Stephan and Kassis, this volume).

While marriage was not the impediment to African-American women that it was to white women, the need for a doctoral degree became a significant barrier to their upward mobility in academe. The employment of faculty with master's degrees was common in black colleges around 1900. However, with the beginning of regional accreditation for many African-American colleges by the 1920s, the doctorate became a more important credential. Issues of access to leading graduate schools, finances, and previous academic preparation limited the number of African Americans who pursued doctorates up until this time. In a study of African-American holders of doctorates, Greene noted that in the half century after the first doctorate was awarded to an African American in 1876, no more than fifty-one African Americans had earned this degree, and only four of this number were female (1946:23).

In 1921, the first three African-American women earned doctorates. Eva Dykes earned her degree in English philology from Radcliffe; Georgianna Simpson earned hers in Germanic languages from the University of Chicago; and Sadie Tanner Mossell (later Alexander) was awarded a degree in economics from the University of Pennsylvania. Dykes and Simpson taught high school in Washington, D.C., after they earned their doctorates. Mossell, unable to find employment as an economist, went South to work for an African-American-owned insurance company (Alexander 1977).

When Mordecai Johnson was appointed the first African-American president of Howard University in Washington, D.C., in 1926, he recruited all three women to Howard's faculty. Dykes and Simpson, both single, accepted offers. However, in 1923 Mossell had married the attorney Raymond Pace Alexander, whom she had met when they were both undergraduate Phi Beta Kappas at the University of Pennsylvania, and was back living in Philadelphia. She decided against a commuting marriage and declined the Howard offer (Alexander 1977).

Sadie Tanner Mossell Alexander recalled that after her husband completed Harvard Law School and passed the bar, he decided to open a practice in Philadelphia. She spent her first year of marriage unable to find employment. After recognizing that her chances of being employed in the white male profession of economics were nil, she and her husband decided that she would go to law school and join him in his law practice. Thus, in 1927, Alexander became the first African-American woman to graduate from the University of Pennsylvania Law School as well as the first African-American woman to pass the Pennsylvania bar. She practiced law with her husband throughout her entire professional career (Alexander 1977). That the Alexanders would chart out a partnership in marriage and careers was again not unusual for African-American couples, especially among those who were college educated. Among their white contemporaries, women who married successful Ivy League trained attorneys, however, would have been expected to relinquish all employment, regardless of their educational attainment.

The Alexanders' relationship was fueled by their dedication to social justice, civil rights, and "race uplift." Raymond was not only supportive of his wife's career but also financed her law school education. While Sadie was unable to work as an economist, her interest in labor issues and civil rights resulted in her serving for twenty-five years as secretary of the National Urban League.

Foundation Support and the Development of African-American Women Academics

From 1928 to 1948, the Julius Rosenwald Foundation awarded fellowships to African Americans between the ages of twenty-four and thirty-five to attend graduate and professional schools. These awards were available to qualified applicants in all fields. The General Education Board (GEB) of the Rockefeller Foundation also began awarding graduate and professional fellowships to African Americans in select fields during this period. With these two sources of financial support, many talented African-American men and women were able to pursue and complete graduate studies. Harry Greene (1946:24) noted that in 1945, four-fifths of the African-American recipients of doctorates had earned them after 1930. The records of these two foundations reveal not only who sought and received these awards but also that the white male foundation officers learned something about the relationships between married African-American academics.

Both fellowships provided stipends for dependent family members. However, in only rare instances did an African-American spouse relocate with the fellowship recipient. The opinion of the foundation on this matter became clear when the GEB inadvertently provided a family stipend to a Howard Medical School faculty member who had received a fellowship for further study in his specialization. The fellowship recipient's wife was also a professional and remained in Washington with her job. When the foundation discovered its error, one of the officers wrote to the dean of Howard Medical School. The foundation officer noted the error and stated that the foundation would not ask for the money to be returned since it was the foundation's error, but added, "It is my personal opinion that a fellow's independent wife should be encouraged to accompany him even if that means a reduction in their double income—I think the fellow is happier, and often his wife profits quite as much from the new environment as he does." He further told the dean that the foundation hoped that he would "keep this in mind" when recommending future fellows (Robert A. Lambert to Dr. Numa P. B. Adams, 19 July 1939, folder 2380, box 236, General Education Board Papers).

Young African-American academic couples managed to enhance their careers and maintain their marriages in a variety of ways. In 1937 and 1939, the Rosenwald Fund awarded graduate fellowships to Bonita Valien and Preston Valien to pursue their doctorates in sociology at the

University of Wisconsin. In 1940, Kenneth Clark and Mamie Phipps Clark received a joint fellowship toward doctoral studies in child psychology at Columbia University. Other couples applied and received separate fellowships. Viola Goins, a 1938 Rosenwald fellow working on a doctorate in bacteriology at the University of Michigan, married another Michigan doctoral student in sociology and 1939 Rosenwald fellow, Edward N. Palmer. Another Michigan doctoral couple, both Rosenwald fellows, were Cornelius Lacy Golightly, philosophy major and 1941 fellow, and his wife, Catherine Cater Golightly, a literature major and 1943 fellow. Cornelius earned his doctorate in 1941 and continued studies in religion at Harvard University. Catherine was employed at Fisk University during this period, but applied for a second fellowship to complete her doctorate while Cornelius was employed on the faculty at Howard University (Fellowship records, Rosenwald Papers).

The Rosenwald Foundation in particular supported African-American couples and demonstrated no apparent bias against them. In fact, the annual report of 1943 commented on the Golightlys as an example of a "talented couple" (Julius Rosenwald Foundation Fellowship Report 1943, exhibit A, folder 6, box 386, Rosenwald Papers). Another "talented couple" was Hugh and Mabel Smythe, who married in 1939 and were both Rosenwald fellows in different years, fields, and institutions. Mabel held fellowships from 1940 to 1042 for work toward her doctorate in economics at the University of Wisconsin. She earned this degree in 1942. Hugh held Rosenwald fellowships during the years 1939–45 and worked on his doctorate in anthropology at Northwestern University. His studies were interrupted by the war, but he earned his doctorate in 1945. After earning her doctorate, Mabel was appointed an assistant professor of economics at Lincoln University in Missouri and by 1944 was associate professor and acting chair of the Department of Economics. By this time, Hugh had been honorably discharged from the army and was teaching at Atlanta University and Morris Brown College, in the same city. The Smythes' commuting marriage finally ended in 1945 when they both obtained positions at Tennessee State University in Nashville. Although the Smythes lived in different cities for a number of years, they coauthored numerous articles and a book (Hugh H. Smythe fellowship folder, folder 7, box 448, Rosenwald Papers; Mabel M. Smythe fellowship folder, folder 8, box 448, Rosenwald Papers).

Margaret and Charles Lawrence also received Rosenwald Fellowships. Margaret Morgan, a Cornell University graduate, married Charles

Lawrence in her second year at Columbia Medical School in 1938. After their wedding they spent the summer together, then began a commuting marriage when Margaret returned to medical school and Charles attended graduate school at Atlanta University. In 1939, Charles was awarded a Rosenwald Fellowship to work on a doctorate in sociology and joined his wife at Columbia. They resumed commuting in 1941 when Charles interrupted his studies to again accept a faculty position in Atlanta. By this time, Margaret had earned her medical degree and was completing her residency at Harlem Hospital. In 1942, both were awarded Rosenwald Fellowships, which resulted in Charles's return to Columbia to join his wife in New York. They subsequently moved to Nashville, Tennessee, where Charles obtained a faculty position at Fisk University and Margaret joined the faculty of Meharry Medical School. In Margaret's memoirs, written by her daughter Sara Lawrence Lightfoot, she describes the daily letters that she and her husband wrote to one another when they were separated and how they cheered each other's ambitions and accomplishments. She also noted that "marriage and professional life had been comfortable companions because she and Charles cared so deeply about both pursuits, and because her husband felt enhanced, not diminished, by her ambition" (Lightfoot 1988:152, 238).

While some African-American academic couples met as students, others met on the job. One such example is Virginia Lacy and Edward Allen Jones. She was a GEB Fellow in library science at the University of Illinois in 1937–38. Because of Lacy's training and degrees she was recruited to Atlanta University as head of cataloging at Arnett Library in 1939. When the School of Library Service opened in 1941, Lacy was a founding member. The same year, she married Edward Allen Jones, a professor of foreign languages at neighboring Morehouse College, but he left shortly after their wedding to complete his doctorate at Cornell University. Upon his return, two years later, Virginia left for two years to complete her doctorate at the University of Chicago. Thus, it was not until 1945 that the couple was reunited in Atlanta. Virginia, the second African American in the nation to earn a Ph.D in library science, was appointed dean of the School of Library Service. Edward became chair of foreign languages at Morehouse College. The Joneses remained at their institutions for the rest of their professional careers (V. Jones 1978).

When Virginia Lacy Jones recalled these events for the Radcliffe Oral History Project in the 1970s, the interviewer was incredulous and apparently did not realize that this personal history was not unusual for African-American academics. When asked questions regarding the couple's loneliness, Jones informed the interviewer that she and her husband had professional goals and recognized that fellowships would enable them to earn the terminal degrees they needed if they were to remain in academe (V. Jones 1978).

Winona Lee also met her husband on a black college campus. A recent master's graduate from the master's program in theater and drama at the University of Iowa, Lee joined the faculty of Kentucky State College (later University) in 1951. Within nine months she married Joseph Grant Fletcher, acting chair of the English department and head basketball coach. In 1962 Winona Lee Fletcher went to Indiana University for a year and a half to begin work on her doctorate. She left her nine-year-old daughter with her husband and a niece who was a student at Kentucky State. During her residency at Indiana she drove the three-hour trip from Bloomington to Frankfort on weekends and later drove back and forth as necessary between the two cities to complete the remaining requirements for her doctorate. She obtained the terminal degree in 1968. In the years between 1964 and 1968, her daughter frequently accompanied her on research trips around the country as she worked on her dissertation. Fletcher believes that this early exposure to scholarly research influenced her daughter's decision to complete a doctorate in clinical psychology at the University of Michigan in 1982 (Fletcher 1994).

Joseph Fletcher, a Rockefeller grant recipient in the 1930s, never completed his doctorate at Columbia University because of family responsibilities. He was eighteen years Winona's senior and encouraged her to complete her doctorate because he knew that her career would be enhanced by the degree. And, indeed it was. In 1971, Winona was invited to Indiana University as a visiting professor for two years. After her husband retired from Kentucky State in 1978 and the institution began to lose its identity as a historically black college, Winona said her husband encouraged her to accept Indiana's invitation. In 1978, Winona Fletcher joined the faculty of Indiana University full-time and from 1981 to 1984 served as associate dean of the College of Arts and Sciences while maintaining her home in Kentucky and commuting on weekends. She retired in 1994 (Fletcher 1994).

Reflecting on the twenty-seven years she spent on the faculty at Kentucky State, Winona Fletcher stated that all black colleges hired married couples and noted that the institutions could not have survived without them. Fletcher also noted, as did another black woman faculty member, that by hiring two persons, the college could get a better financial deal. She remembered that the college campus was like a family and even though faculty members had extremely heavy teaching loads and low pay, the sense of community and commitment to the students made the experience exciting and rewarding (Fletcher 1994).

Fletcher's experiences were mirrored by those of Mildred White Barksdale. She was hired as an assistant professor in 1952 at North Carolina Central University (NCCU) after obtaining her master's degree in counseling psychology from Indiana University, where she also earned her doctorate in 1958. While at NCCU she met Richard K. Barksdale, a member of the English department. Barksdale left NCCU in 1956 to head the English department at Morehouse College in Atlanta. They were married in 1960, and she joined him in Atlanta. Mildred recalled the ease of obtaining a position for which she was qualified at Atlanta University in 1960. She was hired in the newly established department of special education, her area of specialization, on the first day she arrived, after meeting with Horace Mann Bond, the dean of the college, and Rufus Clement, the president. She was chair of the department from 1960 to 1967, when she became the first black professor at Georgia State University (Barksdale 1994).

Mildred Barksdale confirmed Fletcher's observations that faculty couples were the norm on black college campuses and that it was fiscally advantageous to the colleges to hire couples. In addition, she pointed out that the institutions needed the expertise of the women, who frequently were just as well educated as the men on these campuses. Barksdale recalled that when she was an undergraduate at Jackson College (now Jackson State University) in Mississippi during the 1940s at least a third to a half of the staff were couples (Barksdale 1994).

The sense of community and family on black college campuses was so strong and the need for the expertise of all black professionals was so great that even the wives of presidents often worked on campus. Margaret Murray Washington, Booker T. Washington's third wife, had been principal at Tuskegee prior to their marriage and continued in this position after their marriage in 1892.[5] Benjamin E. Mays's wife, Sadie, was a Rosenwald fellow in the 1930s and earned graduate degrees in social work from the University of Chicago. She taught at the Howard University School of Social Work while her husband was dean of Howard's Divinity School in the 1930s. After he became president of

Morehouse College in 1940, she taught at the Atlanta University School of Social Work. Beulah Gloster, the wife of Hugh Gloster, Mays's successor at Morehouse, held a doctorate in English and in 1930 taught in the college's department of English without pay (Sadie Gray Mays fellowship folder, Rockefeller Archives; Carter 1994.

Susie Jones, the wife of David Jones, president of Bennett College in Greensboro, North Carolina, from 1926 to 1956, served as registrar of the college throughout his presidency, also without salary. Even after the death of her husband, she worked in her position until she retired at age seventy-two. A former Rosenwald fellow and the mother of four children, Jones noted that Bennett College was a family affair. Not only did she work to help build the college by establishing the registrar's office but the Jones children also had roles to play in Bennett's development. There was grass to be weeded, trips to the post office and the bank to take, and many other chores that the Jones children did on behalf of the college (S. Jones 1977:16–18).

Winona Fletcher noted that once a couple obtained positions on the same campus or in the same city and started a family, they rarely thought of uprooting to move elsewhere. Black academics did not live in the same world as whites, where there were many opportunities for growth and mobility in higher education. Black academic couples became identified with and committed to an institution and usually spent their entire career there (Fletcher 1994).

Unlike these African-American couples, the Barksdales did move after Richard Barksdale was offered a position at the University of Illinois in 1971. This move, according to Mildred, brought her teaching career to an unexpected end. Although she had been the first African-American faculty member at the institution when she was appointed professor of education and urban life studies at Georgia State University in Atlanta in 1967 there had not been any discussion at the University of Illinois about a position for her. Their move did predate the era when such negotiations were acceptable, but the Barksdales naively assumed that she would find a position in such a large institution, especially since her degree was from a Big Ten institution and since she had nearly twenty years of teaching experience on the college level. It turned out they were wrong (Barksdale 1994).

After two years of unemployment and making it known to university officials that she wanted a meaningful job, Mildred Barksdale was appointed an assistant dean in the College of Liberal Arts and Sciences.

She remained in this position until her retirement in 1988. Barksdale described her job as a glorified counseling position. She earned significantly less than she had earned in her previous position in Atlanta and she said that she felt her talents were wasted. Even so, she never considered a commuting marriage because of their school-age son. She acknowledged that she had sacrificed her career for her family (Barksdale 1994).

Although African-American married women did find employment opportunities on black college campuses, they did not escape some aspects of sexism. Both Fletcher and Barksdale believed that married women earned less, particularly those that came to the campus already married to faculty members. They were quick to point out, however, that the salaries at black colleges in general were low (Fletcher 1994; Barksdale 1994).

Antinepotism rules did exist in some black colleges. Although most administrators at these institutions attempted to get around such rules, some women indicated in their reports to the Rosenwald and Rockefeller Foundations that they were not working due to antinepotism rules. Edmonia Louise Walden Grider, a GEB fellow in 1930, reported to the foundation in 1936 that she had been dropped from the faculty of West Virginia State where she taught home economics because she "married a gentleman working on the same faculty. A rule was passed that no two people in the same family could draw state checks. I was dropped along with several others in 1933" (Grider 1936).

Similarly, Hilda Lawson Reedy, a Rosenwald fellow from 1937 to 1940, reported losing her position at Lincoln University in Missouri due to her marriage in 1941 to another faculty member, Sidney Reedy. As she put it: "Lincoln's Board opposes the employment of wives of faculty members, silly isn't it?" (Hilda Lawson Reedy, follow-up card to the Julius Rosenwald Foundation, 1944, Rosenwald Papers). Authorities at Lincoln did attempt to circumvent this ruling by providing Hilda Lawson Reedy with an "emergency" appointment. Reedy had earned a Ph.D. in English from the University of Illinois in 1939 at the age of twenty-four. She was the first African-American woman to earn a Ph.D. from that institution. She was immediately hired at Lincoln to develop and teach graduate courses in English. As in Reedy's case, West Virginia State College eventually sought to retain Edmonia Walden Grider; she reported that the institution rehired her on a part-time basis in 1936 (Grider 1936).

It is unclear whether these rules concerning nepotism arose due to the depression or whether some black colleges were being put under greater scrutiny on this issue as the number of black academic couples continued to grow. Ruth Brett earned a doctorate from Teachers College of Columbia University in 1945 and served as an administrator and faculty member on numerous black college campuses before marrying Benjamin Quarles, a professor of history at Morgan State College in Baltimore, in 1952. Brett stated that when she was hired by the president of Morgan, he advised her not to use the name Quarles so that she could avoid the antinepotism rules of the state. She noted that other women on campus in similar situations did likewise (Brett 1987).

Mildred Barksdale reported that she never encountered any antinepotism rules on black college campuses where she was employed nor was she aware of them at any others (Barksdale 1994). Winona Fletcher recalled that at Kentucky State, if a woman was single when she was appointed to the faculty and married later, her job was not in jeopardy. However, many highly educated black wives of faculty and staff members were employed in the public school system in Frankfort or in low-paying jobs in town because antinepotism rules prevented them from being hired at the college. Many of these wives later secured jobs on campus as antinepotism rules were relaxed or overlooked. Whether the question of nepotism was raised and how the antinepotism rules were enforced apparently depended primarily upon the administrator at the college who was responsible for enforcing them (Fletcher 1994). In most black colleges administrators generally found ways to disregard or circumvent antinepotism rules.

While it is true that married African-American women had little difficulty obtaining positions on the same campuses with their husbands, gender differences did exist. The women usually advanced more slowly, were paid less, and rarely attained positions of leadership. Virginia Jones, one of these rare exceptions, noted that she never experienced the sexism other women may have because she was the second African American in the country to earn a Ph.D. in library science and there were no African-American men, at that time, with similar degrees (V. Jones 1978). Mildred Barksdale recalled that at North Carolina Central the men dominated faculty meetings because women were not expected to contribute their opinions and were not taken seriously (Barksdale 1994). Inabeth Lindsey, who served as the dean of Howard's School of Social Work from 1944 to 1967 had similar experiences. Lindsey said she was originally appointed acting dean only until the Howard board could find a man to fill the position. She then became dean when the accreditation association told the school it could not be accredited with an acting dean. Although Lindsey served on the President's Council of Deans at Howard, she believed that President Mordecai Johnson never expected any input from her and did not take her suggestions seriously (Lindsey 1978). Even though Rufus Clement, president of Atlanta University, hired many women, Mildred Barksdale found him extremely sexist and maintained he placed demanding workloads on women faculty members (Barksdale 1994). These views regarding Johnson were not universally shared, although experiences with sexism were not uncommon.

Dorothy Boulding Ferebee earned an M.D. from Tufts University School of Medicine in 1924. After completing her internship and clinical training in 1927, she was appointed to the Howard University Medical School faculty in the department of obstetrics. By 1929, she had been appointed head of the University Medical Center and remained at Howard for over forty years (Ferebee 1979).

At Howard, she met her husband, Claude Ferebee, a faculty member in the College of Dentistry. They married in 1930 and subsequently had twins. Her pregnancy did not result in her dismissal from her job or any expectation that she would leave. In fact, she noted, "I worked hard and regularly up until a month before the babies were expected, and did not give up [my job for maternity leave] until I was ready to go to the hospital" (1979:34).

After a personality dispute with the dean of the College of Dentistry, Claude was dismissed from the faculty. Dorothy recalled that after this event, her success at Howard's Medical School, and the growth of her private practice, her husband "became very unhappy and uncooperative, and insisted that I give up my work. Of course, I wasn't going to do that." She stated that her husband believed that her position at Howard gave her more prestige "than he enjoyed" (1979:18). Eventually, Ferebee's decision to remain in her position at Howard and to keep her private practice resulted in the dissolution of her marriage.

Throughout her years at Howard Medical School, Ferebee recalled that many male physicians resented her position at the university but she found an ally in Mordecai Johnson. She noted:

I think that sexism [at Howard] was a very common practice, and still is. . . . I think that, even though I experienced discrimination and a great deal of jealousy on the part of many of the men physicians and the men directors, I had a very stanch ally at Howard University in the person of Dr.

Mordecai Johnson, the president. He was absolutely superb in seeing that both men and women whose qualifications were recognizable received the kind of recognition to which they were entitled. So that for a long time, my service as medical director of Howard University Health Service largely was due to Dr. Mordecai Johnson's approval of me, and the fact that the physicians who were opposing me were a subterranean faction, were never able to reach me because of the citations and recognition given me by the university president." (1979:34)

Merze Tate, a Radcliffe Ph.D. who served on the faculty of the history and political science departments at Howard University during the same period as Ferebee, described the Committee on the Status of Women at Howard that she chaired during the 1960s: "We had salary scales for professors, associates, instructors, and assistants, but the women were always at the lower level of the scale, seldom in the middle, and never at the top." Male faculty members were always given preference for summer school appointments. On this issue, according to Tate, "women were out" (1978:34).

Black colleges needed and employed African-American women, regardless of marital status. Having a spouse on the same campus in most instances was not a liability. Most African-American women faculty members were devoutly committed to their students and their work and except in retrospect did not appear to voice discontent over gender inequities. On this point, Mildred Barksdale reflected that "perhaps the women of [her] generation didn't ask for enough" (Barksdale 1994). Black colleges as well as the students benefited greatly from the contributions of the women on their faculties.

There is little evidence to suggest that black academic women desired to stop working. In fact, they were very proud of their contributions to their institutions. It was unthinkable to them to struggle for an advanced education and then simply abandon it when they got married. Inabeth Lindsey made this point. After obtaining an undergraduate degree and completing one year toward a master's in social work in 1925 she married Arnett Lindsey, her undergraduate sweetheart. Even among some African-American men, an at-home wife was beginning to be perceived as ideal by the 1920s, and Lindsey's husband expected her to stay home. However, she recalled, "I was quite bored, and guilty about not doing anything, because I said my mother worked too hard and spent too much money on my education for me not to be doing something with the education that was made possible" (1978:4). Lindsey convinced her husband that she should work. In 1936, she returned to graduate school at the University of Chicago. After she earned a master's degree in social work in 1937, she was recruited by Howard University to become the director of the Social Work Program while her husband taught at Clark College and Morris Brown College in Atlanta. The Lindseys reunited under one roof after Arnett became ill in 1938 and came to Washington, D.C., for medical care. Deciding to stay in Washington with his wife, he left academe and went into real estate (1978:47).

Margaret Morgan Lawrence, M.D., noted that even though she had three children she never considered not working, because it was too important for her to "make a contribution." Like all of the other women discussed in this chapter, she had worked too hard for the degrees she had obtained not to utilize them (Lightfoot 1988:239).

Mildred Barksdale did resign her position to relocate with her husband, but reported experiencing a profound sense of loss at not finding a teaching position. She recalled having grown up in rural Mississippi in the 1930s, when there were no schools beyond the eighth grade in her county for African Americans. Her parents sent her to live in Meridian so that she could obtain a high school degree from the segregated black high school there. When Mildred went to Jackson College in 1940, she was the first African American in her community to attend college. She recalled that when she went to graduate school at Indiana University in 1950, the Rosenwald and GEB Fellowships no longer existed. Although her job as housemother of a black residence home paid for her tuition as well as room and board, she did not receive a salary or a stipend and had to borrow from her parents. Also, she often did typing into the early hours of the morning, charging $.25 for a single spaced page and $.10 for a double-spaced page. She recalled that her lack of financial support for graduate study delayed the completion of her doctorate by at least a dozen years (Barksdale 1994).

Married African-American women who were employed on black college campuses prior to the 1970s, when possibilities for employment on white college campuses increased, were met with a variety of opportunities and experiences. As African Americans, those who obtained advanced degrees in the early years of the 1920s and 1930s were highly valued and employed instantly and had the opportunity to enjoy enormous influence on black college campuses; as women, however, they often received lesser pay and had less professional mobility than their male colleagues. At Fisk, for example, while Preston Valien was a member of the faculty of sociology, his wife, with the same degree, served as secretary of the department. When Hugh and Mabel Smythe were appointed to the faculty of Tennessee State University in 1945, Hugh was hired as a professor while Mabel, who had held her doctorate for a longer period and had teaching experience, was appointed as an instructor. In other cases of couples who started out in academia together, such as Kenneth and Mamie Clark, the husband became the well-known scholar (Fellowship records, Rosenwald Papers). And, as noted earlier, whenever there was a question of nepotism, the wife automatically lost her position.

Contemporary Black Academic Couples

Today's African-American academic couples experience the same professional and personal dilemmas as other couples. The motivation of "race uplift" is no longer the driving force of African-American professionals. Further, on the one hand, their employment is no longer confined to black colleges; on the other hand, obtaining faculty positions in close proximity to one another can be a challenge. On today's black college campuses, finding a suitable position for a spouse is no longer as easy as it once was. Positions at black colleges, as elsewhere, must now be advertised, and candidates must be considered by a search committee; it is no longer sufficient merely to have a conversation with the president.

For example, Lawrence Carter and Marva Griffin married in 1969 after meeting when he was a graduate student at Boston University and she was an undergraduate student at Boston Conservatory of Music. In 1977, Marva received a fellowship for doctoral study in musicology at the University of Illinois at Urbana. Lawrence was working on his dissertation and was advised not to move until it was completed. Consequently, the couple commuted over the next five years. After Lawrence graduated in 1979, he was appointed the first dean of the Martin Luther King International Chapel at Morehouse College. Three years later, their commuter marriage ended when Marva moved to Atlanta to write her dissertation. She became the organist at the historic Ebenezer Baptist Church for the next decade and taught part-time at Clark College. In 1988, she was the first African American to be awarded a Ph.D. in musicology from the University of Illinois. For the next four years, she served as coordinator of the music program at Morris Brown College in the Atlanta University Center. She is now assistant director of the School of Music at Georgia State University in Atlanta (Carter 1994).

I am also part of an academic couple. When I met Vincent L. Wimbush in 1983, he was completing a doctorate in religious studies at Harvard University and I was employed in an administrative position at Radcliffe College. After Vincent completed his doctorate in 1983, we married and moved to Claremont, California, where he was appointed an assistant professor at the School of Theology at Claremont College (STC). I possessed a doctorate prior to my marriage and had college-level teaching experience. The dean of STC actively assisted me in finding a position before we moved. He circulated my curriculum vitae to all of the divisions of Claremont College and other institutions within driving distance and flew me out for a job-hunting visit. As a result, I found a position within Claremont College several weeks after I arrived. STC took seriously my desire for an academic post and recognized that this issue would be crucial to my husband's stay at the institution.

These efforts made by STC were not unique. As more and more faculty members with academic spouses arrived, all institutions with which I have been associated have made efforts to accommodate them. While I was at Claremont College, at least two academic couples held positions there. And, in one controversial effort, the wife of a highly sought after professor was given a part-time faculty position that apparently was created for her without the benefit of advertisement or a search.

In 1991 I also began a commuting marriage. For two and a half years, my husband and I were employed in different states. The commuting ended when I left my position at the University of Illinois to accept a position at Hunter College in New York. As Mildred Barksdale had found, a small child was the decisive factor in choosing to keep the family under one roof.

As increasing numbers of academic couples of all races have to face issues of commuting, reduced career mobility, and unemployment, we can learn from the accommodations by black colleges for couples during the age of segregation, when the efforts of all talented African Americans were needed. This was a unique period in our history, when these colleges made accommodations and these couples made compromises. The experiences of these colleges in employing faculty couples can be extremely instructive to scholars of women in the labor force—particularly those researching academic couples.

Conclusion: For the Good of the Race

To help the race was the driving motivation for many educated African Americans through the first half of the twentieth century. The small number of formally educated African Americans, women as well as men, were expected to utilize their rare and hard-earned education for the "uplift" of their people. Thus, a well-educated working wife among middle-class African Americans was viewed quite differently than was her counterpart in white America.

The belief that one should contribute to the race was so persistent that in 1946 when Mary Huff Diggs was appointed the first full-time African-American faculty member at Hunter College in New York, she wrote to Charles S. Johnson, the African-American president of Fisk University, that she often wished she could have her job "duplicated in the Negro schools I know best." She added that this feeling "is related, I believe, to the deep convictions I embraced regarding the preparation of myself for serving the Negro race." Johnson assured Diggs that she was "serving the race" by being a member of the Hunter faculty (Diggs to Johnson, 30 Dec. 1946, and Johnson to Diggs, 3 Jan. 1947, folder 22, box 3, Johnson Papers). However, even decades later, many African Americans did not share Johnson's view.

Mildred Barksdale recalled that many African Americans at Atlanta University considered her disloyal to the race and a sellout when she accepted a position at white Georgia State University in 1967. Now, Barksdale points out, many African Americans are students and faculty members at that institution as well as similar ones without their commitment to their race being called into question (Barksdale 1994). Similarly, Winona Fletcher made clear her devotion to the African-American students at Kentucky State University and noted that she left when the institution was no longer identified as a black institution. She transferred her loyalty to the Afro-American Studies Department at Indiana University, which she helped to establish in 1971 (Fletcher 1994).

The current number of African-American academic couples in American colleges and universities is not known. However, it does not appear that the number is nearly as great as it was during the first half of the twentieth century. As schools became desegregated and more African Americans earned advanced degrees, couples increasingly faced difficulties finding jobs at the same institutions, including historically black colleges. The unique period when these colleges not only employed

African-American women but also retained them during and after pregnancy, thus providing them with more opportunities than were available to educated women in the larger society, had come to an end. Even while employing many couples, these institutions were not immune to the sexism and paternalism that permeated the rest of society and had often employed women for utilitarian rather than egalitarian reasons.

Nonetheless, the importance of the path-breaking role of African-American academic women, largely ignored in the scholarly literature, let alone studied or analyzed, must not be underestimated. The separate black college, which was primarily an outgrowth of society's mandated segregation of African Americans, ironically resulted in professional opportunities for African-American women that were often unavailable to other women. African-American women were the first group of academic women in the United States to be employed in large numbers with their husbands; they were also the first to experiment with accommodations such as commuting marriages and sharing academic awards in order to further their professional goals.

Little is known of the African-American academic couple or woman. Imbued with the prevailing philosophy that all talented and educated African Americans should contribute to the "uplift" and good of the race, many African-American academics contributed significantly, at great personal sacrifice, to the growth and development of black colleges. Untold in this story is the enormous role that African-American women—married and single—played in this endeavor. Many questions remain to be answered. What personal and professional sacrifices did they make "for the good of the race"? What impact did the presence of these women, whose contributions were so impressive, have on black college campuses? How expendable were African-American women when race "uplift" no longer became a critical philosophy within African-American communities?

As academia at large is increasingly hiring and retaining couples, much could be learned from the experiences of these African-American pioneers.

Notes

The author would like to acknowledge the Spencer Foundation, the University of California, and the University of Illinois for the financial support of the research on which this chapter is based. I would also like to thank Kathy A. Perkins for her research assistance.

1. For more on this topic see Webber 1978.

2. For more on "true womanhood" see Welter 1966; for African-American women and "true womanhood" see Perkins 1983.

3. On this topic see also Solomon 1985.

4. For Levi Coppin's opinions on his marriage to Fanny Jackson Coppin see L. Coppin 1968.

5. On Margaret Murray Washington's contributions to Tuskegee, see Harlan 1972, 1983.

Bibliography

Alexander, Sadie Tanner Mossell. 1977. Interview with Walter M. Phillips. Philadelphia, Pennsylvania. 12 Oct. Folder 20, box 1. Sadie Tanner Mossell Alexander Papers. University of Pennsylvania Archives, Philadelphia.

Antler, Joyce. 1980. "After College, What?: New Graduates and the Family Claim." *American Quarterly* 32 (Fall): 409–34.

Barksdale, Mildred. 1994. Interview with the author. Urbana, Ill. 18 July.

Brett, Ruth. 1987. Interview with the author. Baltimore. 12 June.

Carter, Marva, and Lawrence Carter. 1994. Telephone interview with the author. 2 Aug.

Clarke, Edward H. 1873. *Sex in Education; or, A Fair Chance for the Girls*. Boston: Osgood.

Coppin, Fanny Jackson. 1913. *Reminiscences of School Life, and Hints on Teaching*. Philadelphia: AME Book Concern.

Coppin, Levi. 1968. *Unwritten History*. 1919. Reprint, New York: Negro Universities Press.

Duster, Alfreda M., ed. 1970. *Crusade for Justice: The Autobiography of Ida B. Wells*. Chicago: University of Chicago Press.

Ferebee, Dorothy Boulding. 1979. Interview. 28, 31 Dec. Women of Courage Collection. Radcliffe Black Women's Oral History Project. Arthur and Elizabeth Schlesinger Library, Radcliffe College, Cambridge, Mass.

Fletcher, Winona Lee. 1994. Interview with Kathy A. Perkins. Chicago. 26 July.

General Education Board Papers. Rockefeller Archives, Pocantico Hills, N.Y.

Graham, Patricia Albjerg. 1970. "Women in Academe." *Science* 169 (Sept.): 1286.

Greene, Harry Washington. 1946. *Holders of Doctorates among American Negroes*. Boston: Meador Publishing.

Grider, Edmonia Louise Walden. 1936. Follow-up Report to the General Education Board. Rockefeller Archives, Pocantico Hills, N.Y.

Harlan, Louis R. 1972. *Booker T. Washington: The Making of a Black Leader, 1856–1901*. New York: Oxford University Press.

———. 1983. *Booker T. Washington: The Wizard of Tuskegee, 1901–1915*. New York: Oxford University Press.

Hileman, Sharon. 1990. "The 'Female-Determined Relationship': Personal and Professional Needs of Academic Women in Commuter Marriages." In *Women in Higher Education: Changes and Challenges,* ed. Lynne B. Welch, 119–25. New York: Praeger.

Isaac, Sara Richardson. 1976. Interview with the author. Philadelphia. 18 June.

Johnson, Charles S. Papers. Fisk University Special Collections, Fisk University, Nashville.

Jones, Susie. 1977. Interview. July 11. Women of Courage Collection. Radcliffe Black Women's Oral History Project. Arthur and Elizabeth Schlesinger Library, Radcliffe College, Cambridge, Mass.

Jones, Virginia Lacy. 1978. Interview. 10 Oct. Women of Courage Collection. Radcliffe Black Women's Oral History Project. Arthur and Elizabeth Schlesinger Library, Radcliffe College, Cambridge, Mass.

Julius Rosenwald Foundation Papers. Fisk University Special Collections, Fisk University, Nashville.

Langston, Phyllis Terrell. 1980. Interview with the author. Highland Beach, Md. 23 Mar.

Lightfoot, Sara Lawrence. 1988. *Bald in Gilead: Journey of a Healer.* Reading, Mass.: Addison-Wesley Publishing.

Palmieri, Patricia. 1983. "Here Was Fellowship: A Social Portrait of Academic Women at Wellesley College, 1895–1920." *History of Education Quarterly* 23 (Summer): 195–211.

Perkins, Linda M. 1983. "The Impact of the 'Cult of True Womanhood' on the Education of Black Women." *Journal of Social Issues* 29 (Fall): 17–28.

———. 1987. *Fanny Jackson Coppin and the Institute for Colored Youth, 1865–1902.* New York: Garland Publishing.

Rossiter, Margaret. 1982. *Women Scientists in America: Struggles and Strategies to 1940.* Baltimore: Johns Hopkins University Press.

Solomon, Barbara Miller. 1985. *In the Company of Educated Women.* New Haven: Yale University Press.

Tate, Merze. 1978. Interview. Women of Courage Collection. Radcliffe Black Women's Oral History Project. Arthur and Elizabeth Schlesinger Library, Radcliffe College, Cambridge, Mass.

Terrell, Mary Church. 1968. *A Colored Woman in a White World.* Washington, D.C.: National Association of Colored Women's Clubs.

Webber, Thomas. 1978. *Deep as the River: Education in the Slave Quarter Community, 1831–1865.* New York: Norton.

Welter, Barbara. 1966. "Cult of True Womanhood: 1820–1860." *American Quarterly* 18 (Summer): 151–74.

4

· · · · · · · · ·

POSSLQs and PSSSLQs:
Unmarried Academic Couples

Dorothy C. Miller and Anita Skeen

MOST ACADEMICS TODAY probably know personally at least one co-habiting unmarried couple in higher education. Sometimes referred to as "spousal equivalents," heterosexual couples of this type are dubbed "POSSLQs," or persons of the opposite sex sharing living quarters (*Futurist* 1991). While some use the same acronym to refer to same-sex couples, we choose to call them "PSSSLQs" (persons of the same sex sharing living quarters), to be pronounced (if one cares) "pisselques."

According to Jonette Duff and George G. Truitt, authors of *The Spousal Equivalent Handbook: A Legal and Financial Guide to Living Together,* there are as many as 8 million POSSLQs living in the United States, and many additional gay and lesbian couples (cited in *Futurist* 1991). A study of heterosexual cohabitors by Bumpass and Sweet (1989) suggests that almost half of all people in their early thirties and half of the recently married have cohabited. They concluded that in the current population, "4 percent are currently cohabiting, about one-sixth cohabited before marriage, and about one-fourth have cohabited at some time" (615). However, they also found that cohabitation among heterosexual couples is generally time-limited, as they tend to marry or break up within a short period. More than half of first cohabitations result in marriage (617). In their late 1970s study of U.S. couples Blumstein and Schwartz (1983) had similar findings. Less than 2 percent of their cohabiting heterosexual couples had been together for as many as ten years and 55 percent had been together two years or less (594). For many of these couples cohabitation seemed to be a "trial marriage" (84). This choice of living together or marrying marks a fundamental distinction between heterosexual and gay and lesbian couples, who are denied this choice.

A commonly held belief is that approximately 10 percent of the population identifies itself as gay or lesbian. It is impossible to put forth any accurate figures for cohabiting gay men and lesbian couples, since there is no information about how many there are or what their living arrangements are. Due to the widespread lack of legal protections against discrimination, most gays and lesbians feel the need to "hide," at least officially, from the public eye. And even though it is illegal in ten states for unmarried opposite-sex couples to cohabit (*Futurist* 1991:47), they are far less likely to lose their jobs or their housing because of their relationship patterns. Since some research indicates that lesbians are better educated than women in general (Larson 1992), it is possible that lesbians are overrepresented in academia and among academic couples.[1] It is likely that the same is true of gay men. Moreover, in gay and lesbian couples both partners are more likely to see their careers as necessary and important parts of their lives. As Blumstein and Schwartz commented, "The gay and lesbian couples show us what happens when historic expectations are absent from a relationship. Each partner is supposed to work and does. There is no assumption about the primacy of one partner's career, and if a conflict arises, it is negotiated between them. Neither job is automatically considered of secondary or of auxiliary importance" (1983:153). Beyond such inferences, however, there is little research data available about either cohabiting same-sex or opposite-sex couples, not to mention research that focuses upon couples in which both partners are employed in higher education.

One reason for this dearth of studies is that it is still extremely difficult to obtain data on gay and lesbian populations using the usual survey methods. This point is well illustrated in the results of the survey by Bellas and Ferber (see Bellas and Ferber and Hoffman, this volume). Only seven women and seven men, or less than 2 percent of respondents, reported ever having lived with a same-sex partner. As long as there is this apparent reluctance to provide information on what is often a stigmatized situation, the statistical analysis many social scientists use is simply not feasible.

In the case of POSSLQs, the number who remain unmarried is very small and may have escaped the notice of researchers as a categorically specific group. Also, to the extent that living together out of wedlock is still stigmatized, and since at this time the political climate seems to be heightening the stigma, this group may also be reluctant to share information. Another explanation may be that they identify themselves as being married when they are not, at least according to legal definitions. We solicited personal narratives from members of heterosexual and gay and lesbian couples concerning significant issues and problems related to their academic and personal lives. We asked for information concerning the couples' treatment by the university, career moves, salary, and collaborative and competitive issues in both teaching and research. We also encouraged them to report success stories. Our call for narratives went out through seven academic e-mail networks and we contacted individuals with whom we are acquainted. The number of responses we received was infinitesimally small. Only eight individuals or couples responded to our request for information over an eighteen-month period. No heterosexual men responded. The responses came from one gay man, two heterosexual women, and five lesbians. Several respondents are personal friends or acquaintances of the authors.

The low response rate itself raises more questions than the answers it provides. Why was the number of responses so small? Are there so few unmarried academic couples cohabiting that the response reflects their small numbers? They are a small minority, but gay and lesbian couples are becoming increasingly visible on campuses across the country and many are actively involved in seeking domestic partner benefits on their campuses. Does this mean that unmarried heterosexual couples believe their situations are not much different from married academic couples and therefore have little to say about what they feel is unique to their situation? We simply do not know.

We had hoped to receive a larger response, one that would have given us a sample that might allow for at least some beginning hypotheses about the experiences and concerns of this group. However, the very reluctance of people to respond to our call shows how important it is to bring the subject into the open and disseminate what anecdotal information we were able to garner. The narratives that we did receive point to issues of concern and suggest avenues for further study. Our discussion is guided by the scant literature, the narratives received, and our individual experiences and observations as lesbians in academia. We cannot draw conclusions or make generalizations, but we can present real stories, suggest ways of thinking about the lives of unmarried academic couples, and recommend directions for research.

Relationships and Family Life

As women have joined the labor force in great numbers and are increasingly entering professional careers, the assumption that a husband's career should take precedence over his wife's has been questioned. Women on average contribute about one-third of family income, probably more among professional couples. Yet there is some evidence that the institution of marriage influences women's and men's behavior in this regard. In a study of cohabiting heterosexual graduate students, Kotkin (1983) found a number of differences between married, engaged, and cohabiting couples. Asked about sacrifices made for a partner's career, he found that 70 percent of the married women had made sacrifices, such as economic support, relocation, postponement of their own careers, or performance of "career adjunct roles," such as typing papers, doing lab work, and so forth. Just 10 percent of the married men had made similar sacrifices. In contrast, 30 percent of the cohabiting men and women had made sacrifices for each other. Evidence regarding greater egalitarianism among cohabiting couples extended also to housework. Only the cohabiting couples distributed household tasks equally, while among married and engaged couples housework was more often performed by the women. However, predictors of conventional household task allocation are male career precedence and percentage of total income contributed by the male.

Overall, "attitudes and strategies favoring the man's career were found in 80 percent of the married couples, 64 percent of the engaged couples, and 44 percent of the nonengaged cohabitors" (Kotkin 1983:981). Some of the women changed their careers because of the anticipated difficulty of the couple finding two teaching positions in the same place.

One might conclude from this that women who are less desirous of making career sacrifices for their mates are also more likely to choose not to marry. Thus marriage per se may not be a determinant of sacrifice as much as the attitudes of persons who decide whether to marry are. However, most of the women in the study indicated a reluctance to make too many sacrifices as long as they were not married, implying that once marriage became a reality, their attitudes would change (Kotkin 1983).

There was evidence of "career leveling" among the cohabiting couples in that the men involved were not as successful as the married or engaged men.[2] Although Kotkin is silent on this issue, presumably the cohabiting women were more successful than the engaged or married women and perhaps less successful than women not encumbered by professionally ambitious partners. Focusing only on male career ambition and success, Kotkin suggests that the egalitarianism may be generated by either a lack of success or ambition among the men or by "nonconventional sex-role attitudes." He quotes a single non-engaged cohabiting male who stated: "'It would be great if *either* of us were successful'" (1983:984; Kotkin's emphasis). Acknowledging that married men with devoted spouses have an advantage over all others, Kotkin does not discuss the mundane fact that equality of housework chores combined with equality of sacrifices for each other's career goals necessitate spending less time and effort on one's own career. Because of the sacrifices and time commitments involved, egalitarian men in relationships would be expected to be less successful than both single men without partners and nonegalitarian married men, regardless of their ambition or lack thereof.

Egalitarian relationship norms seem to be even more prevalent among gay and lesbian couples. In a study that compared ten cohabiting lesbian couples with ten cohabiting heterosexual couples, the lesbian couples were more likely to divide household chores equally (Schneider 1986:237). Other studies report similar findings (Larson 1992:9). Also, lesbians' attitudes about money differed from those of the other couples in the Blumstein and Schwartz study. Money did not establish the "balance of power" in their relationships (Blumstein and Schwartz 1983:53). Among gay men, although both members of a couple thought that the other's work was important, financial success was a factor in the relationship. "The catch-22 for gay men is that each appreciates a partner who earns money, but if the partner is a success, he may become the more powerful person in the relationship" (Blumstein and Schwartz 1983:75).

University Life

Benefits

The institution of marriage conveys numerous privileges that are mostly unavailable to unmarried heterosexual couples and unattainable for gay and lesbian couples:

rights to spousal shares of marital property upon the death of one partner; tax benefits (including joint tax returns, dependency deductions, gift tax exemptions, and exemptions for alimony and property settlements); rights in tort law (including emotional distress, wrongful death actions, and loss of consortium); rights in criminal law (including immunity from compelled testimony and the marital communication privilege); nonexclusion under zoning laws; visitation privileges in hospitals and other institutions; authority to make decisions for an ill spouse; employee benefits for spouses (including health insurance, medical leave, and bereavement leave); government benefits (including Social Security and veterans payments to spouses, workers' compensation, [unemployment compensation] for those whose spouses move for job-related reasons); lower fees for married couples (including automobile and life insurance, family travel rates, and family memberships); immigration benefits; and draft exemptions. (Rubenstein 1993:430–31)

Employee benefits can thus be viewed as just one category among a multitude of privileges enjoyed by married couples. However, since U.S. public policy links health care with employment, such benefits can mean life and death to some people.

A 1990 survey conducted by the National Gay and Lesbian Task Force found that about 25 percent of colleges and universities in the United States were providing some benefits to domestic partners of students, staff, and/or faculty. The benefits most commonly found were "sick and bereavement leave for the illness or death of a partner, parental leave for the care of a partner's child, access to libraries and recreation facilities, access to married student or faculty housing, and access to on-campus health facilities" (Fried 1994:11). It is notable that the benefits of spousal job assistance and child-care centers, which seem to be increasing (see Raabe, this volume), were not commonly listed. Family and spousal health insurance coverage is conspicuous by its absence as well, but rapid change is occurring in this regard.

In 1991–92 Stanford University formed a committee to consider whether the university should extend domestic partner benefits, including health insurance coverage and tuition grants for employees' children, to gay, lesbian, and unmarried heterosexual couples. At the time the report was submitted in 1992, only one school, Albert Einstein College of Medicine, had extended health insurance to domestic partners of faculty and staff (Fried 1994). By 1994 twenty-six colleges and universities, including all schools in the Ivy League, offered health care benefits to lesbian and gay employees' domestic partners. With some notable exceptions (City University of New York, the University of Iowa, Iowa State University, the University of Minnesota, and the University of Vermont) the list was composed of private institutions. Just five schools on the list also extended such benefits to opposite-sex partners (Badgett 1994).

The task of defining what constitutes a domestic partnership generally requires the establishment of a set of conditions that must be met. Typically, institutions require cohabitation; a mingling of financial assets and obligations, with beneficiary status for partners in insurance and pension plans; minimum time requirements in a relationship or between partnerships if one is dissolved; single status for both partners; and no blood relationship. As mentioned, many schools require that the partners be of the same sex. Smith and Dartmouth reportedly require that same-sex partners pledge that they would marry if given the legal opportunity to do so (Badgett 1994).

A recent University of Iowa study on health insurance coverage for domestic partners focused on the costs associated with health care benefits for HIV positive persons, whom it assumed, for purposes of the study, to consist entirely of gay men. Their research on this issue found that the fear of astronomic costs for these benefits was unwarranted, even in San Francisco, a city that is known to have a large gay male population. Moreover, the study found that the number of same-sex couples who have taken advantage of domestic partner benefits, when offered, is quite small (Subcommittee 1991).[3] The Stanford study drew similar conclusions (Fried 1994). Indeed, some insurance providers themselves, including Blue Cross and Blue Shield of Massachusetts and Kaiser Permanente of northern California, extend domestic partner benefits to their own employees (Badgett 1994). Colleges and universities inhibited by the fear of excessive costs will undoubtedly have their fears abated by the experiences of schools who extend health care benefits to same-sex couples.

For unmarried academic couples employed by the same institution, the issue of domestic partner health insurance benefits per se is not immediately compelling because it is more cost effective for both members of the couple to avail themselves of the benefits individually. However, the opportunity to have family leave to care for one's partner's biological child or elderly relative, bereavement leave, and family rates for recreational and academic facilities may be of concern. The existence of health care insurance for domestic partners may be more helpful to couples employed by different institutions. Notwithstanding its use, the extension of such an important benefit as health insurance institutionalizes a recognition of and respect for gay and lesbian relationships, creating a campus climate conducive to collegiality and productivity.

The Stanford study, an internal document that is so comprehensive in its discussion of the issues that it has been published for wider circulation (Fried 1994), addresses what the committee determined to be the two fundamental issues involved with extending domestic partner benefits: "whether the university should treat domestic partnerships as the moral equivalent of marriage, and how it should weigh cost considerations" (Fried 1994:3). To the former issue the committee argued that a failure to treat domestic partnerships as equivalent to marriage would amount to "an imposition of a moral code not universally shared in a pluralistic society" (16) and would be inconsistent with both the university's previously established nondiscrimination policy and the fact that Stanford had already extended domestic partner benefits to students. Interestingly, the committee was less emphatic about extending domestic partner benefits to heterosexual couples, since they have the choice to marry. If one holds to the principle that benefits for married couples are based on the support of intimate, long-term committed relationships, one could make a case that cohabiting heterosexual couples who are unwilling to make a legal commitment do not have relationships equivalent to those of married couples. However, the committee acknowledged that "for at least some heterosexuals, the choice not to marry reflects a political or ideological objection to the institution of marriage" (33). From that perspective it concluded that the university "ought to remain neutral with respect to its employees' beliefs and ideologies, and the practices that flow from them" (33).

The ideological aspect of the issue is one of the subtexts of the debate. Ironically, granting domestic partner benefits to gay and lesbian couples because they cannot marry, and not to cohabiting heterosexual couples because they can, in fact upholds the hegemony of state sanctioned marriage as the ideal status for long-term, monogamous, couple relationships. As Badgett comments, "Until unmarried heterosexual partners are routinely included, the recognition of domestic partners will not constitute a radical redefinition of family" (Badgett 1994:28). It is also somewhat ironic that gays and lesbians, who have more to lose by being "visible," have been most active in fighting for these benefits. Of course they already exist as a separate and identifiable cultural, social, and political interest group. Unmarried heterosexual couples, we surmise, do not see themselves as a group apart from their married peers. But until the latter group fights for these benefits, it is unlikely that gay and lesbian groups will take up the cause for them (Badgett 1994).

Jobs

Institutions are undoubtedly less likely to have formal programs for hiring unmarried partners. Moreover, if POSSLQs and PSSSLQs are more egalitarian in their relationships than married couples and "career leveling" has occurred, many of them may have difficulty finding positions on the same campus because it is less likely that one would be a sought after "star" for whom universities would be eager to make accommodations. On the other hand, "stardom" is hard to define and seemingly many variables are relevant, including whether partners are in the same or different fields, individual scholarly specialties within a field, the prestige or marketability of the disciplines, and the needs of the institution. In any case, it may be harder for gay, lesbian, and cohabiting heterosexual couples to make decisions regarding career moves, not only because of the difficulties in finding places for both but also because the importance of one career over the other is less likely to be assumed.

Five of the eight responses to our call for narratives included some discussion about finding jobs at the same institution. This encouraging story came from one of our respondents, Claire Young:[4]

> We have a rather happy tale to tell, although we're not sure whether this is due to institutional beneficence or timing and fluke.
>
> In 1991, before we got involved, we were both teaching law in Ontario, but in cities 600 kilometers apart (London and Ottawa). Both of us had tenure and no plans to move. That year Susan was invited to apply for a Chair in Feminist Legal Studies at the University of British Columbia Faculty of Law in Vancouver. Because Vancouver was on the other side of Canada far from friends and family, and because she was happy with her teaching job in Ottawa, she declined. Also that year Claire accepted a visiting Chair in tax law for the 1992–93 academic year at the University of New South Wales in Sydney, Australia. Life was simple.
>
> Then we got involved. Suddenly we were faced with the problem of how to get together in the same location. (Claire had previously been involved in a commuting relationship of about the same distance and had no desire to repeat the experience.) The problem seemed intractable. We had jobs that

were not transportable, we desperately wanted to stay in academia, and while Claire was not particularly happy in London and was quite prepared to move, there were no job opportunities in either of the universities in Ottawa, nor was there a job for Susan in London.

At that point Susan decided to apply for the UBC job just to cover her bases. She got an interview and was offered the job in May, having told the Dean at UBC as well as other key people at the university that she had a female partner who would also need a job. By that time Claire had finalized the plans for Australia and Susan had decided to take a one year leave of absence from Carleton to go with her. We were leaving July 1st. UBC had no full-time positions which Claire could apply for. Indeed she faced the problem familiar to so many academics who wish to change institutions: that she was "too senior" as a tenured associate professor. So Susan eventually declined the job offer because of the lack of opportunities for Claire at UBC, her own ambivalence about leaving Ottawa, and the Australia commitment.

But UBC refused to take NO for an answer and continued to pursue various possibilities. Finally, Susan agreed to take the Chair on a visiting basis for one year to try it out and Claire agreed to fill in for a person going on leave for the year. It was made clear at that time that no promises of any future jobs could be made to Claire. So we opted out of Australia, and before we knew it had moved across the country for the year, with very little hope that a "real" position would emerge for Claire (and as a very "out" lesbian couple).

We started July 1 and by October noises were being made that there might be a position for Claire. As a result of considerable lobbying and the mortgaging of a future retirement position, a job in the Faculty of Law came open. As a tax specialist, Claire filled a need on the faculty and as a "senior woman", she fortunately fell into a program at UBC geared towards attracting senior women academics (the percentage of women faculty at UBC was and is low). By Christmas Claire had a tenure-stream job offer, and Susan still had the offer of the Chair on a permanent basis. We accepted within weeks, with considerable trepidation about being so far away from Ontario.

Due to the circumstances, we arrived at UBC as a completely "out" couple. No real choices had to be made about when to tell or who to tell, a new experience for both of us. Although we were nervous about this at the start, we seem to have been received very positively by faculty, staff and students. So far we have had no particularly negative experiences. The UBC law faculty has long had a number of gay men in it, some out and others very much not. To a certain extent some of the groundwork has been laid by those who are out and indeed there is a rather "tolerant" attitude to those who are not out but who the gossip network clearly has identified as gay.

We do, however have some concerns. As far as we know we are the first lesbian partners working as faculty members in a faculty of law in Canada. We wonder from time to time if it is partly BECAUSE we are a couple that we have been received so warmly. In a way, this fact makes us less threatening. We wonder if the faculty might have responded differently had only one of us been appointed and if that one had not come "out" until appointed. We also realise that in many ways we appear to be very "normal". We have bought a house, we attend faculty social functions together, although we have noticed that invitations issued to heterosexual couples as a couple are often issued to us individually. We are also probably less challenging in certain respects than some lesbians. Although our politics are definitely "left", and we are both outspoken feminists, we do not project an image of tough dykes. We are aware of a lesbian who was not appointed and we sense that some of the resistance to her appointment was based on her image as an outspoken dyke.

Nevertheless, we have to describe our tale as a happy one. Unlike so many couples we have been able to find two jobs in academia in the same city (and in our case in the same faculty). We are also able to be open about our relationship and thus out as lesbians, a luxury denied so many. We would like to think that our story is evidence of changing times for lesbians and gay men in academia, but we feel compelled to recognise that it is more a tale of "so far so good". What will the response be if we argue for curricular changes to include gay and lesbian legal issues or indeed teach a course on "queer theory"? How will our Dean and other colleagues view any university wide activities designed to fight homophobia on the campus? We have started to participate at that level and only time will tell.

Another respondent reported a similarly positive story. When Beth Alexander moved from the medical school at the University of Kansas to Michigan State University to become associate chair of the Department of Family Medicine, she informed the university that her female partner, an associate professor of English, would also require a faculty position. She writes:

> Having been in a relationship that was both a married academic relationship, and subsequently, an unmarried academic partnership, it seems to me there were a couple of particular challenges that presented themselves in the latter situation. I understand those issues much better retrospectively than I did at the time they were happening. When I was being recruited for a job at MSU in the Medical School, I was reluctant to move, but clearly hesitant to move without Anita, my partner. She was a poet and writer, entombed in an English department, and would have been happy to move had there been job opportunities available since the particular English department she was in at the time seemed not to value her skills. In the course of my inter-

views at Michigan State, I made it clear who my family was, and that she would need a job also. Anita and I finally agreed that I would go ahead, try the job, and if I liked it, would press forward in finding her a job.

It is not clear to me whether it was because I was a woman, whether it was because the relationship was lesbian, or whether it was because it was not an officially sanctioned relationship, but once I arrived at Michigan State, it seemed as if everyone forgot that I had left family behind and was "temporarily widowed." Ironically, there was a man in my department whose wife was out of the area, and I noted that he was invited for dinner, etc. several times a week. I was simply viewed as a single woman. After six months of reminding my chair gently that I would not stay if Anita did not have a job, I went to tell my Dean that I would be going back to Kansas if there were not a job for her. Quite quickly, he worked out a temporary job in the English department for two years, with the possibility that it might become permanent. And indeed, as I had predicted, the English Department at MSU liked Anita a lot, and wanted her on a permanent basis. She was recently granted promotion to full professor, but had to re-apply for the tenure, although she had been tenured prior to coming to MSU.

Recently, I became interested in a job in North Carolina; I interviewed and was offered the job. Following my previous learnings, I was open about who I was, and clear that my partner would have to move with me were I to come, and that she would need some assistance in finding a job. This time, probably because the institution was much smaller, and there was less flexibility within the organization to create a position for a partner, nothing happened. Again, I had to be repeatedly clear that the career of my partner was just as important an issue as was my own career. Somehow, that message doesn't "take" on the first pass. We didn't move to North Carolina, although it was a location and a job I would have liked. This time, the problems in moving two careers were bigger than before.

A couple of things I am clear about after two job offers, and one move. The first is that my decision to be open from the beginning of the interview process about who I was, and what would need to happen for both of us was preferable to hiding that information until later in the process. Although people had to be told several times, the message did finally get through. The second lesson is that the moving process was easier with a clear definition of whom I had left behind, and the nature of the relationship. I found that I needed to talk about my sense of missing my partner, occasionally at work, and that would not have been possible had I been more closeted. Most recently, being clear that I liked the job in North Carolina, but could not come until the plans for both careers were dealt with, made the withdrawal from the job search more understandable to those who were recruiting me. Finally, I believe that the triple oppression of being female in a male profession, being in a lesbian relationship, and being in a non-sanctioned relationship, made all of this much more difficult. Employers can often deal with one anomaly, but have much more difficulty when the differences add up. Had I been male, or married, the explanations would have not required repeating nearly so many times.

A lesbian professor from New York commented also on this issue of obtaining jobs at the same institution:

> In 1980 (two years after we "got together"—after a fairly long "courtship as friends") my partner moved to my home in Central New York and began a doctoral program in Sociology. (Her lifelong dream had been to teach in college—she had been in housing for financial and "inertia" reasons). We had some difficult years—her status and salary went from fairly high to "zip" and we were in a very small house which was "mine" with friends who were "mine". She had little identity and the cramped situation made life difficult. She also lived the life of a gypsy scholar, teaching at several nearby institutions as an adjunct for a pittance.
>
> In 1983 we decided to move to a larger home which we bought jointly (her graduate student loans helped a lot) and the added space helped us enjoy living together more. My institution began to accept her as "my spouse" as I always responded to invitations (Commencement committee luncheon at the president's house; get togethers) . . . that I was bringing a guest. Finally our President and others got the message and began saying "spouse or guest" on invitations instead of just "spouse". The president could never remember her name (after many invitations—I think it makes him nervous) but his wife, a charming woman, always was gracious to us both. My partner applied for several jobs on my campus, many times getting an interview, but not the job. In one particularly tense situation, a spouse (male) of a newly hired women's studies professor got a "created position". . . my "spouse" applied for the same position and was qualified, but was passed over. It was considered an "affirmative action hire" to hire that male (the women's studies' professor's spouse) but not to hire MY SPOUSE! Of course, I'd been here nearly 20 years—so they were trying to entice the women's studies professor . . . they didn't need to keep ME!
>
> In 1985 my partner defended her dissertation and got a sabbatical replacement job about 81 miles from our joint home. She rented a garage apartment where she would live on Tuesday and Wednesday nights and asked for a Tuesday, Wednesday, Thursday schedule which was a killer. The "family dog" stayed with me and she commuted weekly . . . even through snow storms (we ARE in the snow belt).
>
> We talked by phone nightly when she was away and she enjoyed academe. I think we helped each other politically—by talking about what we knew of

politics on our campuses—but we were kept from COMPETING academically, because we were at two places. At this time, our separation in mid-week
helped us both professionally, also—because we worked VERY HARD when
were apart and tried to keep some weekend time for "play".

Later in her narrative, she adds:

> I applied as an administrator to my partner's college in the Fall of 1992
> and was among the top 6 candidates (none of which they hired). It was prob-
> ably our only chance to get into the same institution—as it appears she
> would not get hired here.
>
> I am not sure we are not better off being in separate places—but the travel
> is beginning to wear. I will retire before she does (longer years of service,
> plus slightly older) so perhaps I will live in her site for awhile before she
> retires.
>
> We enjoy travel—personal and professional, and the life of a dual career
> academic couple. I think it was the dream of both of us to sit in a big pan-
> eled library type "den" and be grading papers, or talking academics with our
> "spouse". Now we are able to do that . . . anytime we want. We have learned
> much from each other and find that enriching. . . .
>
> Actually words don't do our relationship justice. (I am writing this on our
> 15th anniversary).

In contrast, another lesbian respondent reports the following about
a crisis facing her ten-year relationship: "An issue we must face in the
next two to three years (if the relationship survives) is location for a two-
career family. If I remain in this city in my current job, her employment
opportunities [when she finishes graduate school], if she desires to be
geographically closer, are very limited. I have been attempting, confiden-
tially, to obtain a position in a location within or near which numerous
programs in her field are situated." The phrase "if the relationship survives," while parenthetical in this context, may say much about the pressures upon gay and lesbian academic couples. The above narratives tell
us that, in the right circumstances, it is sometimes possible for lesbian
academic couples to be accommodated by the same institution. Unfortunately, it is impossible to predict, or even to speculate about, what
specific circumstances might make a difference.

Climate

Notwithstanding the appearance of increasing liberality on college campuses, gay and lesbian couples must cope with informal and unofficial
rejection in academe. This is not only an issue of individual interactions

among faculty and staff. The presence or absence of recognition in college or university policies can create a "climate" of acknowledgment or disapproval. Psychiatry professor Terry Stein, a gay man from Michigan State University, sent this response:

> I think the most significant thing about being a partner in an unmarried same-sex relationship within the university setting is the pervasive sense of invisibility and denial of the existence of my relationship. Formal recognition of this relationship is totally absent as a result of the exclusion of any official language and policy that would acknowledge its existence to even the slightest extent. In a sense, this erasure is expectable, however, and perhaps less painful because of the very ordinariness of its occurrence. But the ignoring of my relationship at a personal level is more painful and, therefore, less tolerable. It is as though we were talking about some deeply personal event but could only use the third person to describe it.
>
> For me the ignoring occurs all the time because my partner and I frequently function together within the university in meetings that have been called to deal explicitly with issues having to do with gay and lesbian persons. I don't think there is a very exact protocol for managing professional boundaries concerning any intimate relationships, whether they are heterosexual or homosexual, married or unmarried. Within my field of psychiatry, I had teachers and mentors early in my academic career who were husband and wife, and they used their relationship as a vehicle for instruction about families. While I am not certain such "public displays" of relatedness are wholly appropriate, I envy the permission to do so.
>
> In contrast, I feel that I must keep a distance from my partner in professional meetings. Probably this arises in part from personal inhibitions and reflects as well the gender based proscriptions on intimate personal behavior. Since my partner and I are both men, we have been socialized not to be too close to other men and certainly not to be publicly affectionate. We also eschew any association with effeminate homosexual men by being certain our own public personas are appropriately masculine, i.e., somewhat distant and not too expressive. I love my partner very much and think about him throughout the day, but I don't think anyone who knows us solely within the professional setting of the university would have any sense of the depth and the character of our relationship. I am unwilling to take complete responsibility for the invisible personality of our relationship, even after acknowledging that some of the hiding results from our being men and from needs arising from our individual traits and not only from reactions to our sexual orientation.
>
> The university community, and certainly the administration of the university, doesn't want to acknowledge that we are a couple; it would be too threatening to see—really see—two men in an intimate relationship. It is

somewhat permissible, even if it does not appear to be very interesting, to talk about gay and lesbian relationships in the abstract; it is forbidden to be in the same room with the relationship. Like Larry Kramer said in his criticism of the recent film *Philadelphia*, the relationship of the central character portrayed by Tom Hanks and his partner did not really exist in the film. The men did not speak to each other, they did not touch each other, they did not appear to be the primary other in each other's life. The relationship was sterilized and washed out so that the centrality of it as an organizing principle in the characters' (and our) lives simply disappears.

The ignoring is not universal. Some ask me about my partner or convey messages to him through me. While I tend to be uncomfortable in the role of conduit, I know that we are seen as a couple by these people and I feel validated as a person in relation.

Within the university, I think we are successful as individuals and as a couple, and we are both openly gay. Together these factors probably make us less invisible and less subject to verbal and non-verbal harassment. But these same factors also make us vulnerable to tokenism and objectification. We can be outwardly accepted without really being invited into the inner circle.

In ways similar to Terry's experience, one lesbian respondent, a university administrator whose partner of ten and a half years taught at the same university, reported that when her partner left to pursue doctoral studies elsewhere she suffered a kind of isolation that might not have been characteristic for a member of a married couple. However, in her case, her colleagues may well have been ignorant of her need for sympathy and support. Even sympathetic colleagues who recognized her discomfort and its source may have been reluctant to invade her privacy, since she is "closeted" at work.

I think that I, more than D., had a more realistic idea of the stresses of such a program and was concerned what those stresses and an 1100 mile separation would do to the relationship. I also felt very much abandoned and needed the support of my peers, especially at work. But, since I am very much in the closet at work, that support was not forthcoming. I compared my situation to that of a former dean who moved here without his spouse and family. He received overwhelming sympathy, whereas I, through my own timidity, did not. I was reminded of the . . . song which compares the public treatment of a surviving spouse with that of its treatment of a lesbian whose partner has died.

Cohabiting heterosexual couples may have an easier time of it (or at least an experience more similar to married couples) since they can more easily "pass" for married and their status is common in society as a whole. Since most cohabiting heterosexual couples marry within a relatively short time of beginning to live together, perhaps many perceive their unmarried status as temporary and thus not an issue. Longer term heterosexual cohabitors may also lack concern, since their marital status is essentially "invisible" unless they choose to share it.

One heterosexual respondent had this to say:

> As I mentioned when we spoke, I haven't experienced any problems that I think are different from those married faculty members might experience. Nevertheless, here are my thoughts.
>
> For me the biggest issue is whether administrators think that, because I'm in a relationship, I won't leave to take another job. I may have mentioned that my chair once said that he wasn't worried about me leaving, because my partner is here. Although I quickly told him that he was wrong, I still think that he and others in administrative roles think that I am in their pocket. I worry that such attitudes affect the raises and other considerations I might get; the conventional wisdom (meaning I have no idea if it is true) is that they only value you if you're threatening to leave.
>
> I think that being in a relationship does affect decision making about changing jobs—but that would also be true if my partner was not a professor. Single folks simply don't have to consult with live-in others (spouses, significant others, children) when making career moves. This doesn't mean that single folks move more often—the support systems and friendships they have are important too, and it may be harder to move when you are faced with starting somewhere else alone.
>
> A second issue is that of separating work and home. When both of you work at the university (or any other place) it is easy to bring the work home. My partner and I have collaborated on some projects and have continued to discuss them at home, but that hasn't been a real problem. The problem has been when upsetting things are brought home and discussed endlessly. During a recent university upheaval around administrative leadership, it was easy to continue to talk about stuff at home. We finally made a rule for our house: talking university politics was not permitted after 6 p.m.! This gave us time to do a little talking, but helped us stop and get on with other things. By the way, the rule was in force for guests at the house as well. I credit the rule (both inventing it and enforcing it) with keeping us relatively sane during a trying time for our university's profs.

This respondent and her partner have been together for several years and do not plan to marry, but their relationship to the university is in her view no different than that of married couples. This perception of being taken for granted because they are a couple that would face special difficulties in relocating is similar to that found among married couples by Ferber and Hoffman in their study (this volume).

For gays and lesbians there is always the issue of whether and to whom to "come out." Depending on the size of the community it may be possible to live "two lives," remaining closeted and relying on support from the gay and lesbian community. Support from friends is more important to gay and lesbian couples than to heterosexual couples (Kurdek 1988). If a couple is hiding it is harder to obtain support from coworkers and it may therefore be harder to do one's job. One lesbian respondent commented thus:

> Five years ago I ran for school board in the small town where we live. I was sure that someone would "out" me and the election would be humiliating. Actually I had a lot of teacher support and won handily. When people came to our house to interview me, however, I must admit I took down pictures of us together and put up every picture I had of nieces, nephews and friends' children (a cop out?). My partner has teased me ever since. I felt that, in order to be effective, I had to get elected first! I have been reelected once, and do fight for causes like multicultural awareness, equity for women, and other issues for which there is no other voice on our fairly conservative school board.

She goes on to say about her partner:

> She is much more an activist than I (and more free to do it—in an Arts & Sciences discipline). I'm now a quasi-administrator in a professional school and have much less lee-way about my public beliefs and behavior. We team teach once in awhile, which is a big "high". . . and students like our repartee. I think they see the love, as well as the academic respect . . . it HAS to show.
>
> We are not sure whether we are competitive academically or not—we are very competitive on the tennis court, but I think we truly appreciate each other's merits and applaud them. My partner was awarded an "Excellence in Teaching Award" after 6 years at her institution—I had been nominated once, but did not get it for reasons which may be political. That is about the closest we have gotten to "competing" for the same distinction. It does not bother me that she has received that award—in fact I hope she goes "all the way" (there is a Distinguished Teaching Professorship also). I go to most things at her institution which I can make as "her spouse" and she does that at mine.

When gay men and lesbians are not completely out, it is not difficult to understand how these relationships are affected by informal college and university politics, which sometimes requires socializing. If there is a felt need for hiding one's identity and therefore one's relationship with one's partner, there may be inhibitions about doing collaborative work with other faculty members and even participating in conversations or events that occasion customary self-disclosure about one's personal life.

Gay or lesbian faculty couples may wish to use university-sponsored child care but hesitate for fear of being too open. Contrary to common assumptions, many gay men and lesbians have children. The Children of Gays organization estimates that there are more than 6 million children of lesbians and gay men in the United States (Schulenburg 1985). Ironically, among those who are candid about their lives, there may be insufficient recognition of their family roles. Psychiatry professor Terry Stein included comments about the way he feels the university responds to his family:

> No university administrator, outside of my department or college, has ever asked me about my partner, or for that matter about my son. We are not viewed as a couple or as a family. I believe this reflects a deep alienation from family imposed on lesbians and gay men in American society, what Kath Weston (in her book *Families We Choose*) has described as an exile from kinship. I believe every gay man and lesbian suffers from this conceptual and behavioral exclusion; I believe all of us who are in relationships pay a price through added stress on and lack of support for our relationships. The heterosexual person who chooses not to display her or his relationship is not challenging the same set of assumptions about relation because they are in a position to make the choice to disclose or not disclose about their relationship. I think it is helpful for the gay or lesbian person who is in a relationship to come out as a relational person and, ultimately, to demand, explicitly and straightforwardly, recognition and celebration of the relationship. Equality with heterosexual relationships should not be the primary goal for gay and lesbian relationships, but rather we should seek respect and support for the unique and sustaining role that our relationships and families play in our lives.

These narratives illustrate that the rubric of "climate" covers a wide range of issues that are particularly relevant to gay and lesbian couples and goes beyond the issues of obtaining jobs in the same place or health care benefits. There is evidence elsewhere that this is true. The Michigan State University report of the University-Wide Task Force on Lesbian and Gay Issues (1992), for example, addresses a gamut of campus concerns relevant to gay, lesbian, and bisexual faculty, staff, and students.

Its final recommendations represent the work of over a hundred persons who labored for more than a year to assess the treatment and experiences of lesbians and gays at the university. They administered questionnaires and conducted focus groups. They held campus forums to elicit opinions. Their recommendations include the establishment of an antidiscrimination policy that pervades all aspects of university life, but do not stop there. They urge action related to campus safety; employment and benefit issues; lesbian, bisexual, and gay studies and content across the curriculum; outreach; education; mentoring; health and support services; as well as tackling the exclusion policies of ROTC and some campus religious groups that contribute to a hostile, even violent environment for lesbians and gays. The report provides a blueprint for comprehensive action for the prevention of discrimination and movement toward an environment of open acceptance, respect, and inclusion.

Summary and Conclusions

This chapter is meant to be a starting point for more formal research on this topic. The narratives indicate that different individuals appear to have very different stories to tell, depending upon their institution, whether they are heterosexual or gay or lesbian, and whether they are open or closeted about their sexual orientation. These factors need comprehensive study.

The few narratives we collected portray individuals working hard at both their jobs and their personal relationships, struggling to be viewed within their academic communities as contributing members and also as members of a family unit that is often invisible or appears invalid to their peers and colleagues. The "normalization" of such relationships in academic institutions would undoubtedly allow for the construction of a more level playing field for these members of the academic community. Research that clarifies the situations of unmarried academic couples will identify areas that need change and indicate problems that need immediate attention.

Directions for research might include a comparison of married and unmarried couples with regard to institutional accommodations in hiring couples and their salaries, promotions, achievements, and failures within the system. Because of the stigma attached to lesbians and gays and, to a lesser extent, unmarried heterosexual couples, research regarding possible differential treatment in the informal organizational system is also important. The issue of productivity among persons dealing with the emotionally draining tasks of hiding and facing ignorance, hatred, and discrimination merits exploration. A comparison of faculty experiences in "gay friendly" universities versus those without nondiscrimination policies and other mechanisms of acceptance and protection would help in the identification of university policies and practices that are most helpful or harmful to lesbian and gay academic couples.

Finally, while there have been some studies of differences in couples' personal relationships, it would be interesting to learn whether the findings of Blumstein and Schwartz, for example, hold true among academic couples. Finding a sample of couples to study may prove difficult, however. Ironically, as acceptance of unmarried couples in academia increases, the possibility of obtaining such a sample may increase at the same time as the differences between married and unmarried couples decrease.

Notes

1. There is some indication that lesbians earn less for their educational level and work experience than heterosexual women. See Morgan and Brown 1991. This is generally true of women in higher education. A *Wall Street Journal* article, however, reported that lesbian households' average annual income is higher than the U.S. average. See "Leaving the Corporate Closet" 1991.

2. "Career leveling" refers to the resulting circumstance when members of a couple value equally the career demands of each partner and act accordingly. Their careers are "leveled" in that neither partner faces the gains or loses he or she might have experienced had both partners put all their efforts into furthering one career.

3. Subsequent to this study, the university established a policy of extending health care coverage to same-sex domestic partners.

4. Respondents were asked whether they wished confidentiality or open identification in this publication. Some chose to be identified or agreed to identifying information being included. Others chose confidentiality. We have respected their wishes.

References

Badgett, M. V. Lee. 1994. "Equal Pay for Equal Families." *Academe* 80 (May–June): 26–30.

Blumstein, Philip, and Pepper Schwartz. 1983. *American Couples: Money, Work, Sex.* New York: William Morrow.

Bumpass, Larry L., and James A. Sweet. 1989. "National Estimates of Cohabitation." *Demography* 26 (Nov.): 615–25.

Fried, Barbara. 1994. *Domestic Partner Benefits: A Case Study.* Washington, D.C.: College and University Personnel Association.

"Guidelines for Unwedded Bliss." *Futurist.* 1991. (Sept.–Oct.): 47–48.

Kotkin, Mark. 1983. "Sex Roles among Married and Unmarried Couples." *Sex Roles* 9 (9): 975–85.

Kurdek, Lawrence A. 1988. "Perceived Social Support in Gays and Lesbians in Cohabiting Relationships." *Journal of Personality and Social Psychology* 54 (Mar.): 504–9.

Larson, Kathryn H. 1992. "Economic Issues Facing Lesbian Households." Paper presented at the First Conference of the International Association for Feminist Economics, American University, Washington, D.C., 24–26 July.

"Leaving the Corporate Closet." 1991. *Wall Street Journal.* 22 Nov.:R8.

Morgan, Kris S., and Laura S. Brown. 1991. "Lesbian Career Development, Work Behavior, and Vocational Counseling." *Counseling Psychologist* 19 (2): 273–91.

Rubenstein, William B. 1993. *Lesbians, Gay Men, and the Law.* New York: New Press.

Schneider, Margaret S. 1986. "The Relationships of Cohabiting Lesbian and Heterosexual Couples: A Comparison." *Psychology of Women Quarterly* 10 (Sept.): 234–39.

Schulenburg, Joy. 1985. *Gay Parenting: A Complete Guide for Gay Men and Lesbians with Children.* Garden City, N.Y.: Anchor Books.

Subcommittee of the Funded Retirement Insurance Committee. 1991. *Domestic Partner Coverage.* Iowa City: University of Iowa Personnel Services.

University-Wide Task Force on Lesbian and Gay Issues. *Moving Forward: Lesbians and Gay Men at Michigan State University.* 1992. East Lansing: Michigan State University.

5

The Status of Academic Couples in U.S. Institutions

Helen S. Astin and Jeffrey F. Milem

THIS CHAPTER REPRESENTS the third phase in the evolution of a line of research begun by Helen Astin. This research first began in the 1970s in a series of studies examining gender differences in the academic reward structure (e.g., see Astin and Bayer 1972; Bayer and Astin 1975). Some scholars in higher education argued that the differences between men and women in academic rewards were the result of constraints on women that were imposed on them by marriage and not the result of sex discrimination (e.g., see Lester 1974; Sowell 1975). Those who subscribed to this line of thinking argued that "marriage has opposite effects on the careers of male and female academics, advancing the man professionally and retarding the woman's progress" (Sowell 1975: 55). In establishing an argument that gender differences in academic rewards were at least in part caused by sex discrimination, Astin (1978) and Astin and Bayer (1979) examined data from a 1972 national survey of college and university faculty. The findings from their studies suggested that married academic women were actually more like academic men with respect to career advancement and status than were single academic women.

Astin and Davis (1985) and Davis and Astin (1987) followed up on this earlier work by examining the relationship between marital status and "productivity" for women academics. Astin and Davis (1985) argued that being single greatly disadvantaged academic women. They found that academic women who were married were more "productive" than were academic women who were single and attributed these findings in part to the tendency for women academics to be married to other academics. They argued that these women had a relative advantage over academic women without male partners because their partners put them in closer contact with male colleagues and collegial networks to which they might not otherwise have had access. In their words, "women without a male partner may be more likely to be excluded from the 'boys' network, important connections and critical information. Academic women who are married have fewer obstacles to the social networking and collegiality that plays such an important role in facilitating productivity in academe" (Astin and Davis 1985:99). A similar appraisal was offered by Clark and Corcoran (1986), who argue that single women were "excluded from, or have limited access to, informal networks of communication that carry significant professional information" (38). The valuable role played by these collegial networks in enhancing the productivity of academics has been established by Fox (1985) as well. Fox states that "collegial exchange (as opposed to local identification or loyalty) within the unit or department does appear to facilitate productivity. Ongoing, face-to-face contact helps provide ideas, catch errors, and stimulate development" (1985:267).

This chapter signifies the beginning of the third phase of this line of inquiry. Our analyses involve testing whether women faculty members with spouses/partners who are academics are at a relative advantage or disadvantage when they are compared on a range of outcomes with men who have academic spouses/partners. In pursuing this line of inquiry, we have also compared faculty members married to academics with women and men who report that their spouses/partners are not academics. This allows us to test the interpretations offered by Astin and Davis regarding the possible sources of the relative career advantages of married academic women.

Sample and Methodology

Data used in this study were collected as part of a 1989 national survey of college and university faculty and academic administrators conducted by the Higher Education Research Institute (HERI) at UCLA. Surveys were sent to over 91,000 faculty members at 432 institutions across the country during the fall and winter of 1989. After the second wave of surveys were mailed, responses were received from 55 percent of those surveyed, yielding a final sample of 51,574.

To approximate results that would be obtained if all faculty members at all institutions had responded to the survey, a multistage weighting procedure was utilized. This process first compensates for response bias *within* institutions that participated in the survey. It then corrects for response bias *between* institutions in the sample.

The survey gathered information regarding background characteristics, attitudes and values, pedagogical practices, research activities, perceptions regarding the institutions in which they were employed, and other information regarding faculty roles at their institutions. Comparisons made between the 1989 HERI data and data from a national faculty survey conducted by the National Center for Education Statistics indicate that the HERI data are representative of teaching faculty in regard to age, race, academic rank, and highest degree held (for more detailed information on the HERI faculty survey, see Astin, Korn, and Dey 1991).

We have chosen to focus our analyses primarily on those men and women who indicated that their spouses/partners were academics. Our primary question was how women with academic spouses/partners fare compared with men who have academic spouses/partners. Hence, for the analyses and comparisons reported in this chapter, we selected from the total sample of college and university faculty members only those who responded to a survey item indicating whether or not their spouse or partner was an academic (weighted $N = 307,182$).

To assess how faculty members with academic or nonacademic spouses/partners fare, we utilized two types of analyses. First, we provided descriptive analyses of the characteristics and professional status of women and men with academic partners/spouses and those with nonacademic partners/spouses. Moreover, to explore the impact of having an academic spouse/partner on certain professional outcomes we utilized stepwise regression procedures. These analyses, performed separately for men and women, examined four academic status variables: (1) salary; (2) research productivity as measured by publications during the past two years; (3) academic rank; and (4) being employed at a university as opposed to a four-year or two-year college. For each regression analysis we entered relevant control variables such as age, highest degree completed, field of highest degree, parental education, and type of employing institution before we entered the independent variable of key interest in this study—spouse/partner is an academic.

Background Characteristics

As with previous surveys of college and university faculty members, we found that men were more likely than women to report that they were married. During the 1989–90 academic year, 82 percent of men compared with 62 percent of women indicated that they were "currently married" (see appendix 2, table 5-1). At the same time, only 8 percent of men but 17 percent of women indicated that they were single (never married). Women were also twice as likely to report that they were divorced (13 percent versus 7 percent).

Among those faculty members who reported that they were married or with partners, 35 percent of the men (weighted $N = 234{,}264$) and 40 percent of the women (weighted $N = 72{,}318$) indicated that their spouses/partners were academics. American Indian women were most likely to report that their partners/spouses were academics (50 percent) while Puerto Rican–American women were least likely to report so (22 percent; see appendix 2, table 5-2). Among men, African Americans were most likely to report that their partners/spouses were academics (48 percent) while Asian/Asian-American and Chicano/Mexican-American men were least likely to report that they were married or had partners who were in academe (28 percent and 29 percent, respectively).

Faculty women with academic partners/spouses tend to come from somewhat more educated families than do men whose partners/spouses are academic (see appendix 2, table 5-3). Not surprisingly, more men and women with academic partners/spouses report that their partners/spouses have graduate degrees than men and women with nonacademic partners/spouses do. For example, 88 percent of women report that their academic partners/spouses hold graduate degrees, while only 36 percent of women report that their nonacademic partners/spouses hold graduate degrees. Similarly, 70 percent of men reported that their academic partners/spouses had graduate degrees, but only 27 percent of men reported that their nonacademic partners/spouses had them.

Educational Preparation

Men in academia are more likely to hold doctorates than are academic women (see appendix 2, table 5-4). Women with academic spouses/partners are more likely to hold professional degrees or doctorates (53 percent) than women with nonacademic spouses/partners (39 percent).

Differences in Fields

When we examine the fields in which faculty members received their highest degrees, we find patterns similar to those found in previous studies that examined gender differences (see appendix 2, table 5-5). These differences tend to occur independent of a spouse's/partner's employment status. Women were more likely to have received their highest degrees in the traditionally female fields of English, other humanities, education, and allied health. Once again, it is informative to examine the percentage of men and women within each disciplinary area who reported that their partners/spouses were academics (see appendix 2, table 5-6). Men in the fields of education, English, and the fine arts (where women have higher levels of representation) were most likely to report that their partners/spouses were academics. On the other hand, over half of the women in agriculture, mathematics/statistics, other humanities, and history/political science reported that their partners/spouses were academics.

Employment Patterns

Women with academic spouses/partners are more likely to be employed at four-year institutions than are women faculty members with nonacademic spouses/partners (74 percent compared with 64 percent; see table 5-7). Of these four-year institutions, women with academic spouses/partners are more likely to be employed at public universities and four-year colleges. Women with nonacademic spouses/partners, in contrast, are more likely to be employed by public two-year institutions. Men with academic spouses/partners are less likely to be at universities than are those with nonacademic spouses/partners (42 percent of men with nonacademic spouses/partners are employed by universities compared with 34 percent of men with academic spouses/partners). The differential between men and women with respect to employment at universities is greater for those with nonacademic spouses/partners than for those with academic spouses/partners.

Rank

Women with academic partners/spouses fare better with respect to rank than do those with nonacademic partners/spouses (45 percent versus 33 percent are full or associate professors; see appendix 2, table 5-8). The descriptive analyses also reveal that for rank, the gender gap is smaller between men and women with academic partners/spouses than between men and women with nonacademic partners/spouses. However, through the use of basic cross-tabulations, it is not possible to determine whether or not this might be a function of field, degree, or age. In the regression analyses later in this chapter, we do control for the effect of these variables prior to examining the relationship between having an academic spouse/partner and rank, productivity, salary, and place of employment.

Publications

When we examine publication records, we see that in the aggregate women publish less than men. However, our data indicate that the gender differential is much greater between men and women with nonacademic partners/spouses (see appendix 2, table 5-9). For example, the difference between men and women with academic partners/spouses who reported that they had not published anything during the previous two years was only 7 percentage points as compared with the 21–percentage-point difference between men and women with nonacademic partners/spouses. A larger percentage (43 percent) of male faculty members with academic spouses/partners reported that they had not published anything in the previous two years than had men with nonacademic spouses/partners (39 percent). The pattern is reversed for women, however (50 percent for women with academic spouses/partners compared with 60 percent for women with nonacademic spouses/partners). Another way to examine this question is to look at those faculty members characterized as "highly productive." Men with academic spouses/partners tend to be only slightly less productive than men with nonacademic spouses/partners; for example, 15 percent of men with academic spouses/partners claim to have published five or more items during the previous two years compared with 17 percent of those with nonacademic spouses/partners. There seems to be a clear advantage, however, for women with academic spouses/partners. As much as 11 percent of women with academic spouses/partners claim to have published five or more professional writings during the previous two years, as compared with 7 percent of women with nonacademic spouses/partners.

Interests

Women with academic partners/spouses tend to express greater interest in research than in teaching when compared with women who have nonacademic partners/spouses (24 percent compared with 17 percent, respectively; see appendix 2, table 5-10). However, the opposite is true for men; 29 percent with academic partners/spouses claim to lean toward or have strong interests in research but 33 percent with nonacademic partners/spouses claim such interests. Again, we see that the gender differential is greatly reduced between men and women with academic partners/spouses.

Regarding work patterns, more women than men, regardless of whether they have academic partners/spouses, tend to engage in research with others instead of doing it alone (see appendix 2, table 5-11). However, women with nonacademic partners/spouses are even more likely to do so.

Career Patterns

Consistent with findings from a number of other studies of gender differences among college and university faculty (Acker 1994; Chamberlain 1988; Lie, Malik, and Harris 1994; Ries and Stone 1993), women were much more likely to report that they had interrupted their careers than were men. Nearly one-third of the women surveyed reported that they had interrupted their career (29 percent) as compared to less than 4 percent of men. Moreover, there are no differences based upon whether or not their partner was an academic. In past surveys the gender differential was much smaller because of men's interruptions for military service.

Women were more likely than men to report that they had received firm job offers in the previous two years. Women with nonacademic spouses/partners were more likely to have received job offers compared with women who had academic spouses/partners (45 percent compared with 36 percent). However, there was hardly any difference between men with academic or nonacademic spouses/partners (30 percent versus 31 percent). That more women had received offers may be the result of affirmative action efforts. On the other hand, the differential between the two groups of women may be a function of limited academic opportunities for women in dual-career couples.

Stress

The last section of the survey looked at sources of stress. The series of items presented in table 5-12 of appendix 2 provides information about stress resulting from nonprofessional as well as professional experiences and activities. Compared with men who have nonacademic partners/spouses, men with academic partners/spouses report slightly more stress resulting from family concerns (household responsibilities, child care), perhaps because they are more involved in household and child-care responsibilities. However, they are less likely to report stress with professional concerns (promotion process, research and publication expectations). Regardless of the status of their spouse or partner, women report more stress in almost all categories than do the men. Women with academic partners/spouses report more stress from subtle discrimination than women with nonacademic partners/spouses. Women with nonacademic partners or spouses are more likely to report stress that results from family responsibilities and marital friction, suggesting that they assume more responsibility for the household than do their partners or spouses.

Summary of Findings of Descriptive Data

Our analyses of descriptive data suggest that women with academic spouses/partners tend to fare better than do women with nonacademic spouses/partners. Specifically, they are more likely to be employed at four-year institutions, to have a high academic rank, to have published more, and to have reported less relative stress resulting from family responsibilities and marital friction. On the other hand, an opposite pattern emerges when we compare men who have academic partners/spouses with men who have nonacademic partners/spouses. Men with academic partners/spouses were less likely to be employed at universities and to have published extensively and were more likely to report greater relative stress resulting from family concerns.

Regression Results

Thus far in this chapter we have examined the personal characteristics and career experiences of academics who have academic spouses/partners and have compared them with academics who have nonacademic spouses/partners. Our findings, as well as findings from previous studies of gender differences in the academic reward structure, indicate that some of the differences that we observed may be influenced by factors such as age, degree field, research productivity, and department of academic appointment (e.g., see Hamermesh 1988; Scott and Bereman 1992;

Smart 1991; Tolbert 1986). To control for the possible influence of these factors, we conducted a series of regression analyses on four selected outcomes: (1) salary; (2) academic rank; (3) research productivity as represented by the number of items published in the previous two years; and (4) employment at a university as opposed to a four-year or two-year college. The regressions for each dependent variable were conducted separately for women and men. Through these analyses, we provide further information concerning the relative effect of having an academic partner/spouse on career outcomes. In the tables presented in appendix 2 we list only those variables that remained statistically significant at the final solution of the regression equation. Appendix 1 provides the coding schema for all of the independent variables that were used in the regression equations.

Salary

In our regression analysis predicting salary for academic men and women (see appendix 2, table 5-13), we first controlled for background variables that included age, parental education, highest degree attained by the respondent, and field of highest degree. We then controlled for job-related characteristics, including rank and type of institution where respondent was employed. Finally, we entered the dichotomous variable indicating whether or not the spouse/partner of the respondent was an academic.

For both men and women, being older (a proxy for years of experience), having received a high terminal academic degree (such as a doctorate), being at a higher rank, being more "productive" over the previous two years, and being employed at a university all served as positive predictors of higher salary. However, having academic spouses/partners had different effects for men and women. Women with academic spouses/partners tend to fare somewhat better with respect to their salary than do women with nonacademic spouses/partners. The opposite finding is apparent for men. Men with nonacademic spouses/partners tend to receive higher salaries than do men with academic spouses/partners.

There are a number of possible explanations for this finding. First, the academic reward system is such that it still favors men whose partners/spouses are either employed in less lucrative jobs outside of academe or who do not work for pay, perhaps based on the assumption that these men need greater financial resources. Second, men with nonacademic partners/spouses may be better negotiators than men with academic partners/spouses. The third explanation is one that draws from each of the first two. It may be that men with academic partners/spouses are not (or feel that they are not) in a position of strength in salary negotiations because of their concern for the status of their academic partners/spouses. In other words, these men may either be willing to or feel that they must accept lower salaries in exchange for receiving academic appointments at or near the institutions where their partners/ spouses are employed.

When we compare women with men, we find that fields indeed differentiate the genders with respect to salaries. We find that men in the more traditionally female fields of education, humanities, and English fare worse than their male counterparts in other fields. Women in these fields, while not faring as well as women in other fields, show less of a differential in their salaries. In addition, men employed at universities fare much better than their counterparts at other types of institutions.

Rank

For the regression analysis predicting academic rank (see appendix 2, table 5-14), we utilized a three-stage process of entering variables similar to that used in the regressions predicting salary. As with the previous analysis, age, number of publications, and degree attainment served as positive predictors of rank for both men and women. The field of highest degree, number of publications, and employment setting were entered into the equations after controlling for the effects of background characteristics. Men and women who were employed at universities tended to be at lower academic ranks than those who were employed at other types of institutions. Men who were employed at four-year colleges tended to be at lower academic ranks; however, this was not the case for women.

In our test of whether or not being married or involved in an intimate relationship with another academic affected rank attainment we found a pattern of effects similar for men and women. Women and men whose partners/spouses were academics tended to be at higher ranks than men and women whose partners/spouses were nonacademics. However, the relative advantage of having an academic partner/spouse appears to be stronger for women than for men (unstandardized regression coefficient of 0.11 for women versus 0.04 for men). For women the positive effect of being in an intimate relationship with an academic is, in part, a result of greater access to information about how the system works (as was suggested in the earlier work of Astin and Davis). The general finding is that having an academic partner/spouse is more advantageous for women than for men. The advantage for men with academic partners/spouses may be partly offset by greater responsibilities for child care and household chores.

When we examine the unstandardized regression coefficients for men and women with respect to rank attainment, we see a couple of interesting findings. Men in the physical sciences and health-related fields are much more likely to be found in higher ranks than are the women in these fields, even after controlling for the effects of age, degree, and publications. These are fields in which women are in the minority. However, it is interesting to note that women in English also have a harder time attaining the higher ranks than do men. Likewise, women at universities do not fare as well as do men. However, with respect to having an academic partner/spouse, the positive effect is much stronger for women that it is for men.

Publications

In our analysis predicting research productivity we chose to examine the number of items respondents had published during the previous two years (see appendix 2, table 5-15). Once again, a process similar to the previous analyses of entering variables into the regression equation was used. Degree attainment served as a positive predictor of productivity for both women and men. Younger faculty were also more likely to report higher levels of publication during the previous two years. This finding is not surprising given the pressure to publish that is placed on younger faculty members who are trying to obtain tenure or be promoted to full professor. After controlling for the effect of age, academic rank served as a positive predictor of productivity. Faculty at higher ranks are more likely to have access to important resources in various forms, including grants and graduate research assistants, that facilitate productivity. Also, those who are at higher ranks have attained such posts because of their records in research and publications.

Not surprisingly, the findings indicate that levels of research productivity are strongly influenced by the type of institution where faculty are employed. Being employed at a university served as an extremely strong positive predictor for both men and women. However, being employed at a four-year college had a different pattern of effects for men and women. For men, employment at a four-year college had a positive effect on productivity while for women the effect was weakly negative. Of course, one would need to also examine how these differences may play out if we were to employ measures of productivity other than scholarly output.

As with the findings from the regressions predicting salary, the effect of having an academic spouse/partner varies for men and women. Women with academic spouses/partners tend to be more productive than do women with nonacademic spouses/partners. However, the direction of the effect is the opposite for men. Again, it may be that men with academic spouses/partners may not be as productive given their greater household responsibilities. Also, men with nonacademic spouses/partners may benefit from clerical and research support offered by their spouses/partners. On the other hand, women with academic spouses/partners fare better, perhaps because of access to information and networks through their academic spouses/partners.

We observe some gender differences with respect to the factors that affect productivity. Age is a more important factor for men than for women in that within rank, older men are less productive than younger men. Age is less of a factor in women's productivity. Also, men in higher ranks tend to be more productive than women in the same rank. In part, this may be because men who are full professors enjoy more benefits from the support of grants and graduate students than do women.

Once again, fields appear to have differential effects for women and men. Men in the fine arts are less likely to be productive than are men in other fields. However, the fine arts predict relatively high productivity for women. While women in the humanities appear to be quite productive, the opposite is the case with men. A similar pattern can be seen with the agricultural fields.

However, once again, the critical issue in these analyses is the effect of having an academic partner/spouse on productivity. This proves to be a positive factor for academic women, but a negative factor for men.

University Employment

In the final regression analysis we examined what effect having an academic spouse or partner had on the type of institution at which the faculty member was employed (a university versus a four-year or two-year college; see appendix 2, table 5-16). As we would expect to find given the job expectations of faculty employed at this type of institution, faculty who are more productive are more likely to be found at universities. As with each of the other analyses, having a high terminal degree served as a predictor of employment at a university. A rather intriguing finding that appears in the analysis of only this dependent variable is the fact that socioeconomic status (as reflected in father's or mother's level of educational attainment) entered the regression with significant weights. Academic women and men who came from more highly educated families were more likely to be employed at universities. It is not possible to know whether this finding reflects past advantages accrued from the type of institutions that respondents had attended or whether it has to do with higher levels of ambition or expectation that resulted from being raised in more affluent homes. Regardless, the theories of accumulated advantages (Zuckerman 1977; Merton 1968) and anticipatory socialization (Clark and Corcoran 1986) would seem to have some merit in understanding this phenomenon.

Age affected the employment of men and women differently. Younger women were more likely to be employed at universities while among men the older cohorts were more likely to be employed there. This difference may be a reflection of affirmative action practices as well as changes in women's behavior with respect to increasingly higher expectations of employment settings and greater ambition in more recent times. (These behavioral changes appear to have occurred regardless of whether or not a woman's partner was an academic.) Women with academic partners/spouses, however, were less likely to have been employed at universities and so were men with academic partners/spouses.

Summary and Conclusions

This study provides empirical evidence of the positive effect on academic women of having an academic as opposed to a nonacademic partner/spouse. This lends further support to the findings of earlier research indicating that married women were more productive than single women (Astin and Davis 1985; Davis and Astin 1987; Cole and Zuckerman 1984; Davis and Astin 1990). Davis and Astin (1987, 1990; see also Astin and Davis 1985) attribute such findings to the fact that many academic women are married to other academics. Marriages and partnerships with other academics are believed to give academic women a relative advantage over single women by providing them with greater access to academic networks, information, and social support.

Initially, one may be surprised and somewhat dismayed about the effect that marriage or intimate partnership with another academic has for men. However, upon greater reflection, we believe that these findings do make sense. If we think back to our descriptive analyses, we find that men with academic partners or spouses are more likely than men with nonacademic partners or spouses to mention household and child-care responsibilities as sources of stress. These findings are consistent with research on dual-career couples indicating that men are assuming greater responsibility for household tasks and child rearing (Bird and Bird 1985; Gaddy, Glass, and Arnkoff 1983; Gilbert 1985). As long as homemaking and child-care responsibilities take time and energy and as long as women can reach greater equality only if these responsibilities are shared more equally, it is inevitable that men's careers will suffer. On the other hand, men potentially benefit from having a more successful spouse/partner.

Moreover, in the past researchers and writers have speculated about what role women who do not work outside of the home might have in supporting their spouse's/partner's careers (e.g., see Davis and Astin 1990). These women are presumed to absorb more family responsibilities and household chores. In addition, these women are believed to be able to help their spouses/partners socially. Many may also assume much of the work that relates to career demands placed on their spouse/partner by typing manuscripts or doing other clerical or research support tasks.

In closing, it appears that academic partners/spouses have more egalitarian arrangements overall in that egalitarian arrangements at home appear to result in greater equality in the workplace. In other words, the gender gap is smaller for academics who are married to or intimate partners with other academics. Viewed another way, men's professional attainments are apparently not achieved at the expense of their partners in academia.

Appendix 1

Coding Schema for Variables Used in Regression Equations

Academic Fields
  1 = All other fields
  2 = Specific field (e.g., agriculture; biological sciences; business; education; engineering; English; health sciences; history/political science; humanities; fine arts; mathematics/statistics; physical sciences; social sciences)

Age
  1= ≤ 29   2 = 30–34   3 = 35–39   4 = 40–44
  5 = 45–49   6 = 50–54   7 = 55–59   8 = 60–64
  9 = 65–69   10= ≥ 70

Degree
  1 = None   2 = B.A.   3 = M.A.
  4 = J.D., M.D., Ed.D., Ph.D.

Father's/mother's education
  1 = ≤ 8th grade   2 = Some high school
  3 = High school graduate 4 = Some college
  5 = College graduate   6 = Some graduate school
  7 = Graduate degree

Colleges and universities
  1 = All other types of colleges
  2 = College or university

Publications (number of writings accepted in the previous two years)
  1 = None   2 = 1–2   3 = 3–4   4 = 5–10
  5 = 11–20   6 = 21–50   7 = 51+

Rank
  1 = Lecturer, adjunct, other   2 = Assistant professor
  3 = Associate professor   4 = Professor

Salary (base salary in $1,000s)
  1 = ≤ 10   2 = 20–29   3 = 30–39   4 = 40–49
  5 = 50–59   6 = 60–69   7 = 70–79   8 = 80–89
  9 = 90–98   10= ≥ 99

Spouse/partner an academic
  1 = No   2 = Yes

University
  1 = All other types of colleges   2 = University

Appendix 2

TABLE 5-1. Marital Status (percent)

	Men	Women
Currently married	82.1	62.0
Separated	1.4	1.6
Single, never married	7.7	16.6
Single, with partner	1.7	4.2
Single, divorced	6.5	13.1
Single, widowed	0.6	2.6

Note: Data are based on the total sample of teaching faculty.

TABLE 5-2. Academics with Academic Spouses/ Partners by Racial/Ethnic group (percent)

	Men	Women
American Indian	41.5	49.8
Asian American	28.4	43.7
Black/Negro/African American	47.7	40.7
Mexican American/Chicano/Chicana	29.3	36.5
Other	38.5	53.6
Puerto Rican American	40.5	21.6
White/Caucasian	35.0	39.2

Note: Weighted data; *N* of men = 234,264; *N* of women = 72,318.

TABLE 5-3. Educational Attainments of Spouses/Partners and Parents (percent)

	Spouse/Partner		Father		Mother	
	Men	Women	Men	Women	Men	Women
8th grade or less						
Academic spouse/partner	0.0	0.0	21.8	14.6	16.0	9.9
Nonacademic spouse/partner	0.2	0.3	21.7	16.4	16.0	10.4
Some high school						
Academic spouse/partner	0.0	0.0	11.8	10.2	11.4	10.0
Nonacademic spouse/partner	0.6	1.0	11.1	10.0	10.8	10.0
High school graduate						
Academic spouse/partner	0.4	0.1	21.7	21.8	32.5	29.6
Nonacademic spouse/partner	7.9	7.2	22.9	22.5	34.7	35.0
Some college						
Academic spouse/partner	2.8	1.0	14.1	15.1	16.2	17.2
Nonacademic spouse/partner	22.5	16.5	12.5	16.6	15.5	18.1
College graduate						
Academic spouse/partner	13.6	4.1	11.6	13.1	14.5	18.3
Nonacademic spouse/partner	29.8	25.6	12.8	13.4	14.0	15.5
Some graduate school						
Academic spouse/partner	13.3	6.3	4.6	6.0	3.2	5.7
Nonacademic spouse/partner	12.2	13.5	4.6	4.9	3.4	4.0
Graduate degree						
Academic spouse/partner	69.7	88.4	14.4	19.2	6.2	9.2
Nonacademic spouse/partner	26.7	35.9	14.4	16.2	5.6	7.0

Note: Weighted data.

TABLE 5-4. Highest Degree Earned by Academics

	With Academic Spouse/Partner		Without Academic Spouse/Partner	
	Men	Women	Men	Women
Bachelor's	2.0	3.7	2.7	6.1
Master's	24.0	38.2	20.7	47.6
LL.B., J.D.	0.6	0.2	0.7	0.9
M.D., D.D.S.	0.3	0.9	0.5	0.2
Other professional degree	0.7	0.7	0.7	0.5
Ed.D.	6.1	4.9	3.7	4.5
Ph.D.	60.6	46.0	65.3	32.5
Other degree	4.1	3.6	3.8	4.0
None	1.3	1.9	1.9	3.7

Note: Weighted data; *N* of men = 232,702; *N* of women = 71,507.

TABLE 5-5. Major of Highest Degree (percent)

	With Academic Spouse/Partner		Without Academic Spouse/Partner	
	Men	Women	Men	Women
Agriculture	1.5	0.5	2.3	0.3
Biological sciences	7.2	5.0	7.1	3.7
Business	5.5	4.4	7.9	7.5
Education	15.2	23.6	10.0	23.3
Engineering	4.4	0.7	8.8	0.7
English	6.6	10.3	5.0	7.3
Fine arts	10.2	8.4	6.8	6.5
Health related	1.3	7.6	2.1	17.6
History, political science	7.7	4.3	7.8	2.6
Humanities, other	8.5	10.9	7.3	6.5
Mathematics, statistics	6.0	5.2	6.3	3.3
Physical sciences	8.1	2.3	9.5	1.8
Social sciences	12.5	11.0	12.7	10.6
Technical, other	1.6	0.8	1.9	1.4
Other	3.6	5.3	4.5	6.9

Note: Weighted data; *N* of men = 226,133; *N* of women = 69,582.

TABLE 5-6. Academics with Academic Partners by Field of Highest Degree (percent)

	Men	Women
Agriculture	26.1	54.5
Biological sciences	35.4	47.6
Business	27.3	27.9
Education	45.0	40.1
Engineering	21.1	37.7
English	41.4	48.0
Fine arts	44.6	45.9
Health related	25.4	22.0
History, political science	34.7	52.3
Humanities, other	38.6	52.3
Mathematics, statistics	33.9	50.6
Physical sciences	31.4	45.2
Social sciences	34.6	40.6
Technical, other	32.1	28.0
Other	30.5	33.5

Note: Weighted data.

TABLE 5-7. Type of Institution of Employment
(percent)

	Spouse/Partner Not an Academic	Spouse/Partner an Academic
Public university		
Men	30.3	25.5
Women	17.0	19.8
Public four-year college		
Men	25.6	27.7
Women	22.3	25.7
Public two-year college		
Men	16.1	19.7
Women	34.3	24.2
Private university		
Men	11.2	8.7
Women	7.3	7.4
Private four-year college		
Men	16.7	17.4
Women	17.4	21.2
Private two-year college		
Men	0.6	1.0
Women	1.8	1.7

Note: Weighted data; *N* of men = 232,018; *N* of women = 71,262.

TABLE 5-8. Academic Rank (percent)

	Spouse/Partner Not an Academic	Spouse/Partner an Academic
Professor		
Men	42.2	43.2
Women	11.6	19.5
Associate professor		
Men	26.0	27.0
Women	21.0	25.3
Assistant professor		
Men	20.1	17.9
Women	31.5	29.8
Lecturer		
Men	1.2	0.8
Women	4.3	3.1
Instructor		
Men	8.6	9.2
Women	27.0	20.0
Other		
Men	1.9	1.8
Women	4.6	2.2

Note: Weighted data; *N* of men = 234,264; *N* of women = 72,318.

Table 5-9. Publishing Activities (percent)

	Number of Publications													
	0		1–2		3–4		5–10		11–20		21–50		51+	
	M	W	M	W	M	W	M	W	M	W	M	W	M	W
Articles published in academic or professional journals in lifetime														
Academic partner	23.0	37.1	18.6	20.4	13.2	14.2	16.2	14.7	11.9	8.2	11.6	4.4	5.5	1.2
Nonacademic partner	21.6	49.5	16.1	23.3	12.6	11.1	16.1	8.7	13.1	5.0	12.9	2.1	7.5	0.5
Chapters published in edited volumes in lifetime														
Academic partner	62.5	71.6	18.3	16.9	9.0	6.1	6.7	4.0	2.4	1.1	0.9	0.3	0.2	0.0
Nonacademic partner	60.1	79.8	19.1	13.3	9.9	3.9	7.2	2.1	2.5	0.5	0.9	0.2	0.2	0.2
Books/manuals/monographs written or edited in lifetime														
Academic partner	47.8	55.6	31.6	32.9	11.1	7.1	6.4	3.6	2.2	0.7	0.7	0.1	0.2	0.0
Nonacademic partner	48.5	64.8	30.4	25.6	11.4	6.3	7.0	2.6	2.0	0.3	0.5	0.3	0.3	0.1
All professional writings published or accepted in previous two years														
Academic partner	43.2	49.8	25.3	25.6	16.0	13.4	12.3	9.9	2.6	1.1	0.4	0.2	0.1	0.0
Nonacademic partner	38.8	60.2	25.7	23.2	18.4	10.2	13.7	6.0	2.5	0.3	0.7	0.1	0.1	0.1

Note: Weighted data.

TABLE 5-10. Primary Scholarly Interest (percent)

	With Academic Spouse/Partner		Without Academic Spouse/Partner	
	Men	Women	Men	Women
Very heavily in teaching	36.5	43.4	30.8	50.1
Both, but leaning toward teaching	34.2	32.3	36.5	32.9
Both, but leaning toward research	25.3	20.8	28.4	14.3
Very heavily in research	4.1	3.5	4.3	2.7

Note: Weighted data.

TABLE 5-11. Research Working Environment (percent)

	With Academic Spouse/Partner		Without Academic Spouse/Partner	
	Men	Women	Men	Women
Work alone	69.7	65.3	67.0	60.7
Work with others	23.5	25.3	26.5	28.1
Member of group	6.8	9.4	6.5	11.3

Note: Weighted data.

TABLE 5-12. Sources of at Least Some Reported Stress (percent)

	Extent of Source of Stress			
	Somewhat		Extensive	
Source of Stress	Men	Women	Men	Women
Care of elderly parent				
Academic partner	20.4	20.6	7.6	8.8
Nonacademic partner	18.4	19.0	6.5	9.2
Child care				
Academic partner	26.2	20.9	7.3	12.7
Nonacademic partner	24.2	24.8	6.5	15.4
Children's problems				
Academic partner	28.9	24.3	6.1	8.5
Nonacademic partner	29.4	27.6	6.0	9.4
Colleagues				
Academic partner	43.6	44.6	9.8	12.9
Nonacademic partner	42.3	43.8	9.9	11.2
Committee work				
Academic partner	47.0	47.1	11.1	15.6
Nonacademic partner	45.9	49.3	9.5	13.3

Faculty meetings				
Academic partner	41.1	41.6	8.8	10.1
Nonacademic partner	39.8	40.7	7.5	11.4
Fund-raising expectations				
Academic partner	15.8	13.5	5.3	4.8
Nonacademic partner	16.1	14.9	6.7	3.1
Lack of personal life				
Academic partner	46.7	40.9	30.3	50.0
Nonacademic partner	48.1	40.9	28.8	50.2
Long-distance commuting				
Academic partner	10.3	12.7	4.7	9.4
Nonacademic partner	10.6	18.7	3.4	9.6
Managing household responsibilities				
Academic partner	48.5	50.8	13.4	26.1
Nonacademic partner	47.9	52.1	12.8	29.6
Marital friction				
Academic partner	20.9	19.5	3.8	4.1
Nonacademic partner	21.4	24.0	4.7	3.8
Physical health				
Academic partner	30.5	33.0	5.6	6.1
Nonacademic partner	29.5	35.5	5.5	6.3
Research or publishing demands				
Academic partner	33.9	32.2	14.5	17.6
Nonacademic partner	36.6	24.2	16.0	19.9
Review/promotion process				
Academic partner	28.1	30.6	13.6	19.0
Nonacademic partner	28.8	31.7	15.4	20.4
Students				
Academic partner	42.6	46.9	5.1	6.1
Nonacademic partner	42.3	49.3	4.9	6.3
Subtle discrimination				
Academic partner	16.1	33.5	5.8	13.8
Nonacademic partner	15.0	32.8	5.2	10.2
Teaching load				
Academic partner	42.8	43.2	19.0	27.4
Nonacademic partner	44.4	46.0	17.8	27.6
Time pressures				
Academic partner	46.8	35.1	34.8	57.0
Nonacademic partner	46.3	39.5	34.9	53.1

Note: Weighted data.

TABLE 5-13. Variables Predicting Salary (Final Solution)

Variable	Unstandardized regression coefficient		Standardized regression coefficient	
	Men	Women	Men	Women
Age	2.37	1.52	0.26**	0.21**
Degree	1.26	1.83	0.05**	0.10**
Agriculture	−4.40		−0.04**	
Biology	−2.14	1.56	−0.03**	0.02**
Business	7.39	−6.65	0.11**	0.12**
Education	−2.20	−0.43	−0.04**	−0.01**
Engineering	7.64	7.66	0.12**	0.05**
English	−2.73	−1.72	−0.04**	−0.04**
Fine arts	−2.72		−0.04**	
Health-related fields	2.40	0.64	0.02**	0.02**
Humanities	−2.94	−1.08	−0.05**	−0.02**
Mathematics	1.85		0.03**	
Physical sciences	1.50		0.02**	
Social sciences	0.74	1.86	0.01**	0.04**
Rank	5.84	5.15	0.36**	0.40**
University	10.77	7.91	0.31**	0.26**
Publications in previous two years	2.35	1.90	0.17**	0.14**
Four-year college	5.23	5.90	0.15**	0.22**
Spouse/partner an academic	−0.77	0.18	−0.02**	0.01**
Constant	−10.97	−21.81		
R^2 = .5059 (men)	R^2 = .4318 (women)			

** $p \le .001$.

TABLE 5-14. Variables Predicting Academic Rank (Final Solution)

Variable	Unstandardized regression coefficient		Standardized regression coefficient	
	Men	Women	Men	Women
Age	0.25	1.52	0.46**	0.36**
Degree	0.42	0.36	0.27**	0.26**
Agriculture	0.26		0.03**	
Biology	0.15	0.17	0.04**	0.03**
Business	−0.04	−0.09	−0.01**	−0.02**
Education	−0.01	−0.06	−0.00	−0.02**
Engineering	0.07		0.02**	
English	0.02	−0.15	0.01**	−0.04**
Fine arts	0.39	0.42	0.10**	0.10**
Health-related fields	0.12	−0.05	0.01**	0.01**
History	0.18	0.18	0.04**	0.03**
Humanities	0.02		0.01*	
Mathematics	0.14	0.09	0.03**	0.02**
Physical sciences	0.19	0.12	0.05**	0.01**
Social sciences	0.14	0.10	0.04**	0.03**
Publications in previous two years	0.16	0.18	0.19**	0.17**
Four-year college	−0.08		−0.04**	
University	−0.06	−0.14	−0.03**	−0.06**
Spouse/partner an academic	0.04	0.11	0.02**	0.05**
Constant	1.84	−0.93		
R^2 = .3570 (men)	R^2 = .2673 (women)			

* $p \leq .01$.
** $p \leq .001$.

TABLE 5-15. Variables Predicting Research Productivity (Final Solution)

Variable	Unstandardized regression coefficient		Standardized regression coefficient	
	Men	Women	Men	Women
Degree	0.31	0.36	0.17**	0.27**
Age	−0.14	−0.04	−0.22**	−0.07**
Agriculture	−0.14	0.39	−0.02**	0.02**
Biology	0.06	0.10	0.01**	0.02**
Business	−0.12		−0.02**	
Education	−0.21	−0.12	−0.06**	−0.05**
Engineering	0.12		0.02**	
Fine arts	−0.33	0.04	−0.07**	0.01**
Health-related fields	0.07	−0.05	0.01**	−0.02**
Humanities	−0.08	0.20	−0.02**	0.05**
Mathematics	−0.24	−0.21	−0.05**	−0.04**
Physical sciences	0.13	0.18	0.03**	0.02**
University	0.87	0.61	0.35**	0.26**
Rank	0.24	0.15	0.21**	0.16**
Four-year college	0.09	−0.04	0.04**	−0.02**
Spouse/partner an academic	−0.02	0.09	−0.01**	0.04**
Constant	0.40	−1.33		
R^2 = .2981 (men)	R^2 = .3072 (women)			

** $p \leq .001$.

TABLE 5-16. Variables Predicting Employment at a University (Final Solution)

Variable	Unstandardized regression coefficient		Standardized regression coefficient	
	Men	Women	Men	Women
Publications in previous two years	0.15	0.13	0.36**	0.30**
Degree	0.10	0.07	0.14**	0.11**
Age	0.02	−0.01	0.08**	−0.06**
Level of mother's education	0.01	0.01	0.03**	0.04**
Level of father's education	0.01	0.01	0.02**	0.04**
Agriculture	0.23	0.18	0.07**	0.02**
Biology		0.10		0.05**
Education	−0.07	−0.10	−0.05**	−0.09**
Engineering	0.17		0.09**	
English	−0.06	−0.06	−0.03**	−0.04**
Fine arts	0.12		0.06**	
Health-related fields	0.09		0.02**	
History		0.06		0.03**
Humanities	0.03	0.08	0.01**	0.05**
Mathematics	0.02	−0.10	0.01**	−0.03**
Physical sciences	−0.03	−0.10	−0.02**	−0.03**
Spouse/partner an academic	−0.04	−0.02	−0.04**	−0.02**
Constant	0.09	1.08		
R^2 = .2204 (men)	R^2 = .2001 (women)			

** $p \leq .001$.

Note

The authors would like to thank KC Boatsman for her assistance with the data analyses used in this chapter.

References

Acker, Joan R. 1994. "Power, Productivity, and Participation." In *Working in the Twenty-First Century,* ed. J. Glass, 1–28. Los Angeles: UCLA Institute for Industrial Relations.

Astin, Alexander W., William S. Korn, and Eric L. Dey. 1991. *The American College Teacher: National Norms for the 1989–90 HERI Faculty Survey.* Los Angeles: Higher Education Research Institute.

Astin, Helen S. 1978. "Factors Affecting Women's Scholarly Productivity." In *The Higher Education of Women: Essays in Honor of Rosemary Park,* ed. Helen S. Astin and W. Z. Hirsch, 133–57. New York: Praeger.

Astin, Helen S., and Alan E. Bayer. 1972. "Sex Discrimination in Academe." *Educational Record* 53 (1): 101–18.

———. 1979. "Pervasive Sex Differences in the Academic Reward System: Scholarship, Marriage, and What Else?" In *Academic Rewards in Higher Education,* ed. Darrell R. Lewis and William E. Becker Jr., 211–29. Cambridge, Mass: Ballinger Publishing.

Astin, Helen S., and Diane E. Davis. 1985. "Research Productivity across the Life and Career Cycles: Facilitators and Barriers for Women." In *Scholarly Writing and Publishing: Issues, Problems, and Solutions,* ed. Mary F. Fox, 147–60. Boulder: Westview Press.

Bayer, Alan E., and Helen S. Astin. 1975. "Sex Differences in the Academic Reward System." *Science* 188 (May): 796–802.

Bird, Gerald A., and Gloria W. Bird. 1985. "Determinants of Mobility in Two-Earner Families: Does the Wife's Income Count?" *Journal of Marriage and the Family* 47 (Aug.): 753–58.

Chamberlain, Mariam K., ed. 1988. *Women in Academe.* New York: Russell Sage Foundation.

Clark, Shirley M., and Mary Corcoran. 1986. "Perspectives on the Professional Socialization of Women Faculty." *Journal of Higher Education* 57 (1): 20–43.

Cole, Jonathan R., and Harriet Zuckerman. 1984. "The Productivity Puzzle: Persistence and Change in Patterns of Publication among Men and Women Scientists." In *Advances in Motivation and Achievement,* vol. 2, ed. Marjorie W. Steinkamp and Martin L. Maehr, 217–58. Greenwich, Conn.: JAI Press.

Davis, Diane E., and Helen S. Astin. 1987. "Reputational Standing in Academe." *Journal of Higher Education* 58 (3): 261–75.

———. 1990. "Life Cycle, Career Patterns, and Gender Stratification in Academe: Breaking Myths and Exposing Truths." In *Storming the Tower: Women in the Academic World,* ed. S. S. Lie and V. E. O'Leary, 89–107. New York: Nichols/G.P. Publishing.

Fox, Mary F. 1985. "Publication, Performance, and Reward in Science and Scholarship." In *Higher Education: Handbook of Theory and Research,* vol. 1, ed. J. C. Smart, 255–82. New York: Agathon Press.

Gaddy, C. D., C. R. Glass, and D. B. Arnkoff. 1983. "Career Involvement of Women in Dual-Career Families: The Influence of Sex-Role Identity." *Journal of Counseling Psychology* 30 (3): 388–94.

Gilbert, L. 1985. *Dual-Career Husbands.* New York: Academic Press.

Hamermesh, Daniel S. 1988. "Salaries: Disciplinary Differences and Rank Injustices." *Academe* 74 (3): 20–24.

Lester, Richard A. 1974. *Antibias Regulation of Universities: Faculty Problems and Their Solutions.* New York: McGraw-Hill.

Lie, Suzanne S., Lynda Malik, and Duncan Harris, eds. 1994. *The Gender Gap in Higher Education.* The World Yearbook of Education series. London: Kogan Page.

Merton, Robert. 1968. "The Matthew Effect in Science." *Science* 159 (Jan.): 56–63.

Ries, Paula, and Anne J. Stone. 1992. *The American Woman, 1992–1993: A Status Report.* New York: W. W. Norton.

Scott, Joyce A., and Nancy A. Bereman. 1992. "Competition versus Collegiality: Academe's Dilemma for the 1990's." *Journal of Higher Education* 63 (6): 684–98.

Smart, John. 1991. "Gender Equity in Academic Rank and Salary." *Review of Higher Education* 14 (4): 511–26.

Sowell, Thomas. 1975. *Affirmative Action Reconsidered: Was It Necessary in Academe?* Washington, D.C.: American Enterprise Institute for Public Policy Research.

Tolbert, Pamela S. 1986. "Organizations and Inequality: Sources of Earnings Differences between Male and Female Faculty." *Sociology of Education* 59 (Oct.): 227–36.

Zuckerman, Harriet. 1977. *Scientific Elite: Nobel Laureates in the United States.* New York: Free Press.

6

. . . .

The Scholarly Productivity of
Academic Couples

Marcia L. Bellas

THIS CHAPTER ADDRESSES the question of whether faculty members who have had an academic partner differ from other faculty members in their publication patterns. Given the importance of productivity as a measure of success for individual academics and for institutions of higher education, this question would seem to be of interest both to faculty members who are in relationships with others who are employed by academic institutions as well as administrators and members of hiring committees who may view academic couples with some degree of apprehension.

I have divided the chapter into four sections: (1) description of the data; (2) methods and results of an examination of whether or not having had an academic partner influences a composite measure of scholarly productivity; (3) methods and results of an assessment of whether or not having had an academic partner influences specific types of scholarly productivity for a subsample of faculty who had ever had a partner; and (4) summary of findings and conclusions.

Description of the Data

These analyses draw on data from a survey of faculty at public and private colleges and universities in Illinois conducted by Marianne Ferber and myself in the spring of 1993. We selected twenty-two institutions to

represent the nine major categories of the Carnegie classification system of institutions of higher education: research universities I and II,
doctorate-granting universities I and II, comprehensive universities I
and II, liberal arts colleges I and II, and two-year colleges. This classification system is based on Ph.D. production (among alumni in the case
of schools without doctoral programs), programs offered, and the
amount of federal funding received in the sciences (see Carnegie Foundation for the Advancement of Teaching 1987 for additional details). We
chose at random two public and two private institutions from each category, except in cases where two such institutions were not located in
Illinois (e.g., public liberal arts colleges) and in the case of two-year
colleges, where we selected three public institutions because there was
only one private two-year institution in the state.

We mailed questionnaires to two thousand faculty members, whom
we randomly selected from faculty directories (or, in some cases, from
randomly generated lists of names that institutions provided). We over-
sampled women so as to include equal numbers of both sexes. The number of faculty members that we selected at each institution reflected the
percentage of students at that institution relative to the total number of
students at all institutions in our sample. For example, if students at a
particular institution comprised 5 percent of students at all institutions
in our sample, we selected 5 percent of our faculty sample from that
institution. We undersampled faculty from two-year colleges, since these
institutions are such a large segment of the student body within Illinois
and because we wished to obtain adequate representation of all types
of institutions. Eight-hundred fifty-four faculty members, or 43 percent
of our sample, completed the survey after one follow-up mailing. We
subsequently eliminated 88 respondents who were not regular faculty
members (e.g., practicing physicians who occasionally taught a course),
reducing the number of usable questionnaires to 766.

Our questionnaire requested information about the educational and
employment histories of faculty, as well as similar information for any
partners the respondents had ever had. We defined "partner" as a spouse
or someone with whom the respondent had had a relationship for at
least three years. Because we gathered information on multiple partners,
we considered a faculty member who had *ever* had a partner employed
by an academic institution at the same time as the respondent as having been a member of an "academic couple," rather than only those who
were in such a relationship at the time of the survey. Using this defini-

tion, approximately half of our respondents qualified as having had academic partners.[1]

Do Faculty Members Who Have Had Academic Partners Differ from Other Faculty Members in Their Overall Productivity?

When I first considered the question of whether faculty members with academic partners differ from other faculty members in their productivity, I speculated that if there were differences in publication rates between those who have had academic partners and those who have not, the former group would probably be more productive. I reasoned that faculty members with academic partners might benefit from living with people who understand the demands of research and publishing. An academic partner could provide a "sounding board"—someone to read drafts of one's writing and with whom to discuss ideas. Academic couples might also collaborate more formally, especially if both partners are in the same field.

On the other hand, there could be a downside to an academic partnership. Academic partners might compete for research time, especially if children are present in the household. In contrast, a nonacademic partner with a less demanding job might provide support services that facilitate a faculty member's research and publishing. This could include indirect assistance, such as caring for family members, assuming responsibility for domestic chores, and arranging social activities, as well as more direct types of research assistance (Hochschild 1975; Fowlkes 1980). This line of thinking would predict that faculty members with nonacademic partners would be the more productive group, although this might depend on occupations of partners, and any effect could differ for the sexes. A third possibility, of course, is that there are no discernible differences in the publication patterns of faculty members who have had academic partners and those who have not.

The literature relevant to this research question is sparse. A somewhat dated study of psychologist couples addressed the question of the potential effects of a partner's occupation on scholarly productivity. Based on questionnaires completed by 138 members of the American Psychological Association (APA), Bryson and colleagues (1976) concluded that those who were part of a psychologist pair (identified by joint APA membership) published more articles, gave more conference presentations, and received more grant funds than other psychologists. Although

these findings seem reasonable, the study has a number of methodological shortcomings that may limit its generalizability. For example, the
sample mixed both academic and nonacademic psychologists. Yet, psychologist pairs were more prevalent in academic settings, where publications are more likely to be required and rewarded and where resources
to facilitate publishing are probably greater than in nonacademic settings. Bryson and colleagues also found that members of psychologist
pairs were more likely to hold Ph.D.'s than other psychologists in their
sample (i.e., members of the control group), a factor clearly associated
with productivity. Furthermore, members of psychologist pairs received
their degrees at an earlier age, on average, which may reflect motivational
differences between the two groups. The control group also included
both unmarried and married psychologists. Since there is evidence that
unmarried men publish less than married men on average (Astin 1984;
Bellas 1992) and that unmarried women publish fewer journal articles
than married women (Astin and Davis 1985), including unmarried people in their control group may have biased that group's productivity
downward. Despite its methodological limitations, the study's findings
lend some support to the possibility that faculty members with academic
partners publish more than those with nonacademic partners.

One other study is relevant to the research question at hand, although
it too is now rather dated. Examining the effects of the educational level of spouses on career attainment for a sample of Ph.D. recipients, Ferber and Huber (1979) found that men whose wives had Ph.D.'s published
less than men with less-educated wives (this was true both for men
whose wives had bachelor's degrees and for men whose wives had other graduate degrees). This finding is consistent with the possibility that
less-educated wives contribute more to their husband's careers than
more highly educated wives, who most likely attend to their own careers.
Interestingly, the husband's educational level had no effect on women's
scholarly productivity. This suggests that the support mechanisms provided by less-educated wives to their husbands are not, conversely, provided by less-educated husbands to their wives.

My initial approach to addressing the question of whether faculty
members who have had academic partners differ from other faculty
members in their productivity involved examining the effects of an ar-
ray of independent variables or potential predictors of productivity on
a composite productivity measure that combines the number of jour-

nal articles, chapters, and books (excluding textbooks) published. I used regression analysis, a statistical technique that reveals the relationship between each independent variable and the dependent variable by holding constant or controlling for the effects of other independent variables. In addition to the primary independent variable of interest—whether or not a faculty member has had an academic partner—the independent variables in the regression model include factors identified in the literature as influencing faculty productivity (e.g., Fox 1983; Astin 1984). Independent variables pertaining to characteristics of respondents themselves included sex (women publish less than men, on average); experience (the total number of publications increases with years of experience, although the relationship may not be linear; the variable reflects years since highest degree); having a doctorate as one's highest degree (faculty members with doctorates publish more than those without this degree); field of highest degree (academics in some fields publish more than those in others, reflecting such things as variation across disciplines in styles of research, opportunities for collaboration, and journal acceptance rates);[2] type of employer (faculty members at institutions that place more emphasis on research publish more than faculty members at other types of institutions);[3] being a full professor (associated with higher productivity);[4] and amount of grant funds generated by faculty members (also associated with higher productivity). It is likely that these last three variables have two-way relationships with productivity. In other words, being employed by a research university, being a full professor, and generating grant revenues increase productivity, but higher productivity also increases the likelihood of being employed by a research university, being a full professor, and receiving grant funds.

A second set of independent variables pertained to characteristics of respondents' partners. These include total number of years a partner was not employed, whether or not a partner had a doctorate, whether or not a partner's highest degree was in the same general field as the respondent's, and how many miles the current partner lived from the respondent. With the exception of the last variable, these characteristics apply to *all* partners a respondent had ever had. In other words, the number of years that partners were not employed totals these years for all partners, while whether or not a partner had a doctorate and whether or not a partner's highest degree was in the same field as the respondent's apply to all previous partners. For example, if a previous partner had a doctorate but the current partner did not, I considered the respondent to have had a partner with a doctorate.

Table 6-1 shows means and standard deviations for each of the variables included in the analysis.[5] Table 6-2 presents the regression results. Before controlling for the effects of independent variables, I examined whether a bivariate relationship or correlation exists between having had an academic partner and the composite productivity measure. Because of the possibility that any apparent effect of having had an academic

TABLE 6-1. Means and Standard Deviations of Variables in Regression of Productivity on Predictor Variables

	Mean	Standard Deviation
Dependent Variable		
Productivity	9.911	16.662
Independent Variable		
Respondent		
Academic partner	0.553	0.497
Sex (1 = female)	0.533	0.499
Years since highest degree	14.997	9.865
Highest degree is doctorate	0.637	0.481
Field of highest degree		
Arts	0.029	0.168
Biology	0.074	0.261
Education	0.181	0.386
Engineering	0.024	0.152
Health	0.071	0.257
Humanities	0.184	0.388
Physical sciences	0.110	0.314
Professions	0.177	0.382
Type of employer institution		
Doctorate-granting	0.181	0.385
Research university	0.274	0.446
Full professor	0.250	0.433
Grant dollars (100s)	1036.491	2459.539
Partner(s)		
Years not employed	2.481	6.343
Highest degree is doctorate	0.263	0.441
Highest degree in same general		
field as respondent's	0.286	0.452
Number of miles from respondent	36.480	250.898

Note: Articles, chapters, and books were combined; $N = 766$.

TABLE 6-2. Regression of Productivity on Predictor Variables

Independent Variables	Equation 1 b (s.e. of b)	Equation 2 b (s.e. of b)	Equation 3 b (s.e. of b)	Beta
Respondent				
Academic partner	0.402 (1.025)	1.043 (1.105)	0.788 (1.084)	0.024
Sex (1 = female)	−0.967 (1.082)	0.291 (1.154)	2.342[a] (1.287)	0.070
Years since highest degree	0.173††† (0.061)	0.147** (0.061)	0.162††† (0.060)	0.096
Highest degree is doctorate	4.283††† (1.264)	4.600††† (1.266)	4.890††† (1.238)	0.141
Field of highest degree[b]				
Arts	−4.377[a] (3.226)	−4.571[a] (3.199)	−3.507[a] (3.137)	−0.035
Biology	1.591 2.288	1.713 (2.275)	1.700 (2.230)	0.027
Education	−2.766[a] (1.777)	−3.009[a] (1.773)	−2.548 (1.734)	−0.059
Engineering	0.948 (3.510)	1.155 (3.488)	1.909 (3.412)	0.017
Health	−1.071 2.349	−1.330 (2.347)	−0.701 (2.301)	−0.011
Humanities	−0.875 (1.753)	−1.367 (1.747)	−1.477 (1.708)	−0.034
Physical sciences	1.840 (2.007)	1.351 (1.999)	0.956 (1.956)	0.018
Professions	−0.935 1.820	−1.138 (1.807)	−0.775 (1.767)	−0.018
Type of employer institution[c]				
Doctorate-granting	4.508††† (1.409)	4.381††† (1.402)	4.320††† (1.370)	0.100
Research university	10.443††† (1.299)	10.260††† (1.298)	13.173††† (1.829)	0.353
Full professor	8.608††† (1.381)	8.275††† (1.375)	8.206††† (1.344)	0.213
Grant dollars (100s)	0.002††† 0.000	0.002††† (0.000)	0.003††† (0.000)	0.410
Partner(s)				
Years not employed		0.279††† (0.085)	0.229** (0.084)	0.087
Highest degree is doctorate		−1.830 (1.279)	−0.881 (1.262)	−0.023

Highest degree in same		0.896	1.007	0.027
general field as respondent's		(1.175)	(1.149)	
Miles from respondent		0.002	−0.005[a]	−0.070
		(0.002)	(0.003)	
Sex interactions				
Sex / Research university			−5.261*	−0.114
			(2.326)	
Sex / Grants			−0.002†††	−0.138
			(0.000)	
Sex / Miles from respondent			0.011**	0.126
			(0.004)	
Constant	−2.676	−3.621	−5.160	
Adjusted R^2	0.472	0.481	0.505	

Note: Articles, chapters, and books were combined; $N = 766$.
a. $p < .10$.
b. Compared with social sciences.
c. Compared with two-year colleges, liberal arts colleges, and comprehensive universities combined.
* $p < .05$.
** $p < .01$.
††† $p < .001$, one-tailed test.

partner on productivity might be due to including never-partnered people in the group of faculty members who have had only nonacademic partners, I first examined whether productivity differed significantly for never-partnered faculty members and those who have had only nonacademic partners. It did not, so I combined faculty members who have had only nonacademic partners with those who have never had a partner and compared their productivity to that of faculty members who have had academic partners. The regression coefficient of 2.908 ($p < .05$) indicates that faculty members with academic partners published approximately three more articles, books, and book chapters (the composite productivity measure) than other faculty members, before controlling for the effects of other variables in the model (results not shown).[6]

To determine whether the apparent effect on productivity of having had an academic partner simply reflects differences in other characteristics and qualifications of faculty members, such as years of experience and highest degree, I next controlled for their effects. As equation 1 of table 6-2 shows, the effect of having had an academic partner on productivity disappeared after controlling for the effects of respondents' characteristics.[7] Nonetheless, it is worth noting which independent variables significantly influenced faculty productivity. Consistent with previous findings, years of experience and holding a doctorate contributed to higher productivity. In addition, faculty members employed by doctorate-granting or research universities were more productive than those employed by other types of institutions, as were full professors and faculty members who had generated more grant dollars. As previously noted, the latter three variables probably have two-way relationships with the dependent variable. Productivity may in part determine the type of institution at which faculty members are employed, but the stronger effect is probably in the opposite direction (Allison and Long 1990). Similarly, productivity may influence a faculty member's rank and receipt of research grants (funding agencies prefer to invest in applicants with records of success), but rank and grant revenues also affect productivity. I included these variables to control for their effects on productivity, but because of the likelihood of reciprocal, or feedback, effects their coefficients should not be interpreted as representing causal effects.

Equation 2 of table 6-2 adds characteristics of respondents' partners to the regression model. All variables significant in equation 1 retained their significance in equation 2. Only one variable pertaining to partners' characteristics achieved statistical significance. The more years partners were not employed, the higher the number of faculty publications. One possible explanation for this relationship is that a nonemployed partner facilitates productivity indirectly, for example, by assuming the bulk of the household responsibilities, or directly by providing research assistance.

As a final step in the analysis, I tested for interactions between sex and each of the independent variables to determine if the effects on productivity of any of the independent variables differed for the sexes. As shown in equation 3 of table 6-2, this was the case for three variables: employment by a research university; amount of grant funding; and number of miles a current partner lived from a respondent. Both the effects of being employed by a research university and the amount of grant funding on productivity were greater for men than for women. These findings are consistent with the view that research universities may provide an environment that is less conducive to publishing for women than for men. But again, due to the reciprocal nature of these variables, it is not appropriate to interpret the coefficients. The third interaction effect, and perhaps the most interesting, shows that the greater the distance between faculty respondents and their partners, the higher the productivity for women but the lower the productivity for men. Specifically, each additional 100 miles of distance between partners increased women's productivity by approximately one-half of a publication, while decreasing men's productivity by the same amount. One possible explanation for this sex difference is that the greater the distance between partners, the more likely it is that they maintain separate residences for at least part of the week. Such an arrangement probably alleviates some household responsibilities for women (since women do most of the household labor even among highly educated couples), freeing them up to spend more time on research and publishing. This view is consistent with Hartmann's (1981) estimate that men actually create more housework than they contribute. In contrast, men who live away from their partners at least some of the time may by default assume more household responsibilities than they would if they lived with their partners full-time.[8] It is also possible, of course, that causality runs in the opposite direction. Perhaps highly productive women are most likely to assume long-distance relationships.

As equation 3 of table 6-2 also shows, all of the independent variables previously mentioned retained their significance in the full regression model. Controlling for the effects of other variables, each additional year since obtaining one's highest degree translated into approximately one-seventh of a publication. In other words, all else being equal, faculty members produced one additional publication for every seven years of experience. Those with doctorates had nearly five more publications than those without doctorates. Being employed by a doctorate-granting institution or a research university, being a full professor, and generating grant revenues also contributed to higher productivity. Finally, the more years partners were not employed, the greater the number of faculty publications. Each additional year of nonemployment resulted in about one-fourth of a publication. Note that I did not find a significant negative effect of having had a partner with a Ph.D. for either sex, as Ferber and Huber (1979) reported for men. This difference may reflect the increased labor force participation among less-educated women, which has probably reduced the contributions such women make to their partners' careers. In addition, having had a partner whose highest degree was in the same field did not have a significant effect on faculty members' productivity, consistent with the findings of Ferber and Huber, except for faculty members who have had a partner with a Ph.D. For these faculty members, having had a partner in the same field translated into nearly five additional publications, after controlling for the effects of other variables in the regression (results for this restricted sample of Ph.D. couples are not shown).[9]

Do Faculty Members Who Have Had Academic Partners Differ from Faculty Members Who Have Had Only Nonacademic Partners for Specific Types of Productivity?

For the next stage of the analysis, I examined whether faculty members who have had academic partners differed from other faculty members for specific types of productivity. Because there is some evidence that unmarried people publish less than married people and because of the complexity of comparing three groups of faculty—those who have had academic partners, those who have had only nonacademic partners, and those who have never had a partner—I excluded the eighty-six never-partnered people from this stage of the analysis. Thus, I address what would seem to be the more theoretically relevant question of whether faculty members who have had academic partners differ from those who have had only nonacademic partners for specific types of productivity.

Our questionnaire solicited information from faculty members about various types of publications: refereed journal articles, book chapters, textbooks, edited books, other books, other types of publications, and other professional achievements (e.g., productions in the visual and performing arts). We requested the number of each, and for each type, the number authored alone, with a partner, and with other collaborators. Comparing the mean numbers of various types of publications for faculty members who have had academic partners to those who have had only nonacademic partners revealed more similarities than differences between the two groups (see table 6-3). Notably, the mean number of sole authorships did not differ significantly. More notable is the finding that these groups also did not differ in their total productivity (sole

TABLE 6-3. Mean Number of Publications for Specific Productivity Measures

Type of Productivity	Mean	Statistically Significant Difference	
		Nonacademic Partner	Academic Partner
Book chapters			
Sole-authored	0.81		
Co-authored			
With partner	0.11	0.04	0.16*
With other(s)	0.36		
Total	1.28		

Edited books			
Sole-authored	0.04		
Co-authored			
With partner	0.20		
With other(s)	0.09	0.03	0.13[a]
Total	0.34		
Journal articles			
Sole-authored	4.86		
Co-authored			
With partner	0.58	0.31	0.77*
With other(s)	2.94	1.70	3.46**,[b]
Total	8.34	7.18	9.18[a]
Textbooks			
Sole-authored	0.11		
Co-authored			
With partner	0.02		
With other(s)	0.11		[b]
Total	0.24		[b]
Other books			
Sole-authored	0.21		
Co-authored			
With partner	0.06		
With other(s)	0.05		
Total	0.32		
Other publications			
Sole-authored	3.87		
Co-authored			
With partner	0.24	0.08	0.36[a]
With other(s)	1.18		
Total	5.18		
Other professional achievements			
Sole-authored	2.01		
Co-authored			
With partner	0.09	0.01	0.13*
With other(s)	0.17		
Total	2.29		

a. $p < .10$.
b. The effect of having an academic partner differed for the sexes.
* $p < .05$.
** $p < .01$.

and co-authorships combined) for any of the specific types of publications. In other words, although there were some differences in types of co-authorships between faculty members who have had academic partners and those who have not (i.e., co-authorships with partners versus others), these differences did not translate into higher total productivity for any specific types of publication.

As would be expected, faculty members who have had academic partners tended to publish more on average with their partners than faculty members who have had only nonacademic partners.[10] This was true for journal articles (.77 versus .31), book chapters (.16 versus .04), and other professional achievements (.13 versus .01). More unexpected is the finding that faculty members who have had academic partners published twice as many journal articles on average with someone *other* than a partner (3.46 versus 1.70). In addition, for three productivity measures, the effects of having had an academic partner differed for the sexes.

After determining that faculty members who have had academic partners were more productive on average than faculty members with nonacademic partners for four productivity measures (book chapters with partners, other professional achievements with partners, journal articles with partners, and journal articles with persons other than partners), my next step was to determine what factors might account for these differences. That is, I wanted to assess whether the apparent relationships between having had an academic partner and the four productivity measures were due to other variables associated both with having had an academic partner and with higher productivity.

My strategy was to first identify variables that might explain the association between having had an academic partner and the four productivity measures, in order to control for their potential effects on productivity. I constructed a separate regression model for each of the four productivity measures, using as controls those variables correlated with *both* the explanatory variable (having had an academic partner) and the dependent variables (the productivity measure). In table 6-4 I identify the control variables as well as their correlations with the explanatory variable and the four dependent variables. For each of the control variables, Table 6-5 shows the percentages of faculty members with academic partners and with nonacademic partners who have these characteristics.

As the data in table 6-5 indicate, faculty members who have had academic partners were more likely than faculty members who have had

TABLE 6-4. Correlations between Variables Related to Having Had an Academic Partner and Productivity Measures

Control Variable	Explanatory Variable: Academic Partner	Dependent Variable: Other Achievements with Partner	Book Chapters with Partner	Journal Articles with Partner	Journal Articles with Others
Respondent					
Female	.112**	.020	.069	.019	−.077*
Full professor	.090*	−.002	.006	.075	.263**
Highest degree in biology	.086*	−.019	.009	.015	.108**
Highest degree in professions	−.086*	−.018	.059	−.003	−.043
Highest degree is doctorate	.078*	−.041	.060	.135**	.201**
No rank	−.106*	−.035	.025	−.062	−.092*
Partner(s)					
Highest degree in same general field as respondent	.217**	.068	.149**	.165**	−.022
Highest degree is bachelor's or less	−.355**	−.016	−.043	−.094*	−.081*
Highest degree is doctorate	.078*	.017	.142**	.148**	.001
Years employed by any academic institution	.620**	.014	.084*	.046	.039
Years employed by same academic institution as respondent	.460**	.051	.086*	.061	.002
Years not employed	−.183**	−.028	−.052	−.052	.093*

* $p < .05$.
** $p < .01$.

TABLE 6-5. Characteristics of Faculty Members with
Nonacademic and Academic Partners for Control Variables

Control Variable	Nonacademic Partner	Academic Partner
Respondent		
Female	44.0%	55.6%
Full professor	20.6%	28.7%
Highest degree in biology	5.0%	9.9%
Highest degree in professions	21.0%	14.4%
Highest degree is doctorate	58.7%	66.4%
No rank	12.6%	6.4%
Partner(s)		
Highest degree in same general field as repondent	18.7%	39.5%
Highest degree is bachelor's or less	47.4%	14.6%
Highest degree is doctorate	6.6%	36.7%
Years employed by any academic institution	0.0	11.1
Years employed by same academic institution as respondent	0.0	6.4
Years not employed	4.4	1.9

only nonacademic partners to be female (56 percent versus 44 percent), to hold doctorates (66 percent versus 59 percent), to hold their highest degree in the biological sciences (10 percent versus 5 percent), and to be full professors (29 percent versus 21 percent). They were also six times more likely to have had partners with doctorates (37 percent versus 7 percent), twice as likely to have had partners whose highest degree was in the same general field as their own (40 percent versus 19 percent), and, by definition, more likely to have had partners who were employed at academic institutions. Faculty members who have had academic partners were *less* likely than faculty members who have had only nonacademic partners to hold their highest degree in the professions (14 percent versus 21 percent) and to occupy a faculty position without a designated rank (6 percent versus 13 percent), common practice at two-year colleges. In addition, as would be expected, faculty members who have had academic partners were less likely to have had partners who did not have advanced degrees (15 percent versus 47 percent), and their partners spent fewer years out of the labor force on average than the partners of other academics (2 years versus 4 years).

After identifying variables associated both with having had an academic partner and at least one of the four dependent variables, I conducted regression analyses to determine whether the control variables explained the apparent effect of having had an academic partner on each of the four productivity measures. In other words, I determined whether or not having had an academic partner influenced productivity after controlling for the effects of variables correlated both with having had an academic partner and the specific productivity measure.[11] Recall that I excluded from the analysis academics who had never had a partner. Consequently, I adjusted for sample selection bias by including a correction variable in each regression equation.[12]

Dependent Variable 1: Other Professional Achievements Produced with Partners

None of the variables that were correlated with having had an academic partner were also correlated with the number of other professional achievements produced with a partner. Therefore, I could not analyze this relationship further and conclude that the association between having had an academic partner and other professional achievements produced with a partner cannot be explained by other variables in the data set. It appears that having had an academic partner was conducive to producing significantly more other professional achievements with a partner.

Dependent Variable 2: Book Chapters Published with Partners

Table 6-6 shows the findings of the analysis of the effects of the academic partner variable on the number of book chapters published with partners, controlling for the effects of variables associated with both the explanatory and the dependent variable. The positive effect of having had an academic partner on the number of book chapters published with partners, evident in equation 1, disappeared with the addition of the control variables in equation 2. Faculty members who have had academic partners were more likely than other faculty members to have had partners with doctorates and to have had partners in the same field. These characteristics appear to facilitate and to explain the higher numbers of book chapters published with partners among faculty members who have had academic partners.

Dependent Variable 3: Journal Articles Published with Partners

The results of the analysis of the effect of the academic partner variable on journal articles published with partners are similar to those for book chapters published with partners (see table 6-7). The beneficial effect of having had an academic partner on the number of journal articles pub-

TABLE 6-6. Regression Examining the Relationship between Having Had an Academic Partner and the Number of Book Chapters Published with Partners

Control Variable	Equation 1		Equation 2	
	b (s.e. of b)	Beta	b (s.e. of b)	Beta
Sample selection control	1.345[a] (0.826)	0.067	0.684 (0.839)	0.034
Academic partner	0.117* (0.062)	0.078	0.002 (0.071)	0.002
Partner with doctorate			0.162* (0.073)	0.098
Partner in same field			0.189** (0.065)	0.121
Years partner at same institution[b]			0.005 (0.005)	0.044
Constant	−0.113		−0.090	
Adjusted R^2	0.008		0.030	

Note: N = 680.
a. $p < .10$.
b. I did not include the number of years the partner was employed at any institution because it is highly correlated with the number of years at the same institution. Tested separately, neither variable showed a significant effect on book chapters published with partners.
* $p < .05$.
** $p < .01$.

lished with partners, seen in equation 1, disappeared with the addition of the control variables in equation 2. As for book chapters, having had a partner with a doctorate and having had a partner in the same field facilitated publishing journal articles with a partner. Unlike book chapters, however, the number of journal articles published with partners was greater if faculty members themselves held doctorates. This difference in the propensity to publish journal articles with partners may reflect the greater general likelihood of faculty members with doctorates to publish in journals relative to faculty members without doctorates.

Dependent Variable 4: Journal Articles Published with Persons Other Than Partners

Table 6-8 shows the results of the analysis of the effects of having had an academic partner on the number of journal articles published with persons other than partners. These findings indicate that the positive association between having had an academic partner and the number

TABLE 6-7. Regression Examining the Relationship between Having
Had an Academic Partner and the Number of Journal Articles
Published with Partners

Control Variable	Equation 1		Equation 2	
	b (s.e. of b)	Beta	b (s.e. of b)	Beta
Sample selection control	1.899 (3.290)	0.024	−0.354 (3.314)	−0.004
Academic partner	0.445* (0.245)	0.074	−0.006 (0.266)	0.000
Doctorate			0.625** (0.246)	0.104
Partner with bachelor's			−0.151 (0.297)	−0.023
Partner with doctorate			0.670* (0.299)	0.102
Partner in same field			0.793** (0.260)	0.128
Constant	0.088		−0.171	
Adjusted R²	0.003		0.043	

Note: N = 680.
* p < .05.
** p < .01.

of articles published with persons other than partners, seen in equation
1, is explained by the greater likelihood of faculty members who have
had academic partners to be full professors and to hold their highest
degree in the biological sciences, a field with relatively high collaboration rates (equation 2). After controlling for the effects of other variables,
the number of years that partners were not employed also contributed
to the number of articles published with persons other than partners.
Although nonacademic partners spend more time on average out of the
labor force than academic partners do, the advantage in this for faculty
members is not strong enough to offset the disadvantages derived from
the lower average rank and lesser prevalence in the biological sciences
of faculty with nonacademic partners.

Sex Interactions

Equation 3 of table 6-8 indicates that the effect of having had an academic partner on the number of articles published with persons other
than partners differed for men and women. After controlling for the

TABLE 6-8. Regression Examining the Relationship between Having Had an Academic Partner and the Number of Journal Articles Published with Persons Other Than Partners

Control Variable	Equation 1 b (s.e. of b)	Equation 2 b (s.e. of b)	Equation 3 b (s.e. of b.)	Beta
Sample selection control	−35.226*** (10.922)	86.505 (72.683)	79.696 (72.550)	0.297
Academic partner	1.957** (0.815)	1.223[a] (0.867)	2.862** (1.165)	0.143
Sex (female = 1)		−4.888 (4.283)	−2.330 (4.444)	−0.120
Doctorate		1.214 (1.387)	1.139 (1.384)	0.065
Highest degree in biology		8.475* (4.538)	8.024* (4.530)	0.222
No rank		0.350 (1.492)	0.185 (1.490)	0.005
Full professor		6.295*** (1.760)	6.121*** (1.757)	0.276
Partner with bachelor's degree		−0.592 (0.941)	−0.636 (0.938)	−0.029
Years partner not employed		0.101[a] (0.062)	0.116* (0.062)	0.080
Sex / Academic partner			−3.369* (1.618)	−0.165
Constant	5.624	−8.152	−8.587	
Adjusted R^2	0.022	0.090	0.095	

Note: N = 680.
a. $p < .10$.
* $p < .05$.
** $p < .01$.
*** $p < .001$.

effects of other variables in the regression model, men who have had academic partners published nearly three more articles than men who have had only nonacademic partners. For women, however, having had an academic partner did not significantly affect the number of articles they published with persons other than their partners. Thus, for this specific productivity measure, having had an academic partner did not appear to benefit women as it did men.

How might we interpret this finding? Studies of productivity show that informal networks are critical to the collaboration process (Hagstrom 1965; Finkelstein 1982). As Mary Frank Fox (1991:199) observes, "collaboration is both a means to, and an indication of, involvement and integration into the research community." The restricted access of faculty women to informal social networks (as well as more formal channels that enhance research and publishing) may contribute to women's lower rate of publishing articles with persons other than their partners and to their lower overall productivity (Kaufman 1978; Reskin 1978; Astin 1984; Fox 1991). Presumably, having had an academic partner extends a faculty member's social network and exposure to potential collaborators. Among those with academic partners, men may be better able than women to use this extended network for professional purposes. It is also possible that for men, the difference in the number of articles published with nonpartners does not represent true differences in collaboration, but rather differences in publication success (Fox 1991). Even so, the question remains why this is not also true for women.

I found significant sex interactions for two other productivity measures as well: the number of textbooks published with persons other than partners and the total number of textbooks published. For both measures, having had an academic partner did not significantly affect productivity for men, but depressed it for women (.111 fewer textbooks published with persons other than partners and .143 fewer total textbooks) (equations not shown). Thus, unlike the effect on journal articles published with persons other than partners, having had an academic partner does not seem to advantage men in publishing textbooks with nonpartners, although in both cases it does appear to disadvantage women.

Summary and Conclusions

For this sample of Illinois faculty, the effects of having had an academic partner on scholarly productivity appear to be minimal.[13] Comparing faculty members who have had academic partners with those who have not on a composite productivity measure (number of books, chapters, and journal articles, combined) showed that the former group published significantly more than the latter. However, this relationship disappeared after controlling for the effects of additional characteristics of faculty respondents. Although having had an academic partner did not significantly affect productivity after controlling for the effects of other variables, the analysis revealed some significant predictors of faculty productivity. Consistent with existing literature, years of experience, holding a doctorate, being employed by a doctorate-granting or research university, being a full professor, and generating grant revenues were all associated with higher faculty productivity.

Only two variables relevant to the characteristics of partners significantly influenced faculty productivity. The more years that partners were not employed, the more productive the faculty member. Although this suggests that partners contribute to faculty productivity, the actual mechanisms by which this occurs require additional investigation. Finally, greater physical distance between respondents and partners appears to increase productivity for women, while decreasing it for men. This difference may reflect reduced household demands for women and, conversely, increased demands for men.

A more detailed analysis of specific types of productivity for a subsample of partnered people also revealed more similarities than differences between faculty members who have had academic partners and those who have not. The two groups did not differ significantly in the average number of sole-authored publications or in the total number of publications for any of the specific measures. However, faculty members who have had academic partners did exhibit higher productivity than faculty members who have had only nonacademic partners on four measures of productivity: other professional achievements produced with partners, book chapters published with partners, journal articles published with partners, and journal articles published with persons other than their partners. For all but other professional achievements produced with partners, the higher productivity of faculty members who have had academic partners was explained by differences between the two groups in other characteristics associated with scholarly productivity.

For several specific productivity measures, the effects of having had an academic partner differed for the sexes. Men who have had academic partners published significantly more journal articles with persons other than their partners than did other men, while there was no significant difference between the two groups of women. This suggests that having had an academic partner may increase men's professional networks in a way that does not occur for women. In addition, although having had an academic partner did not affect the number of textbooks published with persons other than partners and the total number of textbooks for men, it led to lower productivity in these areas for women. Thus, where sex differences exist, having had an academic partner appears to be less beneficial to women.

In conclusion, the productivity of faculty members who have had academic partners differs little from that of other faculty members for this particular sample. However, I wish to emphasize that this was a preliminary investigation, and additional research is needed to understand the possible links between family status and productivity and how any relationships might differ for women and men. Time-order studies showing publications in relation to life events, such as the formation of relationships, would help unravel the intricacies of any causal relationships. For the moment, however, I conclude that although having had an academic partner does not appear to add significantly to faculty productivity, neither does it appear to detract from it. Thus, these findings suggest that administrators should not view faculty members with academic partners as different from other faculty members in terms of their scholarly potential. And, certainly, the results of this study offer no formula to faculty members for calculating how romantic involvements with other academics might help or hinder their scholarly productivity.

Notes

I thank Neal Ritchey, Lowell Hargens, Marianne Ferber, and Jane Loeb for helpful comments on earlier drafts of this chapter.

1. Although I use a broad definition of "academic couple" and consequently include some non-*faculty* couples, I do explore the potential effects on faculty productivity of the partner's degree level.

2. I created dummy variables to represent nine broad academic fields: *Professions* (agriculture, architecture, business, journalism, law, library science, mathematics, social work, and vocational/technical fields); *biological sciences* (biochemistry, biology, botany, physiology, zoology, and general/other biological sciences); *education* (elementary, secondary, educational administration, educational psychology, foundations, home economics, industrial arts, physical education, and general/other educational fields); *engineering* (aeronautical, chemical, civil, electrical, mechanical, general/other engineering fields); *fine arts* (art, drama, music, other fine arts); *health sciences* (dentistry, medicine, nursing, veterinary medicine, other health fields); *humanities* (foreign languages, English, history, philosophy, religion, general/other humanities); *physical sciences* (mathematics, chemistry, earth sciences, general/other physical sciences); and *social sciences* (geography, anthropology, economics, political science, so-

ciology, psychology, general/other social sciences, and related interdisciplinary studies). A dummy variable means I gave each respondent a value of "1" for his/ her field of highest degree and a value of "0" for all other fields. Social sciences is the omitted reference category in the regression equation. That is, any effect of faculty members' field on productivity is interpreted in relation to the effect of having been in the social sciences.

3. I created dummy variables for five institutional categories based on the Carnegie classification system. Research institutions combine public and private research universities I and II; doctorate-granting institutions combine public and private doctorate-granting colleges and universities I and II; comprehensive institutions combine public and private comprehensive college and universities I and II; liberal arts institutions combine public and private colleges I and II; and two-year institutions combine public and private community, junior, and technical colleges. I added to the reference category (liberal arts colleges) institutional categories that did not differ significantly in their effects on productivity. Thus, I included only doctorate-granting and research universities in the final regression model. All other types of institutions serve as the omitted reference category.

4. I tested the effects on productivity of each rank separately, but only the effect of being a full professor differed from the reference category of assistant professor. Therefore, I added instructors and associate professors to the reference category.

5. Standard deviations are a measure of the dispersion or range of responses. Large standard deviations reflect greater variation in responses while small standard deviations reflect a clustering of responses around the mean.

6. A regression coefficient (b) refers to the amount of change in the dependent variable (number of publications) that is associated with a one-unit change in an independent variable. I show variables significant at the $p < .10$ level in the tables, but do not discuss them in the text. $P < .10$ is generally considered to be "borderline" in significance, and indicates that there is less than a 10 percent chance that the observed relationship is due to chance. $P < .05$ is the customary standard of statistical significance in the sociological field, meaning that there is less than a 5 percent chance that an observed relationship is the result of chance.

7. I explored the potential effects of number of years with an academic partner and number of years employed at the same institution, but neither variable significantly affected productivity so I retained the simpler measure of whether or not a respondent had ever had an academic partner. In addition to examining the data for any effect of having had an academic partner on productivity, I also looked for a possible relationship with grant dollars, but the two variables were not even correlated.

8. Studies of satisfaction in commuter couples report that the ability to

compartmentalize aspects of their lives and to focus intensely on their jobs while separated from their partners is a positive aspect of long-distance relationships (see, e.g., Bunker et al. 1992).

9. Restricting the regression to faculty members with doctorates did not otherwise substantively change the results.

10. It is possible, however, that faculty members received assistance with their publications from nonacademic partners, but that this was less likely to result in acknowledged co-authorships than when faculty members collaborated with academic partners.

11. Note that this approach differs from trying to explain variance in the dependent variables, the more common use of regression analysis. I did not include many variables known to affect productivity in the analysis because they were not associated with having had an academic partner and thus could not explain away the apparent relationship between having had an academic partner and higher productivity.

12. This adjustment corrects for bias that may result from excluding a portion of the total sample from one's analyses. For example, because faculty women are less likely to be partnered than men, they are less likely to be included in a subsample of people with partners. This may influence regression coefficients since women publish less than men on average. The actual sample selection adjustment is calculated by first using a logit technique: $P(O)=1-P(PAR)$, where $P(O)$ is the probability of being omitted from the subsample, and $P(PAR)$ is the probability of having had a partner. I predicted the probability of having had a partner by first regressing partner status (ever/never partnered) on the independent variables relevant to the subsequent subsample analyses (excluding variables that applied only to partnered people). The logit analysis yielded a regression equation from which I computed predicted values for each partnered person. I transformed these into probabilities of being excluded from the subsample of partnered faculty. The specific equation for these transformations is $\text{Log}\,[P(PAR)/1-P(PAR)] = f$ (sex, highest degree in the biological sciences, highest degree in the professions, having no rank, having a doctorate, being a full professor). $P(O)$ then constitutes a new variable (sample selection control), which I entered into the productivity regressions for the subsample of partnered people (see Berk 1983; and, for an example of the method's implementation, Hoffman and Ritchey 1992).

13. For a different conclusion about the relationship between having an academic partner and productivity, see Astin and Milem, this volume. Based on data from a large national survey of faculty, Astin and Milem conclude that having an academic partner is beneficial to women but detrimental to men. These inconsistent findings may be due to differences in the size and composition of our samples, as well as differences in analytical approaches.

References

Allison, Paul D., and J. Scott Long. 1990. "Departmental Effects on Scientific Productivity." *American Sociological Review* 55 (4): 469–78.

Astin, Helen S. 1984. "Academic Scholarship and Its Rewards." In *Advances in Motivation and Achievement,* vol. 2, ed. Marjorie W. Steinkamp and Martin L. Maehr, 259–79. Greenwich, Conn.: JAI Press.

Astin, Helen S., and Diane E. Davis. 1985. "Research Productivity across the Life and Career Cycles: Facilitators and Barriers for Women." In *Scholarly Writing and Publishing: Issues, Problems, and Solutions,* ed. Mary F. Fox, 147–60. Boulder: Westview Press.

Bellas, Marcia L. 1992. "The Effects of Marital Status and Wives' Employment on the Salaries of Faculty Men: The (House)wife Bonus." *Gender and Society* 6 (4): 609–22.

Berk, Richard. 1983. "An Introduction to Sample Selection Bias in Sociological Data." *American Sociological Review* 48 (June): 386–98.

Bryson, Rebecca B., Jeff B. Bryson, Mark H. Licht, and Barbara G. Licht. 1976. "The Professional Pair: Husband and Wife Psychologists." *American Psychologist* 31 (Jan.): 10–16.

Bunker, Barbara, Josephine Zubek, Virginia Vanderslice, and Robert Rice. 1992. "Quality of Life in Dual-Career Families: Commuting versus Single-Residence Couples." *Journal of Marriage and the Family* 54 (May): 399–407.

Carnegie Foundation for the Advancement of Teaching. 1987. *A Classification of Institutions of Higher Education.* Princeton: Carnegie Foundation for the Advancement of Teaching.

Ferber, Marianne A., and Joan Huber. 1979. "Husbands, Wives, and Careers." *Journal of Marriage and the Family* 41 (May): 315–25.

Finkelstein, Martin. 1982. "Faculty Colleagueship Patterns and Research Productivity." Paper presented at the annual meeting of the American Educational Research Association, New York, Mar.

Fowlkes, Martha R. 1980. *Behind Every Successful Man: Wives of Medicine and Academe.* New York: Columbia University Press.

Fox, Mary Frank. 1983. "Publication Productivity among Scientists: A Critical Review." *Social Studies of Science* 13 (May): 285–305.

———. 1991. "Gender, Environmental Milieu, and Productivity in Science." In *The Outer Circle: Women in the Scientific Community,* ed. Harriet Zuckerman, Jonathan R. Cole, and John T. Bruer, 188–204. New York: W. W. Norton.

Hagstrom, Warren. 1965. *The Scientific Community.* New York: Basic Books.

Hartmann, Heidi I. 1981. "The Family as the Locus of Gender, Class, and Political Struggle: The Example of Housework." *Signs* 6 (3): 366–94.

Hochschild, Arlie. 1975. "Inside the Clockwork of Male Careers." In *Women and the Power to Change,* ed. Florence Howe, 47–80. New York: McGraw-Hill.

Hoffman, Constance A., and P. Neal Ritchey. 1992. "Assessing the Differences in Distance of Interstate Migration, 1980." *Sociological Focus* 25 (3): 241–55.

Kaufman, Debra Renee. 1978. "Associational Ties in Academe: Some Male and Female Differences." *Sex Roles* 4 (1): 9–21.

Reskin, Barbara F. 1978. "Sex Differentiation and the Social Organization of Science." In *The Sociology of Science: Problems, Approaches, and Research*, ed. Jerry Gaston, 6–37. San Francisco: Jossey-Bass.

7

Are Academic Partners at a Disadvantage?

Marianne A. Ferber and Emily P. Hoffman

THE CENTRAL QUESTION EXPLORED in the previous chapter was how the productivity of male and female faculty members may be influenced by their varying histories as members of different households. In this chapter we ask whether and how these histories influence their professional success directly, as well as indirectly via their productivity. Historically, this question has not been of great interest because a large majority of male faculty members had wives who were full-time homemakers (see Stephan and Kassis, this volume) and the few women who had faculty positions were often single.[1] Today, this has changed, and it is widely believed that differences in marital and parental status, as well as differences in the employment status of their partners, may exert direct influences on the career progress of women and men, ranging from the type of institution where they are employed to the rank and salary they attain, mainly because these factors may influence mobility and bargaining power and perhaps also administrators' perceptions of their needs.[2] Existing studies have shed light on some of these questions,[3] but leave many of them unanswered.

Review of the Literature

A large number of researchers have investigated hiring, ranks, and salaries of male and female faculty. They have, however, paid very little attention to the possible effects of household arrangements, direct or indirect, on academic careers. Instead, they focused almost entirely on gender discrimination, usually defined as the unexplained portion of differences in rewards. For instance, the portion of the earnings gap that cannot be accounted for by differences in such variables as highest degree earned, years of experience, numbers of various types of publications, dollars of grants received, and so forth is frequently used as a rough measure of salary discrimination, although it is clear that it is far from a perfect one. This is true not only because it is impossible to measure all potentially relevant characteristics but also because there is disagreement about the explanatory variables that should be included. One example of this is using rank as an explanatory variable to predict faculty salaries, as many studies do. This has been found to result in a smaller unexplained male-female wage gap and hence lower estimates of discrimination (Hoffman 1976). However, critics point out that the determination of rank itself may be as much subject to discrimination as the determination of salary (Loeb and Ferber 1973). Another example is that virtually everyone accepts discipline as an explanatory variable, although there is evidence that salary differentials between disciplines are themselves influenced by the proportion of women in the field (Bellas 1994). We shall return to this issue later.

One of the few direct measures of discrimination is found in Fidell (1970), a study that provides direct evidence of discrimination in hiring. Descriptions of ten fictitious individuals were sent to executive officers of psychology departments, with requests to indicate what position each of these individuals would be qualified for. The results of this survey showed that a candidate was considered qualified for a higher position when the respondent believed the applicant was male rather than female. Most other research concerned with discrimination also found that through the 1960s and 1970s women were at a disadvantage in a variety of ways.

All else being equal, women were less likely to be hired (Szafran 1984), especially at the most highly ranked institutions (Moore and Newman 1977; Kolpin and Singell 1994) and for tenure-track positions (Ferber and Green 1982). They were also likely to be promoted more slowly (Ahern and Scott 1981; Bayer and Astin 1975; Szafran 1984). Most notably, a large number of investigations suggested that women were paid less than men with equally measured qualifications (Ferber and Kordick 1978; Loeb and Ferber 1973; Fox 1981; Gordon and Morton 1974; Hoffman 1976; Lee 1981;

Malkiel and Malkiel 1973; Megdal and Ransom 1985; Reagan and Maynard 1974; Richman 1984; Szafran 1984). According to Hirsch and Leppel (1982), this was true even at a historically female institution. Barbezat (1988) concluded that the unexplained portion of male-female salary differentials declined by about half during the 1960s and 1970s, but estimated that it was still about 30 percent by the end of that period.

More detailed investigations at times revealed that there was discrimination against some, but not all women. For instance, Bayer and Astin (1968) reported that men and women were hired at equal rank and promoted equally in the physical sciences, but not in the social sciences. Farber (1977) found evidence of gender differences in percentage raises only for younger women, but recognized that as a result they would remain behind their male colleagues in absolute earnings for the remainder of their careers.

A far smaller number of researchers reported finding no evidence of discrimination during the 1960s and 1970s. Among these are Cartter and Ruhter (1975), who indicated that there was no discrimination in first placement. Cole (1979), while noting that in much earlier days women in science, including those who made substantial contributions, had been largely treated as invisible, went on to claim that by the 1970s the scientific community distributed its rewards in an extremely equitable fashion. Lester (1974) was equally convinced that the existing system during these years was entirely impartial. Johnson and Stafford (1974) noted that women were paid somewhat less than men with similar measured qualifications, but ascribed this to more frequent career interruptions and the greater likelihood that they were, or had been, working part-time; hence they also concluded that there was no discrimination.[4]

More recently, the preponderance of the evidence shows that discrimination has declined substantially. Thus, not only do O'Neill and Sicherman (1990) indicate that both parts of the earnings gap—the part explained by gender differences in relevant characteristics and the part that is not explained—have declined among economists, but McCrate and Livingston (1993) found that for a sample of all professionals under forty years of age in Vermont with master's degrees or Ph.D.'s, sex was not a significant factor in determining salary.[5] Willis and Pieper (1993) detected no significant differences in promotions of women and men, once publications, field, and year of Ph.D. were accounted for.[6] Formby, Gunther, and Sakano (1993), as well as Singell and Stone (1994), concluded that differences in first placement of women and men had disappeared as a general phenomenon, although the latter also concluded that there was evidence women had been hired in lower-ranked departments. Finally, while McMillen and Singell (1994) found that rewards for positive characteristics were smaller for women than for men, penalties for negative attributes of women were smaller as well. This would be consistent with the widely held perception that members of "out-groups" are often seen as being "all alike," but does not constitute discrimination in the usual sense.

Even so, some recent research suggests that discrimination has not entirely disappeared. Ransom and Megdal (1993), as well as Barbezat (1988), reported that the gender gap in academic pay declined during the 1960s and early 1970s but also that it has not changed since then and that women's salaries remain substantially lower than those of equally qualified men.[7] Bellas (1994) similarly showed that women are paid less, in significant part because salaries are lower as the proportion of women in a field rises. Kahn (1993) produced evidence of persistent, albeit declining, gender differences in achieving tenure, as did the Committee on the Status of Women in the Economics Profession (1993). At the same time, this committee also noted that a greater proportion of female than male Ph.D.'s in economics had been hired recently, but Kolpin and Singell (1994) pointed out that higher-quality institutions continued to be less likely to hire women,[8] and Broder (1993b) detected evidence of salary discrimination among older cohorts even in the late 1980s.

In spite of the considerable diversity of findings and conclusions, these studies collectively provide useful information about the history of gender differences in hiring, promotions, and salaries. However, as previously noted, they shed little light on the effects of marital and parental status on the careers of women and men in academia and less on the possible effects of the employment status of their partners. Among the existing studies of dual-career couples, most focused on potential effects of partners on productivity, rather than on career outcomes as such.[9] Bryson and Bryson (1980) did report that both partners in married couples considered the woman's career secondary, which would be expected to give the man the advantage, but that study may be dated by now. More recently, Rubenson and Decker (1992:abstract) found that the careers of such individuals are not very much affected "by the complexity of their family settings—a clear departure from popular wisdom." To the extent that policies of universities and colleges have often been influenced by ad hoc opinions about women's career commitment, there may be little factual basis for them.[10]

Campus lore has long suggested that individuals who were hired when their partners were already faculty members and candidates who received offers after their partners did were likely to be less competent than faculty members who had no such connections when they were first employed.[11] Such negative perceptions of secondary hires, justified or not, lent respectability to the widespread antinepotism rules of earlier days. In spite of the lack of hard evidence to support these opinions, they may well be at the root of some of the remaining resistance to programs for couples today.[12] Concern that highly regarded scholars may use their influence to obtain more favorable treatment for their partners also appears to be rather widespread, albeit equally undocumented.

There is somewhat more evidence to support the common concern of academic couples that one or both of them may receive lower rewards than would be the case if their partner were not employed by the same institution. Ferber, Loeb, and Lowry (1978) found that both women and men with faculty spouses had somewhat lower salaries than others with comparable qualifications. The most common explanation for this is that it is generally difficult to obtain attractive outside offers for both partners, and when only one of them receives a good offer, the other is less likely to be willing to move.[13] This view is supported by Ferber and Kordick (1978), who found that lack of willingness to move to further one's own career had a modest, but significant, negative effect on earnings. The same study also showed that women were considerably more likely than men to permit their location to be determined by their partner's career. One would expect this to be less true today, but considerably more recent research (Bielby and Bielby 1992; Preston 1993) confirmed that this gender difference has not yet disappeared.[14]

In spite of the evidence that professional couples tend to be at a disadvantage, there appears to be considerably more concern about the possibility that partners of academics may get preferential treatment. As already suggested, it is likely that some individuals may be hired, retained, and perhaps relatively well rewarded because colleges and universities are eagerly competing for the services of their more distinguished partners. Inasmuch as it is the junior partner who is more likely to benefit from such a situation, women may be expected to be the chief beneficiaries of such situations, as long as they often continue to be predominantly younger than the men they live with. Thus it is not clear whether academic couples in general, and the female partners in particular, are likely to be at a disadvantage or may, on the contrary, tend to enjoy special advantages.

Obviously, a great deal remains to be learned about the growing number of academic couples who, for good or ill, are destined to be a permanent feature of campuses. This chapter helps to shed light on some of the important questions that concern these couples and their colleagues, as well as the institutions that deal with them as potential or actual faculty members.[15]

Data and Methods

As noted earlier, in the preceding chapter Bellas investigated how the productivity of faculty members may be influenced by their varying histories as members of diverse households, including the effect of being a member of a faculty couple. Like Bellas, we used the data collected for this purpose from a representative sample of institutions of higher learning in Illinois, ranging from major research-oriented universities to others largely or entirely oriented toward teaching, including two-year colleges.[16] Our task was made easier because we could focus on the direct effect of having an academic partner on a faculty member's career progress beyond the effect on productivity, which has already been investigated by Bellas. Even this is not, however, a simple matter. We are still confronted by the fact that people enter relationships at different stages of their careers and of their partners' careers, remain in relationships for varying lengths of time, and may or may not enter new ones. Nor is it always possible to disentangle cause and effect. For instance, we focus on the impact of personal arrangements on careers, but clearly careers also influence personal lives. Nonetheless we provide some evidence that can be useful both to institutions making personnel decisions and to scholars making career decisions.

Our basic approach was to use standard regression and logit analyses[17] to investigate career progress as indicated by the type of employer, as well as the ranks and salaries of respondents. Although we are particularly interested in the possible direct effects of having a partner who is a member of the same faculty,[18] we are also more generally concerned with the effect of various household and professional characteristics of respondents on the type of institutions where they are employed and on their ranks and salaries. The former include such variables as the total number of years spent with partners, the level of education of these partners, the number of years the partners were employed at the same institution, the geographic distance from the current partner, whether respondents were married to their partners, the number of children, and the number of years the children spent in the household. The latter include age, race, highest degree earned, years of professional experience, field, number of various types of publications, administrative experience, part-time status, and dollar amounts of grants obtained.

As it turned out, many of the variables we investigated were consistently found not to have a significant effect on the outcomes, and were consequently discarded.[19] Beyond that, some variables that were not significant for particular relationships often had to be eliminated from individual logit regressions in order to get them to converge.[20] Table 7-1 provides the definitions for those variables that were used in the final regressions reported on below. We examine all relationships separately for female and male faculty, so that we can determine whether the effects of the different variables are the same for women and men.[21]

TABLE 7-1. Variables Used in Final Regression

Admininstration	Ever had an administrative position, yes = 1; no = 0
Age	Age of respondent
Black	Black = 1; Other = 0
Experience	Total years with present employer, plus previous employer
Fields	
Arts	Art, art history, dance, drama and speech, music, other fine arts
Biology	Anatomy, bacteriology, biochemistry, biology, botany, ecology and evolution, genetics, microbiology, molecular biology, plant pathology, physiology, zoology, other biological sciences
Education	Dietetics, education, home economics and family research, library science, nursing, physical education, physical therapy, social work
Engineering	Engineering
Health	Dentistry, pharmacology, speech and hearing, veterinary medicine, other medicine
Humanities	English, foreign languages, history, philosophy, religion and theology, speech communications, other humanities
Physical science	Astronomy, chemistry, earth sciences and geology, mathematics, physics, statistics, other physical sciences
Professions	Business, law, medicine (omitted category)
Social science	Anthropology, archeology, economics, geography, international relations, political science, psychology, social studies, sociology

Grants	Dollar amount
Household-related variables	
Distance	Distance from current partner (in miles)
Number of children	Number of children
Number of children times age	Number of children times their ages
Partner on same faculty	Sum of years all partners were employed on the same faculty
Years with partners	Years with all partners
Ph.D.	Doctoral degree
Part-time	Part-time = 1; full-time = 0
Publications	
Journal articles	Number of journal articles
Edited books	Number of edited books
Textbooks	Number of textbooks
Other books	Number of other books
Chapters	Number of chapters in books
Other publications	Number of other publications
Rank	
Assistant	Assistant professor = 1; otherwise 0
Associate	Associate professor = 1; otherwise 0
Full professor	Full professor = 1; otherwise 0
Other	Lecturers, instuctors, and faculty with no rank
Salary	Natural logarithm of nine-month equivalent salary
Top-ranked university	Research or doctoral university, category I

In view of forces working in both directions, it is not clear whether having a partner who is a member of the same faculty should be expected, on balance, to have positive or negative effects.[22] On the one hand, there are lingering prejudices against faculty couples and, in spite of the greater openness to hiring two academic partners, they clearly continue to be at a disadvantage with respect to mobility. On the other hand, there has been increasing recognition that faculty couples are here to stay, and most institutions of higher learning have begun to realize that they cannot do without them. Further, both partners have the compensating advantages of having a potentially influential ally[23] and having access to a larger network of friends among their colleagues. Similarly, given a good deal of evidence that the status of women in academia has been improving considerably, we do not necessarily expect the present reward structure for women to be significantly different from that for men.[24]

Analysis

Before discussing the results of our research, a few explanations are in order for those not accustomed to this kind of statistical analysis. Logit regressions are used when the dependent variable is dichotomous, such as the employer being a research or doctoral university, as opposed to all other institutions of higher education, or achievement of full professor rank, as opposed to other lower ranks.[25] When the dependent variable is continuous, such as salary, ordinary least squares regressions are used; for these, the adjusted R^2 indicates the proportion of the variation of this (dependent) variable that is explained by all the other (independent) variables used in the regression.[26]

The data in table 7-2 show the influence of various factors on whether a respondent was employed at a research or doctorate-granting university, generally regarded as being the most prestigious, or at another type of university or college.[27] As would be expected, for both men and women, having a doctoral degree had a significant positive effect on the probability of being employed at one of the top-ranked institutions. So did

TABLE 7-2. Determinants of Employment at
Research and Doctoral Universities

Variable	Men b	Men t	Women b	Women t
Age	0.023	1.67[a]	−0.031	3.61**
Experience	−0.025	2.10*	0.015	1.55
Ph.D.	0.481	2.82**	0.350	2.91**
Partner on same faculty	0.173	0.97		
Years with partners	−0.018	2.15*	−0.005	0.98
Journal articles	0.044	5.43**	0.029	3.02**
Other books	0.062	1.11	−0.001	0.01
Chapters	0.013	1.18	0.113	2.81**
Constant	3.912		5.814	
Chi square	305.88		583.67**	
Probability	0.692		0.000	
Sample size	328		447	

a. $p < .10$.
* $p < .05$.
** $p < .01$.

a larger number of journal articles published, the most valued type of publication in most fields. Somewhat surprisingly, for women book chapters were significant as well and, as we shall see later, they were also found to play a part in determining a woman's rank and salary. It is generally assumed that chapters are not as highly regarded as articles because they tend not to be refereed as rigorously. That may explain why this variable was not significant for men. Nonetheless, being invited to contribute a chapter to a book suggests that the author is likely to be relatively well known and well regarded. This might be more highly valued in the case of women, perhaps because a substantial reputation even now is less likely to be taken for granted in their case. There may also be differences in weights for different types of publications by field, and there continue to be substantial gender differences in distribution by field. For instance, women are more highly represented in the humanities and far less in the physical sciences than are men.

Several additional findings are also worth noting. First, for women, but not men, greater age has a negative relation to being employed at research or doctoral institutions, showing that older women are less likely to be employed at the most highly ranked institutions than are younger women. This suggests that at these prestigious universities discrimination against women has been declining or that affirmative action pressures on these institutions to increase their previously very low representation of women has been working, at least to some extent. Second, years of experience have a negative effect for men.[28] It appears that while men at research universities are more likely to have doctoral degrees, men at lesser institutions are likely to have more years of work experience than men in the same age range at top universities.

Finally, the total number of years men had partners has a significant negative effect on the likelihood of their being at a research or doctoral university.[29] Because productivity is controlled for, this might be ascribed to lesser mobility, presumably because partners often prefer not to move, so that men with partners have less bargaining power than those who have no such attachments; or it could be that very ambitious, professionally committed young men, who are most likely to be employed at these universities, are also likely to postpone making commitments to partners. It is, however, surprising that this effect does not show up for women, because we would expect both these effects to be far more important for them. In fact, contrary to what might be expected, none of the variables relating to partners or children are significant for women in this regression,[30] or, as we shall see, in the regressions for rank and salary.[31]

Further, it should be noted that in a comparable single logit regression for men and women together, the coefficient for a dummy variable for female was not significant, and the sign was actually positive. This clearly suggests that sex by itself, apart from possible interactions with other variables, no longer plays a consequential part in determining whether a person is employed at a research or doctoral university as opposed to another type of institution. On the other hand, the logit model displayed in table 7-2 successfully predicts employment at a research or doctoral university for men but not for women, as indicated by the chi square.[32] That is not particularly surprising in view of the continued tendency for women to be the second partner hired.

Logit estimates of attainment of the rank of full professor are shown in table 7-3.[33] Again, only two variables have a positive effect for both men and women at the 5 percent significance level or better: having a Ph.D. and additional years of experience. Administrative experience, grants, and

TABLE 7-3. Determinants of Attaining Full Professorship

Variable	Men b	Men t	Women b	Women t
Admininstration	0.117	0.77	0.413	2.50*
Experience	0.059	6.12**	0.082	7.03**
Grants	0.000	0.01	0.0001	2.13*
Ph.D.	0.881	4.33**	0.795	3.78**
Years with partners	0.013	2.06*	−0.007	1.20
Journal articles	0.019	3.09**	0.006	0.97
Chapters	0.019	1.80[a]	0.083	2.39*
Edited books	0.015	0.65	−0.063	0.61
Other books	0.091	1.80[a]	0.027	0.32
Other publications	0.001	0.21	0.005	0.74
Constant	2.162		2.096	
Chi square	328.81		449.16	
Probability	0.872		0.298	
Sample size	370		445	

a. $p < .10$.
* $p < .05$.
** $p < .01$.

chapters in books have a significant positive effect at that level only for women, although book chapters are also weakly significant for men at the .10 level; journal articles and the number of years spent with all partners are, on the other hand, significant for men. No other variables were significant for either female or male faculty, showing once again that personal relationships tend to have little effect on academic careers and that this is particularly true for women. That having had a partner does prove to be an asset for men is consistent with the assumption that women often provide support for their husbands in a variety of ways; at times they function as "research assistants," entertain colleagues, and most commonly, even today, take care of a very large share of household chores. It is also the case, however, that for men the number of years with a partner is likely to be highly correlated with age.

It is also interesting to note that in a logit regression that estimated attainment of rank for the whole sample, we found, once again, that the dummy for sex was not significant; hence there is no evidence that gender per se plays a role in promotions either, although in this instance the sign for female was negative. Finally, unlike the model for employment at top universities, the model in table 7-3 does successfully predict rank for both women and men.

The third dependent variable to be examined, and the one that has received the most attention from other researchers, is salary.[34] The results, shown in table 7-4, indicate that we were reasonably successful in accounting for differences in this variable, for we were able to explain 52 percent of the variation in men's salaries and 63 percent of the variation in women's salaries.[35] Once more, having earned a doctoral degree and having accumulated more years of experience have a significant positive effect for both sexes, as does working full-time; having chapters in books and having had an administrative position also have a positive effect for women. The lack of greater importance of publications may, in part, be attributable to the fact that a large proportion of respondents in this survey are employed at schools where faculty are not generally expected to publish, and some of those employed at institutions that do stress research are in fields where publications are not necessarily emphasized either, such as clinical medicine and librarianship.[36] Nonetheless, these findings are unexpected, and contrary to the results of other studies. We shall return to this point later.

Among the variables noted above to be significant is, first of all, part-time status.[37] This is not unexpected because pay for part-time employ-

ees is generally reduced considerably more than would be expected simply in terms of their reduced work time. Second, we found that salary
varies considerably by discipline. Many fields are significantly less well
rewarded than the omitted category of professions, which includes the

TABLE 7-4. Determinants of Salary (Including Publications)

Variable	Men		Women	
	b	t	b	t
Administration	−0.013	0.28	0.137	3.55**
Black	−0.145	0.91	0.104	0.68
Experience	0.015	4.56**	0.016	6.02**
Fields				
Arts	−0.138	1.36	−0.183	2.39*
Biology	−0.084	0.90	−0.134	1.59
Education	−0.122	1.54	−0.209	3.48**
Engineering	−0.103	0.78	−0.009	0.06
Health	0.115	1.02	0.055	0.90
Humanities	−0.285	3.74**	−0.299	4.98**
Physical science	−0.158	1.97*	−0.086	1.03
Social science	−0.138	1.77[a]	−0.179	2.66**
Grants	0.00001	1.91[a]	0.00001	1.24
Household-related variables				
Distance	0.0001	1.47	−0.0001	1.34
Number of children	−0.080	1.15	−0.005	0.09
Number of children times age	0.001	1.03	0.00003	0.03
Years with partners	0.0003	0.16	−0.0004	0.26
Ph.D.	0.228	4.20**	0.259	6.61**
Part-time	−1.286	13.84**	−0.905	16.86**
Publications				
Chapters	0.0002	0.06	0.021	2.35*
Edited books	−0.0001	0.02	0.013	0.64
Journal articles	0.001	0.59	0.002	1.09
Other publications	0.0003	0.21	0.00004	0.003
Other books	0.010	0.63	−0.019	0.82
Textbooks	0.013	0.42	0.001	0.17
Constant	10.336		10.195	
Adjusted R^2	0.519		0.631	
Sample size	327		394	

a. $p < .10$.
* $p < .05$.
** $p < .01$.

highly paid areas of business, law, and medicine. Because we use field as one of the determinants of salary, we implicitly accept existing pay differentials among disciplines, which are quite large. In fact, as noted previously, these differences may well be related to the proportion of women in the field (Bellas 1994). Unfortunately, however, our data do not permit us to test this hypothesis. Third, women who have ever had an administrative position receive a higher salary than would otherwise be predicted, perhaps because to date mainly rather exceptional women have achieved such positions. It may also be that, to the extent that administrators are paid on a higher scale than faculty, this means a larger increment for women who, as we shall see, are less likely to experience regular salary increases with promotion in rank.

As mentioned previously, the relatively small effect that publications have on salaries is rather surprising. Publications were, however, found to have some effect on the probability of being employed at a research or doctoral university and on the person's rank. To the extent that these variables, in turn, do influence salaries, their full effect may be somewhat greater than appeared initially, although the effect is mainly indirect. This is suggested by the slightly larger R^2 value for the men's regression in table 7-5, which does not include publications but does include the type of employer and the rank of the individual, than in table 7-4, which includes publications but not the other two variables.[38]

A closer examination of table 7-5 shows that employment at a research or doctoral university has a significant positive effect on salary, but the results with regard to rank are considerably more mixed. For both men and women, the coefficient for positions not on the tenure track, including lecturer, instructor, and other faculty positions without specific titles, is negative and significant as compared with the omitted category of full professor. For assistant professors, however, the negative coefficient is significant only for men, although it is also weakly significant (.10 level) for men who are associate professors. For women, the sign for associate professor is not even negative. One may speculate that this could be the result of salary compression. That is to say that recently salaries for assistant professors have risen more rapidly than those of other faculty, with the result that salaries for full professors are sometimes only a little higher than those of more recently hired associate professors. Among women, associate professors, who were generally hired more recently than full professors, may additionally have benefited from a decline in discrimination or by affirmative action.

TABLE 7-5. Determinants of Salary (Including Employer and Rank)

Variable	Men		Women	
	b	t	b	t
Administration	−0.017	0.38	0.131	3.44**
Black	−0.109	0.75	0.089	0.57
Experience	0.007	2.07*	0.014	5.06**
Fields				
Arts	−0.078	0.78	−0.210	2.79**
Biology	−0.047	0.53	−0.110	1.34
Education	−0.070	0.92	−0.169	2.82**
Engineering	−0.009	0.07	−0.018	0.12
Health	0.085	0.78	0.056	0.94
Humanities	−0.266	3.63**	−0.279	4.66**
Physical science	−0.091	1.18	−0.073	0.88
Social science	−0.090	1.20	−0.129	1.93[a]
Grants	0.00001	1.63	0.00001	1.79[a]
Household-related variables				
Distance	0.0001	1.12	−0.00004	0.68
Number of children times age	0.003	1.98*	0.0003	0.28
Number of children	−0.136	2.08*	−0.014	0.26
Years with partners	−0.0001	0.09	−0.00002	0.01
Part-time	−1.185	13.02**	−0.901	16.28**
Ph.D.	0.167	3.04**	0.228	5.37**
Rank				
Associate professor	−0.105	1.95[a]	0.015	0.31
Assistant professor	−0.243	3.64**	−0.053	1.10
Other	−0.488	4.16**	−0.145	2.41*
Top-ranked university	0.141	3.02**	0.105	2.90**
Constant	10.548		10.217	
Adjusted R^2	0.553		0.630	
Sample size	338		408	

a. $p < .10$.
* $p < .05$.
** $p < .01$.

With respect to fields, the results are somewhat different from the regressions that do not use employment at a top university as an independent variable, perhaps because pay differentials by field may vary by type of institution. For the most part, however, the same fields tend to have lower salaries for women and men. Two differences between men and women are, however, similar to those noted before. Women are re-warded for having held administrative positions, and both are penalized for being in fields other than the highly paid professional fields, albeit for men the negative coefficient is significant only for the humanities, while for women it is significant for the arts and education as well as the humanities.[39]

Considerably more surprising is the negative effect on men, but not women, of the number of children. For while young men today are spending a good deal more time with their children than did men in earlier days, women continue to do so to a far greater extent. It should also be noted that for older men the positive effect of the interaction term with age slightly more than compensates for the negative effect of the number of children alone. While additional children have a nega-tive effect on younger men's salaries, older men (those above fifty) with more children tend to have higher salaries than those with fewer chil-dren. More likely than not this is, at least in part, a cohort effect, because the older man of today who had more than one or two children was also most likely to be married to a full-time homemaker. Such a wife would not only largely have taken care of the children but, as discussed previ-ously, was often helpful to her husband's career in various other ways as well. Further, he may also to some extent have been compensated on the basis of perceived need, especially in earlier years when this was often deemed an acceptable practice.

In order to determine the net effect of the various differences in these two salary regressions, we used Oaxaca's (1973) technique of comput-ing the average salary for women by using the mean values of their char-acteristics with the regression coefficients obtained from the model for men's salaries. With this method, using the data from the salary regres-sion with publications (table 7-4), the mean earnings of women would have been 3 percent higher ($33,056 as opposed to their actual mean earnings of $31,984), although still only 84 percent of the mean earn-ings of men ($39,498). Interestingly, however, the mean computed sal-ary for men would also be higher, by 4 percent ($40,945 compared with the actual earnings of $39,498), if they were paid according to the fe-male salary structure and their own characteristics. Using the results from the salary regression that includes both rank and institution but not publications raises women's salaries by 4 percent ($33,392 compared with $32,080), and again is only 84 percent of men's salaries. Men's sal-aries, on the other hand, would decline, but only marginally, by 1 per-cent (from $39,696 to $39,473). Like our other findings, these results show no convincing evidence of gender discrimination, once differences by field are accounted for.[40] It appears that the lower mean salary for women is caused by differences in the relevant characteristics of women and men, rather than by gender differences in how those characteristics are rewarded.

Conclusions

Overall, we can obviously conclude that there is remarkably little evidence that the careers of faculty members, and especially women, are influenced by any of the household-related variables, including their partners' level of education and employment status (variables which, along with a good many others, were omitted from the regressions shown in the tables because they consistently failed to be significant). In fact, for women the presence of children has no significant effect, although it has a negative effect for younger men. On the face of it, this failure to uncover significant relationships might appear to be disappointing. It must be remembered, however, that we essentially set out to discover whether institutions tend to get a bad bargain by employing couples or whether individuals are unfairly disadvantaged by having partners who are also academics. Viewed in that light, it is reasonable to conclude that "no news is good news." That respondents with partners on the faculty are about equally likely to be hired by research universities, are promoted to full professor at about the same rate, and are paid about the same as other faculty with comparable qualifications may be seen as encouraging.

Similarly, the failure to find any substantial direct effect of sex on an individual's professional career should be seen as evidence of considerable progress over earlier years when women were generally found to be at a substantial disadvantage in hiring, promotion, and salary, well beyond the difference that could be explained by the available measured indicators of merit.[41] Under the circumstances one may even want to forego raising the question of whether this suggests that women were discriminated against in the past or that women have more recently been able to acquire all the unmeasured virtues men have had all along.[42]

It is, nonetheless, probably premature to expect the day to arrive soon when the remaining differences in the status and the reward structures of academic women and men will disappear as well.[43] The continued segregation by field, as well as the far greater proportion of women who work part-time and in ranks that are not on the tenure track, tells us something about that. So does the strikingly larger percentage of men than women who have doctoral degrees, 71 percent compared with 54 percent (as noted in the introduction). While academia continues to be, for the most part, male-dominated, and is by no means always welcoming to young women scholars (Fox 1995), most of the differences noted above are primarily caused by conditions in society at large, rather than merely by the situation in academia, and are likely to continue changing only slowly. These issues deserve more attention from researchers, including the question of whether the substantial salary differentials explained by gender differences in any or all of these respects are fully warranted or are, in fact, a lingering form of discrimination.

Meanwhile, the representation of women in academia continues to rise, no doubt contributing to the growing numbers of academic couples, and the growing acceptance of academic couples undoubtedly facilitates the continued growth in the numbers of women in academia. The research presented here does not show that this process has been, or could be, frictionless. But it should help to dispel the fears of those who expected the gates would open to large numbers of unqualified people, as well as of those who thought the institutions would have the opportunity to exploit hapless couples who are not willing to sacrifice togetherness for greater professional progress.

Notes

1. This was apparently less true of black faculty women (see Perkins, this volume).

2. The argument that women do not need as much money as men because they have someone to support them was commonplace at one time. It is not beyond possibility, therefore, that such considerations as a man having a dependent wife and children or a woman not having a husband may still play a part in salary decisions, although it is no longer acceptable to admit this.

3. Most notably, these issues have been addressed in Helen S. Astin's work; they are examined further in Astin and Milem (this volume). In a number of instances their findings are different from ours. The explanation for such differences, not unusual among different research studies (Bentley and Blackburn 1992), may be both the diverse samples and the different methodologies used.

4. In later papers, however, Johnson and Stafford (1975, 1979), perhaps in response to such critics as Strober and Quester (1977), acknowledged that the possibility of discrimination cannot be eliminated.

5. In more technical terms, in a salary regression, the coefficient for a dummy variable for sex was small and usually not significant. There was a significant, but very small gap, 5 percent or less, among older men and women (McCrate and Livingston 1993). As noted in Bellas (this volume), relationships are regarded as not significant when the probability is greater than one in ten ($p <$ .10) that a difference as large as that found could occur by chance; many researchers employ the more rigid standard of not accepting a relationship as significant when the probability is greater than one in twenty ($p < .05$). Although variables that are only significant at the 10 percent level are indicated in the tables, they are generally not discussed in the text.

6. Some of the studies that reported discrimination, such as Broder (1993a), did not control for publications.

7. Ransom (1990) also found that segregation by field did not decline any further in the 1980s and may even have increased slightly for doctoral degrees awarded.

8. Interestingly, they also provide evidence that discrimination is costly, because in departments that continued to hire fewer women in recent years, faculty members published relatively less.

9. See, for instance, Astin and Davis (1985), who found that in academia, rather surprisingly, married women were more productive than single women.

10. These issues are discussed at some length in Hornig (this volume).

11. The prevalence of this belief may not be entirely unrelated to the fact that women used to constitute a substantial majority of "trailing spouses." Weissman et al. (1973) found that every faculty wife in their sample had been hired after their partners.

12. Ferber and Green (1982) compared the performance of "faculty wives" with that of other faculty women and provided no support for the notion that the former are less qualified than the latter. Further, as already noted, Astin and Davis (1985) found that married women tended to be more productive than single women.

13. Some couples do, under such conditions, opt for a commuting relationship. This does not, however, appear to be common. In our sample of 851, only 20 reported working/living at a distance of more than 200 miles from their partners. This is too small a number to permit any firm conclusions about their distinguishing characteristics, but it may be noted that they were younger, which suggests that this phenomenon may be on the increase; they were also less likely to be married, had fewer children, and were more likely to have doctoral degrees.

14. This probably also helps to explain why women academics have been more likely to locate in big cities (Marwell, Rosenfeld, and Spillerman 1979), where it is likely to be easier for both partners to find jobs within reasonable commuting distance.

15. Some of the same questions are also investigated by Astin and Milem (this volume).

16. This sample is described in some detail in the previous chapter. It should be noted that we used a different definition for "education" and "professions" than Bellas did. We included the traditionally female professions, such as library science, nursing, and social work, with other "female" fields, such as education and home economics, because salaries are very similar in these groups. Bellas, on the other hand, was concerned with different issues and combined all the professions.

17. The models for type of institution where the respondent is employed and for rank of the respondent are estimated using logit rather than the more usual ordinary least squares regressions (OLS) because the dependent variables are dichotomous (0, 1). Economists prefer to use logit analysis because, unlike OLS, it constrains the predicted value of the dependent variable to be between 0 and 1.

18. The variable used to test this is the number of years spent with any partner on the same faculty.

19. Because some of these were also the questions that respondents were most likely not to provide answers for, eliminating them had the advantage of increasing the sample size appreciably. Some variables, such as a dummy for race, were nonetheless retained in the salary regressions, as were all fields and all indicators of productivity, because some of these were significant.

20. Logit is a maximum likelihood estimation method, which uses an iterative procedure. Convergence of the model is necessary, for it indicates that estimates improved with successive iterations, while failure to converge may show that the model is inappropriate for the data (Greene 1990). Therefore, models that did not converge are not reported here.

21. It would have been most interesting to examine as well similarities and differences for same-sex and opposite-sex couples, but only 14 out of 864 respondents indicated having ever had a same-sex partner. This number is obviously far too small to make a meaningful statistical analysis possible.

22. It will be remembered that Rubenson and Decker (1992), one of the few studies that examined similar questions, found little impact of personal relationships on careers. Astin and Milem (this volume), on the other hand, found that having an academic partner tended to have distinctly favorable effects on faculty women, but predominantly unfavorable ones for men.

23. Their help may often be useful, in spite of the commonly employed rules against faculty, and particularly administrators, being directly involved in decisions concerning their partners.

24. Evidence on these subjects is provided in the introduction as well as in some of the other chapters in this volume.

25. As previously noted, one disadvantage of this approach is that some variables had to be omitted from the logit regressions because of the failure to achieve maximum likelihood convergence when they were included.

26. The meaning of different probabilities was explained in note 5.

27. We ran separate regressions for women and men, on the assumption that some of the variables might have a different effect on female and male faculty. It would be entirely appropriate to run separate regressions for racial and ethnic groups and for faculty who have partners they are or are not married to, but the small number of minorities and the even smaller number of respondents who reported they were living with partners they were not married to precluded this possibility.

28. To the extent that at a given age men at top universities tend to have fewer years of experience, this may be because they are more likely to have spent some years as postdoctoral fellows, which are not counted as "years of experience." It should also be noted that women are not as likely as men to be in fields where postdoctoral fellowships are most common.

29. Perhaps the men who acquire additional credentials by accepting postdoctoral fellowships, which help them get jobs at highly ranked institutions, are also inclined to marry later. On the other hand, we also found that for men, the sum of years with partners employed at the same institution, although not statistically significant, has a positive sign, suggesting that they are somewhat more likely to be at highly ranked universities, possibly because their partners may be more highly qualified or because such institutions are more willing and able to make some accommodation for their partners. This variable, however, had to be omitted for the women's regression in order to get it to converge.

30. As previously noted, not all the variables initially examined ended up being in the final regression.

31. That does not necessarily mean that none of these factors have any effect; it may be, rather, that there are offsetting positive and negative effects. For instance, a woman with a faculty partner may do more housework than one who does not have a partner, but this may be offset by the benefits of more networking with colleagues, emphasized by Astin and Milem (this volume).

32. The Chi square test of goodness of fit for the model has a probability level of .692 for men, which indicates there was no significant difference between the logit model's prediction and the actual data for men. However, for women there is a statistically significant difference between the distribution of the data and the logit model's predictions of employment at a research or doctoral university. In other words, the logit model is unable to successfully predict whether or not women are employed at top universities.

33. Increasingly, at private research universities, this is also when faculty members achieve tenure.

34. As is customary, we use log of salary.

35. This is somewhat higher than the comparable R^2 of Astin and Milem (this volume) of 43 percent and 51 percent. This difference, as well as some other differences in results, may be explained by the fact that we were able to use years

of experience rather than age, which is widely used as a proxy for experience but, particularly for women, is not an entirely satisfactory one. We also used lifetime publications, while they used publications for the last two years, and included two additional variables that turned out to be significant, dummies for working part-time and for having had an administrative position.

36. We did try to take out people in fields that we thought belonged to this group, but did not find that this made any difference, perhaps because we did not succeed in eliminating the right group of people.

37. To the extent that this status is chosen voluntarily, this does not necessarily raise any questions, even though, on the one hand, a substantially larger proportion of women than men work part-time and, on the other hand, men appear to be penalized more when they do. Unfortunately, we do not know to what extent people choose to work part-time or accept part-time positions because they cannot find other work.

38. Remember that the adjusted R^2 shows how much of the variation in salaries is explained by the regression.

39. It is worth noting that as many as 56 percent of women are employed in these poorly paid fields.

40. Mean salaries differ somewhat because of small differences in sample size, caused by some respondents not answering all questions.

41. It should, however, be noted once again that there may well be indirect effects and that we hope that researchers will in the future turn their attention to those, particularly the apparent effect the proportion of women has on salary differentials by field.

42. We must confess, however, that this is still a quite intriguing question to some of the old warriors in the battles about discrimination.

43. Even the fact that no men in our sample were hired under special programs for partners, compared with seven women who were (although that, too, is a very small number), is interesting.

Bibliography

Ahern, Nancy C., and Elizabeth Scott. 1981. *Career Outcomes in a Matched Sample of Men and Women Ph.D.s: An Analytical Report.* Washington, D.C.: National Academy Press.

Astin, Helen S., and Diane E. Davis. 1985. "Research Productivity across the Life and Career Cycles: Facilitators and Barriers for Women." In *Scholarly Writing and Publishing: Issues, Problems, and Solutions,* ed. Mary F. Fox, 147–60. Boulder: Westview Press.

Barbezat, Debra. 1988. "Gender Differences in the Academic Reward System." In *Academic Labor Markets and Careers,* ed. David W. Breneman and Ted I. K. Youn, 138–64. New York: Folmer Press.

Bayer, Alan, and Helen S. Astin. 1968. "Sex Differences in Academic Rank and Salary among Doctorates in Teaching." *Journal of Human Resources* 3 (Spring): 191–200.

———. 1975. "Sex Differentials in the Academic Reward System." *Science* 188 (May 23): 796–802.

Bellas, Marcia. 1994. "Comparable Worth in Academia: The Effects on Faculty Salaries of the Sex Composition and Labor Market Conditions of Academic Disciplines." *American Sociological Review* 59 (Dec.): 807–21.

Bentley, Richard J., and Robert T. Blackburn. 1992. "Two Decades of Gains for Female Faculty?" *Teachers College Record* 93 (Summer): 697–709.

Bielby, Denise D., and William T. Bielby. 1992. "I Will Follow Him: Family Ties, Gender-Role Beliefs, and Reluctance to Relocate for a Better Job." *American Journal of Sociology* 97 (Mar.): 1241–67.

Broder, Ivy. 1993a. "Gender Differences in Promotion and Turnover in Top Economics Departments." Ms.

———. 1993b. "Professional Achievement and Gender Differences among Academic Economists." *Economic Inquiry* 31 (Jan.): 116–27.

Bryson, Jeff B., and Rebecca B. Bryson. 1980. "Salary and Job Performance Differences." In *Dual-Career Couples,* ed. Fran Pepitone-Rockwell, 241–59. Beverly Hills: Sage Publications.

Cartter, Alan M., and Wayne E. Ruhter. 1975. *The Disappearance of Sex Discrimination in First Job Placement of New Ph.D.s.* Los Angeles: Higher Education Research Institute.

Cole, Jonathan R. 1979. *Fair Science: Women in the Scientific Community.* New York: Free Press.

Committee on the Status of Women in the Economics Profession. 1993. Report. *American Economic Review* 83 (May): 508–13.

Farber, Stephen. 1977. "The Earnings and Promotion of Women Faculty." *American Economic Review* 67 (Mar.): 199–206.

Ferber, Marianne A., and Carole A. Green. 1982. "Traditional or Reverse Sex Discrimination?: A Case Study of a Large, Public University." *Industrial and Labor Relations Review* 35 (July): 550–64.

Ferber, Marianne A., and Betty Kordick. 1978. "Sex Differentials in the Earnings of Ph.D.'s." *Industrial and Labor Relations Review* 31 (Jan.): 227–38.

Ferber, Marianne A., Jane W. Loeb, and Helen M. Lowry. 1978. "The Economic Status of Women Faculty: A Reappraisal." *Journal of Human Resources* 13 (Summer): 385–401.

Fidell, L. S. 1970. "Empirical Verification of Sex Discrimination in Hiring Practices in Psychology." *American Psychologist* 25 (Dec.): 1094–98.

Formby, John P., William D. Gunther, and Ryoichi Sakano. 1993. "Entry Level Salaries of Academic Economists: Does Gender or Age Matter?" *Economic Inquiry* 31 (Jan.): 128–38.

Fox, Mary F. 1981. "Sex, Salary, and Achievement: Reward Dualism in Academia." *Sociology of Education* 54 (Apr.): 71–84.

———. 1995. "Women in Higher Education: Gender Differences in the Status of Students and Scholars." In *Women: A Feminist Perspective,* ed. Jo Freeman, 220–37. Mountain View, Calif.: May Field Publishing.

Gordon, Nancy, and Thomas E. Morton, with Ina Braden. 1974. "Faculty Salaries: Is There Discrimination by Sex, Race, and Discipline?" *American Economic Review* 64 (June): 419–27.

Greene, William H. 1990. *Econometric Analysis.* New York: Macmillan.

Hirsch, Barry, and Karen Leppel. 1982. "Sex Discrimination in Faculty Salaries: Evidence from a Historically Women's University." *American Economic Review* 72 (Sept.): 829–36.

Hoffman, Emily P. 1976. "Faculty Salaries: Is There Discrimination by Race, Sex, and Discipline?: Additional Evidence." *American Economic Review* 66 (Mar.): 196–98.

Johnson, George E., and Frank P. Stafford. 1974. "The Earnings and Promotion of Women Faculty." *American Economic Review* 64 (Dec.): 888–903.

———. 1975. "Women and the Academic Labor Market." In *Sex Discrimination and the Division of Labor,* ed. Cynthia B. Lloyd, 201–19. New York: Columbia University Press.

———. 1979. "Pecuniary Rewards to Men and Women Faculty." In *Academic Rewards in Higher Education,* ed. Darrell R. Lewis and William E. Becker Jr., 231–43. Cambridge, Mass.: Ballinger Publishing.

Kahn, Shulamit. 1993. "Gender Differences in Academic Career Paths of Economists." *American Economic Review* 83 (May): 52–56.

Kolpin, Van, and Larry D. Singell Jr. 1994. "The Gender Composition and Scholarly Performance of Economics Departments: A Test for Employment Discrimination." Ms.

Lee, Linda K. 1981. "A Comparison of the Rank and Salary of Male and Female Agricultural Economists." *American Journal of Agricultural Economics* 63 (Dec.): 1010–24.

Lester, Richard A. 1974. *Antibias Regulation of Universities: Faculty Problems and Their Solutions.* New York: McGraw-Hill.

Loeb, Jane W., and Marianne A. Ferber. 1971. "Sex as Predictive of Salary and Status in a University Faculty." *Journal of Educational Measurement* 8 (Winter): 235–44.

———. 1973. "Representation, Performance, and Status of Women on the Faculty at the Urbana-Champaign Campus of the University of Illinois." In *Academic Women on the Move,* ed. Alice S. Rossi and Anne Calderwood, 239–54. New York: Russell Sage Foundation.

Malkiel, Burton G., and Judith A. Malkiel. 1973. "Male-Female Pay Differentials in Professional Employment." *American Economic Review* 63 (Sept.): 693–705.

Marwell, Gerald, Rachel Rosenfeld, and Seymour Spillerman. 1979. "Geographic Constraints on Women's Careers in Academia." *Science* 205 (Sept. 21): 1225–31.

McCrate, Elaine, and Joy Livingston. 1993. *A Study for the Governor's Commission on Women*. Burlington, Vt.: Governor's Commission on Women.

McMillen, David P., and Larry D. Singell Jr. 1994. "Gender Differences in First Jobs for Economists." *Southern Economic Journal* 60 (Jan.): 701–14.

Megdal, Sharon B., and Michael R. Ransom. 1985. "Longitudinal Changes at a Large Public University." *American Economic Review* 75 (May): 271–74.

Moore, William J., and Robert J. Newman. 1977. "An Analysis of the Quality Differentials in Male-Female Academic Placements." *Economic Inquiry* 15 (July): 413–34.

Oaxaca, Ronald. 1973. "Sex Discrimination in Wages." In *Discrimination in Labor Markets*, ed. Orley Ashenfelter and Albert Rees, 124–51. Princeton: Princeton University Press.

O'Neill, June, and Nachum Sicherman. 1990. "Is the Gender Gap in Economics Declining?" Ms.

Preston, Anne. 1993. "Occupational Departure of Employees in the Natural Sciences and Engineering." Ms.

Ransom, Michael R. 1990. "Gender Segregation by Field in Higher Education." *Research in Higher Education* 31 (Oct.): 477–94.

Ransom, Michael R., and Sharon B. Megdal. 1993. "Sex Differences in the Academic Labor Market in the Affirmative Action Era." *Economics of Education Review* 12 (Mar.): 21–43.

Reagan, Barbara B., and Betty J. Maynard. 1974. "Sex Discrimination in Universities: An Approach through Internal Labor Market Analysis." *American Association of University Professors Bulletin* 60 (Spring): 13–21.

Richman, Bill D. 1984. "Faculty Salaries at a Small University: Does Sex Matter?" *Quarterly Journal of Business and Economics* 23 (Spring): 47–57.

Rubenson, George C., and Wayne H. Decker. 1992. "Dual Career Couples in Higher Education: An Empirical Study of the Relationship between Family Status and Career Progress." Paper presented at the National Conference on the Dual Career Couple in Higher Education, Lexington, Ky., Oct.

Singell, Larry D., Jr., and Joe A. Stone. 1994. "Gender Differences in the Careers of Ph.D. Economists." Ms.

Strober, Myra, and Aline O. Quester. 1977. "The Earnings and Promotion of Women: Comment." *American Economic Review* 67 (Mar.): 207–13.

Szafran, Robert F. 1984. *Universities and Women Faculty: Why Some Organizations Discriminate More than Others*. New York: Praeger.

Weissman, Myrna M., Katherine Nelson, Judith Hackman, Cynthia Pincus, and Brigitte Prusoff. 1973. "The Faculty Wife: Her Academic Interests and Qualifications." In *Academic Women on the Move*, ed. Alice S. Rossi and Ann Calderwood, 187–95. New York: Russell Sage Foundation.

Willis, Rachel A., and Paul J. Pieper. 1993. "Gender Differences in Promotion for Academic Economists." Paper presented at the annual meeting of the Western Economic Association, Lake Tahoe, Nev., June.

8

. . . .

Work-Family Policies for Faculty: How "Career- and Family-Friendly" Is Academe?

Phyllis Hutton Raabe

Employment assistance for dual-career partners, extensions of the tenure clock, tenure for part-time faculty—these are some of the policy initiatives higher educational institutions in the United States have made in response to faculty career and family commitments.

As in other professions, and as discussed in the introduction, women today comprise a much larger proportion of faculty in the United States, women with doctorates are more likely to marry and have children, and male faculty increasingly have partners with careers (Lomperis 1990). In academe, as elsewhere, both women and men in dual-career couples combine high commitments to work and career success with those to family, including partners, children, and aging parents (Galinsky and Stein 1990; Kimmel 1993; Schultz, Chung, and Henderson 1988; Voydanoff 1987). Much research has documented the difficulties Americans frequently experience in integrating family and work activities and the ways that work-family conflicts and stress can impair work productivity, career achievement, and retention in the labor force (e.g., Ferber and O'Farrell 1991; Fernandez 1986; Galinsky, Friedman, and Hernandez 1991; Raabe 1990). While these difficulties continue to impact primarily women, they are also increasingly experienced by men as they become more involved in family roles (Gerson 1993; Menaghan and Parcel 1990; Pleck 1993). Overall, two of every five employees (both men and women) report problems in managing the conflicting demands of job and family (Galinsky, Friedman, and Hernandez 1991; Galinsky, Bond, and Friedman 1993).

While individual coping strategies can help (Voydanoff 1987), societal and employer policies are important to help integrate caring for a family with work and career achievement (Friedman and Galinsky 1992; Milliken, Dutton, and Beyer 1990). The difficulties of meeting both family caring needs and prevailing work and career expectations has led many Americans to question the assumptions and practices of "standard work" in the design of jobs, required work times, criteria of work success, and career path profiles (Bailyn 1993; Schor 1991; F. Schwartz 1992). In the words of one report, "most believe they could make greater contributions and go farther in their own careers—despite family obligations—if it weren't for rigid scheduling, open-ended expectations, and outmoded career definitions" (Rodgers and Rodgers 1989:126). For some, the realization that prevailing job and career specifications are social-historical constructions that can be reconfigured bolsters interest in alternative work arrangements—such as part-time work, job sharing, and home-based work—and in flexible career paths (with leaves and reduced work time components) that can facilitate combining family involvement with career success (Bailyn 1993; Galinsky, Bond, and Friedman 1993; Hinrichs, Roche, and Sirianni 1991; D. Schwartz 1994).

In response to these work and family concerns, some U.S. employers are providing alternative work schedules and arrangements, child-care assistance, maternity, parental, and family leaves, and other programs (Ferber and O'Farrell 1991; Galinsky, Friedman, and Hernandez 1991; Pleck 1992; Bureau of Labor Statistics 1988, 1992, 1994). In varying ways these different policies can lessen conflicts and stress both by providing time for family caring (for example, through leaves and reduced work schedules) and facilitating the productive use of work time (for example, through child-care supports and flexible schedules) (Lambert 1993; Raabe 1990; Schor 1991). Many managers endorse work-family policies in terms of mutual benefits: such practices help the organization as well as the work force since improved integration of family and work activities can facilitate work productivity, career development, and retention (Galinsky, Friedman, and Hernandez 1991; Lambert 1993; Lambert et al. 1993; McColl 1988; Starrels 1992). Similarly, academic administrators are interested in the contribution of various work-family policies toward improving faculty recruitment and retention, as well as supporting faculty productivity and professional development (Galinsky and Stein 1990; Gee 1991). As one university president put it: "We must identify means to reconcile the professional goals of gifted, energetic people with their equally important commitment to stability in personal relationships" (Gee 1991:45).

In terms of child care, high quality on-campus centers accessible to faculty provide an important support of career and family integration. Such centers can facilitate earlier return to work from maternity/parental leaves and can contribute to better work concentration and productivity (Mangan 1988). Viable maternity and child-care leaves, reduced work loads for family reasons, extension of the tenure clock for parents, and tenure for part-time faculty are features of alternative work and career arrangements that support the compatibility of family caring and developing an academic career. While these policies have been especially relevant for the retention and recruitment of women faculty, they are germane to both men and women who are actively involved in parenting and other family commitments (Kimmel 1993; Pleck 1993; Rosse 1988).

Part-time work has been a common way for women to combine family and work commitments, but it often has involved significant career penalties, including disproportionately lower wages and benefits and constrained work and career opportunities (American Association of University Professors 1981; Barker 1993; Tilly 1992). However, part-time schedules can constitute a positive, alternative career path if they are linked to career success either through short-term part-time work with viable reentrances to standard career tracks or through part-time career formulations—such as part-time law partners or tenure-track part-time academic positions (*Flexible Work* 1993; Hall 1989; Lomperis 1990; Raabe 1993). Development of such reduced work time arrangements that are compatible with career achievement is essential for their greater and more viable use by women and men who are trying to integrate family and career commitments (Bailyn 1993; Parker and Hall 1993; Pleck 1993).

Since work and career commitments typically are high for both members of dual-career couples, securing appropriate jobs for both is an important issue for such couples and for successfully recruiting and retaining them in faculty positions. For these reasons, many colleges and universities are developing programs to assist dual-career partners in finding appropriate employment (Snyder 1990; Gee 1991; "Dual-Career Program" 1991).

Given increasing numbers of faculty members concerned with both family involvement and career success, and the relevance of such policies as those discussed above, including job assistance for partners, what is the availability of work-family policies at academic institutions, and how does it compare with policy availability in other sectors of the economy?

Work-Family Policies for Faculty: Research Methodology

To ascertain the extent of work-family supportive policies for faculty at U.S. academic institutions, a questionnaire was mailed in 1991 to provosts and academic vice presidents at 300 colleges and universities. A stratified random sample of four equal groups of 75 institutions—large public (10,000 or more students), small public (fewer than 10,000 students), large private (2,500 or more students), and small private (fewer than 2,500 students)—was derived from an initial list of 2,200 higher educational institutions in the United States. The response rate was a very respectable 63 percent (76 percent of large public, 57 percent of large private, 62 percent of small public, and 59 percent of small private institutions). The survey asked about 12 policies, including job assistance for spouses, maternity and parental leaves, expansion of time to achieve tenure to accommodate maternity/parental responsibilities, reduced work schedules to meet family needs, job sharing, tenure for part-time faculty, on-campus child-care centers available to faculty, financial assistance for child care, and elder-care programs. Academic administrators were asked to indicate for each policy whether it was currently available, they were planning to implement it in the near future, they were presently considering it, or they were not considering it.

Frequencies of twelve policies were summarized for the total sample and separately for large public, large private, small public, and small private institutions. To make overall comparisons of institutional policy supportiveness possible, summary policy scores were computed for each institutional type. (The summary score is the mean over the twelve policies of the percentage of institutions of each type which report that these policies are available.)

If a policy existed at their institutions, respondent administrators also were asked to indicate the level of utilization or practice (1—widely practiced; 2—in some cases; 3—very rarely) for five of the policies for which they were likely to have ready knowledge (job assistance for spouse, expansion of time for achieving tenure, accommodative scheduling to meet family needs—such as reduced teaching loads and limited student advising—tenure for part-time faculty, and faculty job sharing). Recent research on employer work-family policies has disclosed that learning about the existence of formal policies is only a first step toward learning about their real impact, because the extent of policy utilization can vary widely (Galinsky, Friedman, and Hernandez 1991; Lambert 1993; Raabe 1990). While administrator assessments of policy practice are not necessarily entirely accurate, they do provide more information than simply knowing that formal policies exist. This is particularly true to the extent that in many instances policies are only practiced in some cases or very rarely.

Work-Family Policies for Faculty: Prevalence, Plans, and Comparative Frequencies

How prevalent are various work-family supportive policies for faculty at U.S. colleges and universities? To what extent are there differences among types of academic institutions? Table 8-1 includes data about these questions.

Among all policies, maternity/maternal leaves are the most frequently available, with large majorities of institutions providing such leaves. With 74 percent providing paid maternity leaves and 84 percent providing unpaid maternity or subsequent parental leaves for women, it is clear that maternity/parental leaves with paid and unpaid components are available to faculty mothers at most institutions. It is important to note that in the United States, the existence and forms of childbirth and parental leaves are highly variable across the states and among employers (Ferber and O'Farrell 1991; Galinsky, Friedman, and Hernandez 1991), in contrast with most Western European countries, which have national laws mandating leaves, generally with pay, for women and often for men as well (Kamerman 1991). The Pregnancy Discrimination Act of 1978 did specify that pregnancy must be included as a covered disability in work organizations that provide a paid disability leave program. However, many organizations do not have such programs, and most employed women do not receive paid maternity leave through disability coverage. The majority of women have to piece together sick leave and vacation time if they are to have paid leave at all. Fathers are in an even more precarious situation when attempting to take childbirth and parental leaves, both because of the existing policy structure and the prevailing culture. They lack the disability foundation for childbirth leave, although, like women, they potentially can use accrued paid leaves

TABLE 8-1. Available Work-Family Policies for Faculty, 1991 (percent)

Work-Family Policy	Large Public (N = 57[a])	Large Private (N = 43[a])	Small Public (N = 47[a])	Small Private (N = 44[a])	Total (N = 191[a])
		Institutional Type			
Job assistance for spouse*	58	43	38	32	44
Expansion of time for achieving tenure	35	32	28	17	29
Accommodative scheduling*	35	42	22	49	36
Tenure for part-time faculty	11	12	15	7	11
Job sharing	23	28	11	16	20
Paid leave for mothers at childbirth	64	76	73	86	74
Unpaid leave for mothers at childbirth	89	87	84	73	84
Paid leave for fathers at childbirth**	21	7	26	0	14
Unpaid leave for fathers at childbirth	42	51	40	26	40
On-campus child-care center (available to faculty)**	54	49	57	23	47
Financial assistance for child care**	21	40	11	14	21
Elder-care programs	9	12	6	7	8
Overall policy scores (average percentage)	38.5	39.9	34.3	29.2	35.7

a. Total numbers differ slightly by item.
* $p < .05$.
** $p < .01$.

in some organizations, and several universities in this sample allowed the use of paid sick leaves for any of the purposes for which family leave is available. However, even when such opportunities are technically possible, there frequently are cultural constraints on their use by men (Pleck 1993). In the past, *unpaid* maternity and parental leaves similarly varied in existence and extent among employers. However, the recent Family and Medical Leave Act (1993) mandates unpaid parental and family leave for both men and women employed at organizations with a work force of fifty or more (U.S. Department of Labor 1993), and on this basis, unpaid leaves currently are available at all colleges and universities (the percentages for these policies given in table 8-1 now would be 100).

None of the other policies studied are in place at the majority of the colleges and universities surveyed, but many are provided by one-fifth to one-half of them. Thus, child-care centers and job assistance for spouses are available at 47 percent and 44 percent of educational institutions, respectively. Other moderately widespread work-family policies are accommodative scheduling to meet family needs (36 percent of all institutions), expansion of time for tenure (29 percent), job sharing (20 percent), and financial assistance for child care (21 percent). The least available policies are elder-care programs, tenure for part-time faculty, and paid leave for fathers at childbirth.

Academic institutions vary greatly in the availability of these policies. For example, one public university in this sample provides job assistance for spouses, expansion of time for achieving tenure, accommodative scheduling, tenure for part-time faculty, job sharing, paid and unpaid leaves for mothers and fathers, and one child-care center with another budgeted. Other colleges and universities provide few work-family policy supports. Types of educational institutions also differ in policy implementations. Among the four types of institutions there is significant variation in the availability of five policies: spousal job assistance, accommodative scheduling, paid paternity leave, on-campus child care, and financial assistance for child care.

As seen in table 8-1, large private universities have the highest implementation levels for four policies: unpaid childbirth/parental leaves for fathers (51 percent), financial assistance for child care (40 percent), job sharing (28 percent), and elder-care programs (12 percent). Large public universities are relatively generous in making available job assistance for faculty spouses (58 percent) and on-campus child-care centers (54 percent). They also are most likely to offer extended time for achieving tenure (35 percent) and to provide unpaid maternity/maternal leaves (89 percent), but lag in offering paid leaves. Small public institutions are comparatively advanced in providing on-campus child care (57 percent), paid paternity leaves (26 percent), and tenure for part-time faculty (15 percent). Small private colleges are most likely to offer paid maternity leaves (86 percent) and accommodative scheduling (49 percent), but strikingly lag behind the others in the availability of on-campus child-care centers (23 percent).

In summarizing work-family policy availability by institutional type, composite frequency scores show that large public and private universities have the most policies (policy implementation average levels of 39 and 40, respectively), followed by small public colleges (34), with small private colleges having the lowest overall policy frequency level (29).

When policies exist, how widely are they utilized? While the existence of formal policies is an important foundation of a "career- and family-friendly" environment, other aspects of the organizational structure and culture of the institution are also important. For instance, particular programs may only be available in some parts of the organization or people may be made to feel uncomfortable about taking advantage of policies that are offered; as a result, they may not be widely used (Bailyn 1993; Hall 1989; Raabe and Gessner 1988; Starrels 1992). To gain some indication about policy usage, respondent administrators were asked about the frequency of use for five work-family policies: job assistance for spouses, expansion of time for achieving tenure, accommodative scheduling, tenure for part-time faculty, and job sharing. As the data in table 8-2 indicate, the modal response generally was "in some cases" or

TABLE 8-2. Extent of Utilization When Policies Exist
(percent)

Work-Family Policy	Institutional Type	Widely Practiced	In Some Cases	Rarely
Job assistance for spouse	Large public	13	70	17
	Large private	24	41	35
	Small public	6	69	25
	Small private	8	85	8
Expansion of time for achieving tenure	Large public	25	50	25
	Large private	17	58	25
	Small public	23	39	39
	Small private	17	33	50
Accommodative scheduling	Large public	12	53	35
	Large private	13	56	31
	Small public	0	29	71
	Small private	6	56	39
Tenure for part-time faculty	Large public	33	33	33
	Large private	0	40	60
	Small public	20	0	80
	Small private	0	100	0
Job sharing	Large public	0	25	75
	Large private	0	40	60
	Small public	0	0	100
	Small private	0	0	100

"rarely." However, among large private universities that provide spousal job assistance, 24 percent reported that the policy is widely used. Among large and small public universities that permit expansion of time to achieve tenure, 25 percent and 23 percent, respectively, said that the policy is widely practiced, and 33 percent of large public universities that permit tenure for part-time faculty said it was widely used. These findings are significant in indicating that at some institutions, spousal job assistance, expansion of time to achieve tenure, and tenure for part-time faculty not only exist but are fairly common practices.

At colleges and universities where various work-family policies are not currently available, respondents were asked if they were planning to introduce them in the near future, and if not, whether policies were being considered (see table 8-3). In addition to those institutions currently providing spousal job assistance for faculty, another 12 percent are planning to begin such programs in the near future. Assuming that they follow through on these intentions, spousal job assistance then will be available to faculty at a majority (56 percent) of higher educa-

TABLE 8-3. Educational Institutions Planning to Implement Work-Family Policies in the Near Future (percent)

Work-Family Policy	Large Public	Large Private	Small Public	Small Private	Total
Job assistance for spouse	12	12	11	14	12
Expansion of time for achieving tenure	5	7	2	7	5
Accommodative scheduling	9	12	2	7	8
Tenure for part-time faculty	0	2	0	2	1
Job sharing	4	5	4	2	4
Paid leave for mothers at childbirth	6	5	0	0	3
Unpaid leave for mothers at childbirth	4	3	0	3	2
Paid leave for fathers at childbirth	4	2	0	2	2
Unpaid leave for fathers at childbirth	2	5	2	0	2
On-campus child-care center	11	2	2	5	5
Financial assistance for child care	2	2	2	2	2
Elder-care programs	4	2	2	2	3

tional institutions. If plans for additional child-care centers are implemented, more than half (52 percent) of all institutions will offer this service. In terms of types of institutions, an additional 12 percent of large private universities plan to implement a policy of accommodative scheduling for faculty to meet family needs, which would make this policy available at 54 percent of such institutions, and an additional 2 percent plan to introduce on-campus child-care centers, which would raise this total to 51 percent. The addition of such centers at 11 percent of large public universities would result in centers being available to faculty at an impressive 65 percent of such institutions. Finally, the introduction of accommodative scheduling at an additional 7 percent of small private institutions would make this option available at 56 percent of these campuses.

Employer Comparisons and the Relevance of Pluralistic Work and Career Arrangements

In providing work-family policies, how do academic institutions compare with other U.S. employers? Table 8-4 compares this study's findings about policy availability for faculty with policy frequencies found at large U.S. companies in a 1991 survey (Galinsky, Friedman, and Hernandez 1991), with Bureau of Labor Statistics findings for full-time employees, and with a subset of this group, professionals in medium and large establishments, the category most comparable to faculty. While the different surveys did not always ask about identical policies, the survey results provide some information about comparative policy frequency.

As table 8-4 indicates, data about leaves have to be compared across categories because both survey researchers and organizations themselves sometimes use different terminology for paid and unpaid leaves. For example, responses to this survey and other research indicate that either accrued paid sick leave or disability insurance may constitute "paid maternity leave" at some workplaces, and unpaid "personal leaves" may be the mechanism for unpaid maternity or parental leaves (National Council of Jewish Women 1993; Raabe and Gessner 1988).

As the data in table 8-4 show, academic institutions collectively appear to lag behind large corporations in guaranteeing paid maternity leave since all do not provide the disability coverage found at large corporations. Nonetheless, in terms of actual practice, academic institutions are fairly comparable since the large majority permit the use of other

TABLE 8-4. Work-Family Policy Availability in the United States, 1991
(percent)

Work-Family Policy	Colleges/ Universities (for Faculty) ($N = 191$)	Large U.S. Corporations ($N = 188$)	Full-time Employees	Professionals in Medium and Large Private Establishments
Leaves				
Paid maternity leave for mothers (various formulations)	74	100	—	—
Paid sick leave (often used for maternity)	—	—	65	87
Paid sickness insurance (disability)	—	—	33	32
Unpaid maternity/ parental leaves (mothers)	84	—	32	43
Unpaid childbirth/ parental leaves (fathers)	40	—	21	31
Personal leaves of absence	—	70	38	29
Other work-family policies				
Workplace child-care centers	47	13	—	—
Financial assistance for child care[a]	21	50	28	48
Employer child-care assistance[b]	—	—	5	11
Job assistance for spouse	44	52	—	—
Accommodative scheduling	36	—	—	—
Flexible work schedules (flextime)	(100?)	77	43[c]	15
Expansion of time for achieving tenure	29	—	—	—
Part-time tenure	11	—	—	—
Job sharing	20	48	16[c]	—
Elder-care programs	8	21	7	11

a. Predominantly pretax dollar accounts.
b. Facilities and child-care subsidies.
c. Bureau of Labor Statistics 1988.
Sources: For colleges and universities: 1991 survey data; for large U.S. corporations: Galinsky, Friedman, and Hernandez 1991; for full-time employees: Foster 1994; for professionals in medium and large private establishments: Bureau of Labor Statistics 1992.

accrued paid leaves for paid maternity leave. In relation to fathers, however, the availability of paid childbirth and parental leaves is unclear. Most of the respondents at the 14 percent of academic institutions with paid leave for fathers at childbirth stated that fathers used paid vacation or sick leaves, but the extent that such use of leaves is possible at other work organizations is not indicated by the available data, so this category was omitted from table 8-4. Since the 1993 Family and Medical Leave Act, the incidence of unpaid parental leaves is no longer as shown in table 8-4, but is 100 percent, as noted earlier.

Spousal job assistance is more widely available at the largest U.S. corporations (52 percent) than in academe generally (44 percent), however, the rate at large public universities (58 percent) surpasses the corporate rate. Large corporations are also more likely than higher educational institutions to allow job sharing and to provide elder-care programs.

Compared with other employers, higher education institutions are strikingly advanced in providing on-site child-care centers. While only a small minority of both American employers in general and large corporations specifically have on-site child care, the rate is significantly higher at universities and colleges—with about half of large private and large and small public institutions having child-care centers available to faculty children. Large corporations are more likely than higher educational institutions to provide financial assistance for child care, but the level of subsidy varies widely and is typically a modest benefit through the use of pretax salary child-care accounts (Galinsky, Friedman, and Hernandez 1991).

The wide variability found among academic institutions in providing work-family policies is also characteristic of U.S. employers in general—as is a low level of availability of most work-family policies. While more employers are instituting such policies and some companies are renowned for their work-family policies and constitute highly supportive environments ("*Working Mother*" 1994), even among the largest U.S. corporations the extent and caliber of work-family policies are generally low (Shellenbarger 1993). For example, Galinsky, Friedman, and Hernandez (1991) found that out of a maximum of 610 points on their Family-Friendly Index, the highest score was 245, and only four companies attained the highest policy level. The majority of companies had low policy levels: 46 percent of companies had "several policies, but not a packaged response" and 33 percent had "few policies, barely aware of issues" (1991:15–16).

Among those employers that implement more work-family policies, the process seems to begin with a profound organizational realization that the work force is changing and is increasingly diverse not only in ethnicity, race, and gender but also in work-family situations (Galinsky, Friedman, and Hernandez 1991; Galinsky, Bond, and Friedman 1993; Lambert 1993). Not only are women and men more likely to have commitments to active involvement with family (children, elderly parents, other relatives) as well as work and careers; these multiple commitments are expressed in different emphases simultaneously and sequentially over the life course (*Work-Family Roundtable* 1994; Voydanoff 1987). Thus, at a given point in time, members of the work force differ from each other in their work-family situations, and the situation for individuals changes over time.

It is clear, therefore, that organizational norms and practices that assume the only or even primary commitment is to work are out of sync with the changed work force (Bailyn 1993). Concomitantly, given the present diverse work force, insistence of organizations on traditional patterns of work is likely to be counterproductive, particularly for knowledge-based and "post-industrial" work in general, where the caliber of work commitment and performance is especially crucial (Hage and Powers 1992; Parker and Hall 1993).

Policy responsiveness to these understandings is particularly challenging for organizations because it involves restructuring of work and careers (Friedman 1994). That is, in contrast with organizational supports of child care and elder care, which are very important components of work-family integration but which enable workers to work in accustomed ways (Lambert 1993), workers' interests in time for family caring through leaves, reduced work, and other flexible and alternative work arrangements involve changes in work itself. Further, faculty and others with career commitments are very eager that these adjustments not be made at the expense of their professional success.

Currently, work organizations are facing the challenge of moving from traditional, established work patterns to flexible work arrangements and career paths that better meet the varied needs of their employees (Bailyn 1993; Parker and Hall 1993; Raabe 1996). In fact, higher educational institutions appear to have certain strengths in this respect that may provide the foundations for "career- and family-friendly" employment. Faculty traditionally have had a comparatively high degree of autonomy and relatively flexible schedules. Such flexibility can make it easier to meet both work and family responsibilities. On the other hand, the demands of academic careers typically have led to long hours of work (Bailyn 1993). In addition, the rigid promotion and tenure systems can cause great stress for those who are combining family and career commitments.

The survey results presented in table 8-1 indicate that some pluralistic work and career arrangements are already available at academic institutions. Together with family leaves, part-time work, and job sharing, short-term reductions in work loads provide time for family caring. The question remains, however, whether taking advantage of such programs is damaging to a faculty member's career or is compatible with career success. In the past, the outcome frequently was the marginalization of the individual who opted for a reduced work schedule (AAUP 1981; Lomperis 1990). Although other employers offer job sharing and part-time positions to professionals and managers (Raabe 1993), career penalties and derailments of those who used such nontraditional paths has led to advocacy of more explicit legitimation and incorporation of part-time work and other alternative work arrangements and leaves into viable career advancement paths (*Flexible Work* 1993; Parker and Hall 1993; Schwartz 1994). In this regard, expanding time to achieve tenure and extending tenure to part-time faculty are significant policies because they modify the rigid tenure-track pattern and offer alternative paths for career achievement that may be more compatible with family involvement.

While current evidence points to the relevance of career-and-family policies for positive personal and organizational results, further longitudinal research is needed on the effects of supportive policy environments in comparison with those that are less supportive. For example, *is* the use of on-campus child-care centers and other career-family policies associated with increased career achievement, less family stress, heightened faculty retention, and increased productivity? Greater knowledge of these processes is important for understanding the personal and organizational outcomes of career-family policy development.

Conclusion

Today's academic dual-career couples typically combine career commitments with active involvements in caring for family members, which vary over the life course. A variety of work-family policies from child-care services to flexible alternative career paths can support the integration of family and work activities. A 1991 survey of current and planned work-family policies at academic institutions reveals great variation among individual institutions and among types of colleges and universities in their policies. Some institutions constitute highly supportive environments while others lack most policies. Overall, in comparison with other kinds of employers, higher educational institutions are particularly advanced in providing child-care services, flexible and reduced work schedules, and adjustments in career paths, such as expansion of time to achieve tenure and tenure for part-time faculty. A major organizational development issue for academic institutions is whether existing work flexibilities will be further expanded and incorporated into viable pluralistic work arrangements and career paths that better meet the diverse work-family situations of today's faculty.

Insofar as faculty are "the heart and soul of the University" (Flawn 1990:67) and are interested in integrating family involvement with career achievement, colleges and universities may increasingly recognize that facilitating such integration is in their interest. If they heed a recent warning by two organizational experts that "ignoring issues of diversity and of work/family balance can be hazardous to organizational health" (Parker and Hall 1993:122), more of them are likely to institute family-friendly policies to enhance both the careers and personal lives of their faculty and promote organizational development.

Note

This is an extension and revision of a paper presented to the 1993 meeting of the Southern Sociological Society in Chattanooga and is partially derived from "United States Higher Education and Work-Family Policies for Faculty," an unpublished manuscript by Phyllis Hutton Raabe and John Mangieri written in 1992.

Bibliography

American Association of University Professors. 1981. "The Status of Part-Time Faculty." *Academe: Bulletin of the AAUP* (Feb.–Mar.): 29–39.

Bailyn, Lotte. 1993. *Breaking the Mold.* New York: Free Press.

Barker, Kathleen. 1993. "Changing Assumptions and Contingent Solutions: The Costs and Benefits of Women Working Full- and Part-Time." *Sex Roles* 28 (Jan.): 47–71.

Bureau of Labor Statistics. 1988. "BLS Reports on Employer Child-Care Practices." *News.* Washington, D.C.: U.S. Department of Labor.

———. 1992. "BLS Reports on Employee Benefits in Medium and Large Private Industry Establishments, 1991." *News.* Washington, D.C.: U.S. Department of Labor.

————. 1994. "BLS Reports on Employee Benefits in Small Private Industry Establishments, 1992." *News.* Washington, D.C.: U.S. Department of Labor.

"Dual-Career Program Helps Recruit Faculty and Administrators." 1991. *Administrator* 10 (12): 1–2.

Ferber, Marianne A., and Brigid O'Farrell, with La Rue Allen, eds. 1991. *Work and Family: Policies for a Changing Work Force.* Washington, D.C.: National Academy Press.

Fernandez, John P. 1986. *Child Care and Corporate Productivity. Resolving Family-Work Conflicts.* Lexington, Mass.: D.C. Heath.

Flawn, Peter T. 1990. *A Primer for University Presidents.* Austin: University of Texas Press.

Flexible Work Arrangements II: Succeeding with Part-Time Options. 1993. New York: Catalyst.

Foster, Ann C. 1994. *Employee Benefits in the United States, 1991–92.* Washington, D.C.: U.S. Bureau of Labor Statistics.

Friedman, Dana. 1994. "The Appropriate Role for Business in Addressing the Work-Family Issue." Keynote address to "Work, Family, and Community in the Twenty-First Century," Drexel University Fifth International Stein Conference, Philadelphia, Pa., Nov. 16.

Friedman, Dana, and Ellen Galinsky. 1992. "Work and Family Issues: A Legitimate Business Concern." In *Work, Families, and Organizations,* ed. S. Sheldon Zedeck, 168–207. San Francisco: Jossey-Bass.

Galinsky, Ellen, J. T. Bond, and D. E. Friedman. 1993. *The Changing Workforce.* New York: Families and Work Institute.

Galinsky, E., D. E. Friedman, and C. A. Hernandez. 1991. *The Corporate Reference Guide to Work-Family Programs.* New York: Families and Work Institute.

Galinsky, Ellen, and Peter Stein. 1990. "The Impact of Human Resource Policies on Employees: Balancing Work/Family Life." *Journal of Family Issues* 2 (Dec.): 355–67.

Gee, E. Gordon. 1991. "The Dual-Career Couple: A Growing Challenge." *Educational Record* (Winter): 45–47.

Gerson, Kathleen. 1993. *No Man's Land: Men's Changing Commitments to Family and Work.* New York: Basic Books.

Googins, Bradley K. 1991. *Work/Family Conflicts: Private Lives—Public Responses.* New York: Auburn House.

Hage, Jerald, and Charles H. Powers. 1992. *Post-Industrial Lives.* Newbury Park, Calif.: Sage Publications.

Hall, Douglas T. 1989. "Moving beyond the 'Mommy Track': An Organizational Change Approach." *Personnel* (Dec.): 23–29.

Hinrichs, Karl, William Roche, and Carmen Sirianni. 1991. *Working Time in Transition.* Philadelphia: Temple University Press.

Kamerman, Sheila B. 1991. "Child Care Policies and Programs: An International Overview." *Journal of Social Issues* 47 (2): 179–96.

Kamerman, Sheila B., and Alfred J. Kahn. 1987. *The Responsive Workplace.* New York: Columbia University Press.

Kimmel, Michael S. 1993. "What Do Men Want?" *Harvard Business Review* (Nov.–Dec.): 50–63.

Lambert, Susan J. 1993. "Workplace Policies as Social Policy." *Social Service Review* (June): 237–60.

Lambert, Susan J., Karen Hopkins, George Easton, Janet Walker, Heather McWilliams, and Moo Sung Chung. 1993. *Added Benefits: The Link between Family Responsive Policies and Job Performance.* A University of Chicago Study of Fel-Pro Inc.

Lomperis, Anna Maria Turner. 1990. "Are Women Changing the Nature of the Academic Profession?" *Journal of Higher Education* 61 (Nov.–Dec.): 643–77.

Mangan, K. S. 1988. "In Response to Growing Demand, Colleges Are Starting to Offer Child Care as a Benefit for Their Employees." *Chronicle of Higher Education* (Feb. 17): A13–14.

McColl, Hugh. 1988. "What a Caring Company Can Do." *Across the Board* 25 (7–8): 38–42.

Menaghan, Elizabeth G., and Toby L. Parcel. 1990. "Parental Employment and Family Life." *Journal of Marriage and the Family* 52 (Nov.): 1079–98.

Milliken, Frances J., Jane E. Dutton, and Janice M. Beyer. 1990. "Understanding Organizational Adaptation to Change: The Case of Work-Family Issues." *Human Resource Planning* 13 (2): 91–107.

National Council of Jewish Women. 1993. *The Experience of Childbearing Women in the Workplace: The Impact of Family-Friendly Policies and Practices.* Washington, D.C.: U.S. Department of Labor Women's Bureau.

Parker, Victoria, and Douglas Hall. 1993. "Workplace Flexibility: Faddish or Fundamental?" In *Building the Competitive Workforce,* ed. Philip Mirvis, 122–53. New York: Wiley.

Pleck, Joseph. 1992. "Work-Family Policies in the United States." In *Women's Work and Women's Lives,* ed. Hilda Kahne and Janet Z. Giele, 248–75. Boulder: Westview Press.

———. 1993. "Are 'Family-Supportive' Employer Policies Relevant to Men?" In *Men, Work, and Family,* ed. Jane C. Hood, 217–37. Newbury Park, Calif.: Sage Publications.

Raabe, Phyllis Hutton. 1990. "The Organizational Effects of Workplace Family Policies: Past Weaknesses and Recent Progress toward Improved Research." *Journal of Family Issues* 2 (Dec.): 477–91.

———. 1993. "Part-Time Professionals and Managers: Work and Career Innovations—and Lessening the 'Mommy Track/Trap?'" Paper presented at the annual meeting of the Eastern Sociological Society, Boston, Mar. 26.

———. 1996. "Constructing Pluralistic Work and Career Arrangements." In *The*

Work Family Challenge: Rethinking Employment, ed. Suzan Lewis and Jeremy Lewis. London: Sage.

Raabe, Phyllis H., and John Gessner. 1988. "Employer Family-Supportive Policies: Diverse Variations on the Theme." *Family Relations* 37 (2): 196–202.

Raabe, Phyllis Hutton, and John Mangieri. 1992. "United States Higher Education and Work-Family Policies for Faculty." Ms.

Rodgers, Fran S., and Charles Rodgers. 1989. "Business and the Facts of Family Life." *Harvard Business Review* 67 (Nov.–Dec.): 121–29.

Rosse, James N. 1988. "University Maternity Policies for Faculty Women." Memo. Stanford University.

Schor, Juliet. 1991. *The Overworked American.* New York: Basic Books.

Schultz, J. B., Y. L. Chung, and C. G. Henderson. 1988. "Work/Family Concerns of University Faculty." *Journal of Social Behavior and Personality* 3 (4): 249–64.

Schwartz, Debra B. 1994. *An Examination of the Impact of Family-Friendly Policies on the Glass Ceiling.* New York: Families and Work Institute.

Schwartz, Felice. 1992. *Breaking with Tradition: Women and Work, the New Facts of Life.* New York: Warner.

Shellenbarger, Sue. 1993. "So Much Talk, So Little Action." *Wall Street Journal,* June 21:R6.

Snyder, Julie K. 1990. "Comparison of University Practices on Dual Career Couple Issues." *Virginia Polytechnic Institute and State University Institutional Research and Planning Analysis* 89–90 (53a).

Starrels, Marjorie E. 1992. "The Evolution of Workplace Family Policy Research." *Journal of Family Issues* 13 (2): 259–77.

Tilly, Chris. 1992. "Dualism in Part-Time Employment." *Industrial Relations* 31 (Spring): 330–47.

U.S. Department of Labor. 1993. *Compliance Guide to the Family and Medical Leave Act.* Washington, D.C.: Employment Standards Administration, Wage and Hour Division.

Voydanoff, Patricia 1987. *Work and Family Life.* Newbury Park, Calif.: Sage Publications.

Work-Family Roundtable: Lifecycle Support. 1994. New York: Conference Board.

"*Working Mother* Magazine Names Top One Hundred Companies for 1994." 1994. *National Report on Work and Family* 7 (18): 3–4.

9

· · · · · · · · · ·

From Antinepotism Rules to Programs
for Partners: Legal Issues

Elaine W. Shoben

MANY EMPLOYERS HAVE RULES concerning the employment of spouses or other relatives of current workers. Some practice nepotism and grant favoritism to relatives, whereas others have antinepotism rules that expressly prohibit the employment of relatives. Both of these practices have been the object of legal challenges against various employers, but courts have not yet provided clear guidelines on the circumstances that justify either practice under modern law. Employers who adopt either nepotism or antinepotism practices should be aware of the possibility that either rule may violate state or federal employment law, especially if the effect of the practice is to disadvantage a group defined by race, gender, national origin, or age. Moreover, the law in some states prohibits employers from discriminating against employees or applicants on the basis of "marital status," and some antinepotism rules have run afoul of this protection.

University employers have rarely been defendants in suits involving either nepotism or antinepotism practices. The few recorded cases of such challenges do not provide good discussions of the legality of such practices because their outcomes turned upon other issues.[1] Thus the legality of university practices favoring or disfavoring spouses or other relatives remains an open question.

This chapter will explore the general principles of employment discrimination and relate them to modern practices that may be subject to suit. It explores in particular the legality of "programs for partners," which many university employers have adopted. These programs are a new form of nepotism under which the university gives employment preference to the partner of an academic employee. The preference may be an advantage with respect to an existing opening or it may be the creation of a special position. No lawsuit has yet addressed the legality of these programs, so it is necessary to examine related cases to predict the outcome of any such future litigation.

The chapter concludes that universities should monitor carefully any such programs, like any employment practices, to avoid potential liability under state and federal employment law. Even if the practice has an adverse effect on a protected group, however, there are substantial arguments for its business necessity. If an employer can establish the business necessity of a rule that adversely affects a group, the rule is permissible to use despite its effect. On the other hand, universities should also monitor the application of the partner preference program in individual cases. Even in the absence of an adverse effect on a group defined by race, gender, national origin, or age over forty, a claimant may prevail if the employer acted intentionally to disadvantage a single individual on one of these prohibited grounds. Intention is broadly defined in this context. It could be intentional discrimination, for example, to give hiring preference to the wife of one employee but not to the husband of another, if the gender of the individuals plays any part in the decision. Notably, the presence of an affirmative action plan is not a defense regardless of who is benefited by it because the program is not likely to be a bona fide part of that plan.

Nepotism: Challenges and Justifications

Before the advent of the Civil Rights Act of 1964,[2] nepotism was widely practiced in some industries and especially in the trade unions as a primary means of recruiting new workers. The practice is disappearing in the trade unions, largely as a result of the racially exclusionary effect of the practice in unions that were historically all white.

By definition, nepotism in hiring refers to a preference for the relatives of current employees to the disadvantage or exclusion of other applicants. Modern usage encompasses spouses as well as nonmarital partners, although historically nepotism referred to preferences for sons and nephews. Indeed, the term *nepotism* derives from the Latin word for *nephew.* A nepotistic preference may be an absolute one that grants priority over other applicants regardless of qualifications, or it may be simply one factor in favor of an applicant. The most frequently articulated defense of nepotism is its efficiency. Although it is unfair from an applicant's perspective for someone else to have an advantage because of a familial relationship with another employee, from an employer's point of view the practice can be very efficient. Nepotism provides a stream of new workers who have anticipated employment in the industry, who have a general familiarity with the work before employment, and who receive special attention from co-workers during apprenticeship. A new lumberjack, for example, who comes from a lumberjack family has grown up in an environment that prepares one for the job. Moreover, once on the job, crew members are especially interested in the safety and training of new recruits who are related to them and their co-workers. This justification has passed the "rationality" test in a constitutional challenge, but it has not prevailed under the more stringent "business necessity" defense under the Civil Rights Act of 1964.

The modern form of nepotism in universities is generally preferential treatment of partners. Unlike the old trade unions, modern universities generally do not have an all-white work force that nepotism perpetuates. Although this difference does not insulate universities from challenge, it distinguishes them from the defendants in cases successfully attacking union nepotism.

The justification for the practice in universities is also different. Administrators are generally motivated to adopt such programs to recruit promising faculty whose choice among universities includes consideration of employment for a professional spouse. There may be some further argument that hiring the spouse assures a form of professional mentoring by the academic partner, like the apprentice lumberjack, but any such effect is incidental to the primary purpose of the program. Thus, although the programs for partners bear superficial similarity to the old nepotism cases, their outcome will not necessarily be the same. The history of challenges to nepotism nonetheless remains important in assessing the legality of the modern university practice.

Constitution-Based Challenges to Nepotism

The Supreme Court considered a challenge to nepotism and the efficiency justification in its 1947 case *Kotch v. Board of River Port Pilot Commissioners.*[3] The plaintiffs challenged the constitutionality of a Louisiana state law that restricted river pilot licenses to those who were certified by the State Board of River Pilot Commissioners. The board, composed of incumbent pilots, was allowed to certify whomever it chose, and it chose only the relatives of current pilots. The plaintiffs, who were fully qualified for the license but rejected by the board, challenged this requirement as violative of the constitutional guarantee of equal protection of the laws.

The Supreme Court did not agree and found the state's practice rational for the promotion of safety and efficiency. The majority opinion noted that in the pilot towns "young men have an opportunity to acquire special knowledge of the weather and water hazards of the locality and seem to grow up with ambitions to become pilots in the traditions of their fathers, relatives, and neighbors." Moreover, they benefit from the "morale and esprit de corps which family and neighborly tradition might contribute."

The issue before the Court in *Kotch* was solely the rationality of the legislation. The standard of "rationality" is not a demanding one, and the Court found that the effect on safety and the efficiency of nepotism in this context met that standard. Invidious discrimination was not at issue, either with respect to the motivation of the legislature or to the application of the principle to these plaintiffs.

The constitutional basis for the claim in *Kotch* was the Fourteenth Amendment, which guarantees that no state "deny to any person within its jurisdiction the equal protection of the laws." This right is enforced through a statutory provision known as section 1983, which prohibits any person acting under state law from depriving any person of "any rights, privileges, or immunities secured by the Constitution and laws."[4]

State universities are subject to the equal protection requirement of the Fourteenth Amendment. The equal protection guarantee of that amendment does not apply to private universities because state action is necessary, so only those universities who are acting as state employers are concerned with this particular legal requirement. The question is whether the efficiency justification for partner preferences meets the rationality test. *Kotch* suggests that it does, in the absence of invidious discrimination. The issue is not free from doubt because there is no safety issue for the university as there was for the riverboat pilots. In another employment case[5] the Court found rational the use of a general aptitude test to screen applicants for a police department, but safety was again a component of the justification. This precedent also serves to underscore the weakness of the standard; the practice was "rational" even though the defendant could not prove the validity of the test to predict job performance.

Even if a state university survives a constitutional challenge to partner preferences, however, statutory requirements still apply. A plaintiff may bring a variety of claims against a particular employment practice and need establish only one of them to prevail.

Statutory Challenges and the Effects Test

Both public and private universities are subject to statutory requirements of equal employment opportunity that are more stringent than constitutional requirements. The standards of the Civil Rights Act of 1964 and the Age Discrimination in Employment Act[6] are more favorable for plaintiffs both with respect to the evidence a plaintiff needs to produce and with respect to the degree of a defendant's burden to establish a defense.

Most notably, a plaintiff suing under these federal statutes may survive a dismissal of the claim simply by demonstrating that the effect of an employment practice is to exclude individuals disproportionately on the basis of race, gender, national origin, or age forty and over.[7] It is not necessary for the plaintiff to establish that the defendant intended the disparate result. Once the plaintiff demonstrates the adverse impact of any practice, including nepotism and antinepotism, the burden shifts to the defendant to demonstrate the "business necessity" of the practice.

The Supreme Court established the expansive coverage of the Civil Rights Act of 1964 to include this "disparate impact" concept in its landmark opinion *Griggs v. Duke Power Co.*[8] *Griggs* involved the use of educational requirements and aptitude tests that disproportionately excluded applicants on the basis of race for any position in the power company except those in the Labor Department. The Court held in a unanimous opinion by Chief Justice Burger that employers may not use devices that disproportionately disadvantage on the basis of race unless the employer can demonstrate that the devices are job-related and governed by principles of business necessity. The employer had made no such effort in *Griggs* and had adopted these selection procedures when the Civil Rights Act of 1964 became effective simply in an effort to upgrade the existing work force. The effect was to perpetuate the all-white character of the work force in these jobs. The employer had adopted the requirements despite the fact that many of the incumbent employees, who were performing their jobs satisfactorily, could not satisfy the new requirements themselves. No study was undertaken to validate the tests for job performance or to establish in any way the relationship of the requirements to the jobs.

The Supreme Court held in *Griggs* that the act covers not only an employer's invidious motive to discriminate but also the use of practices that are "fair in form but discriminatory in operation." Since that case, courts have applied this principle in many contexts, including nepotism practices. Nepotism has an exclusionary effect when the employer's work force is not well integrated racially at the outset. Because individuals tend to marry people from the same racial group, preferences for relatives will perpetuate the racial composition of the work force. A plaintiff must present actual evidence of that effect in the defendant employer's work force, however, and cannot rely upon assumptions or even upon general segregation in the employer's work force.[9]

In *E.E.O.C. v. Steamship Clerks Union*[10] a group of African-American and Hispanic plaintiffs successfully challenged the nepotism practice of the union controlling the employment of steamship clerks in Boston. The clerks, who checked cargo against inventory lists during the loading and unloading of vessels, were required to join the union, and the union limited membership to individuals who were sponsored by current members. In the six-year period prior to trial the union admitted thirty new members, each of whom was the relative of an existing member. Because all the members were white, the court found that the practice had a racial effect.

Once the plaintiff establishes the disparate impact of a practice, the burden shifts to the defendant to demonstrate business necessity. In cases challenging nepotism, employers have generally not been successful with the defense, but there is remarkably little case law on the subject. The numerous cases discussing the disparate impact of nepotism practices also involve other issues, such as intentional discrimination claims, that dominate the cases. Employers have rarely tried to establish any specific justification for the practice in this context. A general objection that nepotism helps apprenticeship has not sufficed.[11] In the case of the steamship clerks, the union was similarly unsuccessful with a defense that nepotism maintains a "family tradition" without tying that rationale to a business necessity.[12]

One employer did make a spirited defense of its nepotism in *Bonilla v. Oakland Scavenger Co.*[13] This employer preferred members of several large families who were connected to the founders of the company. The company hired two groups of employees, family members and nonfamily members, and gave preference in promotion to the family members. Because the family members were white and most of the other employees were not, the nepotism in promotion had a disparate impact on the basis of race and national origin. The company defended on the grounds that family members would have more concern for the company and a greater interest in promoting its general welfare. The court rejected this argument as insufficient to meet the standard of business necessity.

These precedents are generally unfavorable to employers, but they do not apply well to the university's position with respect to partner preference programs. No case has considered the use of nepotism as a device to acquire a particularly desirable employee. *Bonilla* is the closest parallel to the university situation, and it is clearly distinguishable. The university must argue that its partner program is necessary to attract the most highly qualified academic employees.

Consider, by way of argument, that the university had two positions for which it took applications. For the first position it targeted an outstanding candidate whom we will rank hypothetically as a 10 on a scale from 1 to 10. This targeted candidate had a spouse who applied for the second position. The spouse was qualified and was ranked as a 6 on this hypothetical scale. It was not possible to attract the 10 without hiring the spouse, so the university made an offer to them both. They accepted. If they had not accepted, the next candidate for the first position and the best candidate for the second position were both ranked as 7.

Assume further that the university was sued by a disappointed applicant for the position awarded to the spouse. This applicant was ranked slightly better as a 7 but lost the position because of the partner preference program. If the plaintiff can establish that the program has a disparate impact on the plaintiff's group as defined by race, gender, national origin, or age,[14] the question is whether the university can defend with business necessity. The argument in general, as illustrated by this hypothetical example, is that a university needs the most highly qualified people it can find to achieve productivity and national recognition. The result of the partner preference program was to acquire two qualified academics with an average ranking of 8. If it had not been possible to hire this couple, the university would have filled the positions with two individuals whose average ranking would have been 7. Moreover, the targeted 10 candidate had the potential for making a truly major academic contribution. All the other candidates, although themselves highly qualified, did not have the same special potential.

It is uncertain whether this kind of argument could establish a "business necessity" defense to a disparate impact claim because no existing precedent makes any similar argument. The unique position of university employers may be sufficient for the argument to prevail.

Antinepotism: Challenges and Justifications

Antinepotism rules adversely affect the employment of more than one family member in the same company or unit. The disadvantage may take various forms, but the most common is the prohibition on any form of employment. Other forms include the demotion or transfer of one spouse to avoid marital conflict[15] or the loss of management responsibilities, although perhaps without any loss in grade or pay.[16]

Numerous state and federal statutes prohibit nepotism in various aspects of government employment, such that incumbent employees cannot use nepotism to favor their relatives. A self-imposed prohibition on hiring relatives, particularly spouses, was common among universities in the early part of the twentieth century. Although universities have largely abandoned the practice, some other employers still use the rule. In one interesting case[17] an electric utility operating on land in the Navajo Nation had an antinepotism rule that violated Navajo employment discrimination law but not the federal law of the United States.

The common justification for antinepotism rules is efficiency, specifically the potential for conflict in the fair evaluation and utilization of employees. It is ironic that efficiency arguments are advanced to justify both nepotism and antinepotism, but the key is an appreciation of the contexts in which the rules emerge. Problems of recruitment and safe apprenticeship are not universal; employers without these problems would find no efficiency advantage in nepotism. Conversely, performance evaluations are more subjective and difficult for some jobs than others. Antinepotism rules are most justifiable in those employment situations.

Universities are in the unusual position of an employer that suffers from both types of problems: recruitment has become difficult and the evaluation of academic jobs is inherently difficult and subjective. It should not be tremendously surprising, therefore, that at different times in history universities have employed both rules. The antinepotism rules of the past have disappeared and nepotistic partner preferences have emerged. The future may produce some modified combinations of the two rules as a reflection of the special problems of employing academics. The history of past legal challenges of antinepotism rules, like those of nepotism, should inform future litigation as well.

Constitutional Challenges to Antinepotism

The equal protection guarantee in the Fourteenth Amendment is relevant to antinepotism as it is to nepotism, because both practices categorize applicants and employees and treat them as different on the basis of familial relationship. State universities, but not private ones, are public employers subject to the clause and must defend their noninvidious classifications with their rational purpose.

Another constitutional basis for challenging antinepotism practices is their infringement on the right of association. This right, derived from the first amendment, again restricts the power only of state employers, including state universities. Because the right to marry is a fundamental right of association under the Constitution, a rule that unduly burdens this right must submit to the "strict scrutiny" of the court—a more difficult test than rationality.

There have been several unsuccessful constitutional challenges of antinepotism rules. In *Parsons v. County of Dell Norte*,[18] for example, the sheriff's department did not allow family members to work in the same department. The plaintiff's husband took an opportunity for a better job in the same department where she worked, but then the couple encountered the antinepotism rule. One of them had to quit or transfer to another department. The wife's job paid less than the husband's, so she was the one to quit. The court held that this rule did not unduly burden the right of marital association. Therefore, it was necessary only to examine the rational basis of the rule. Finding such basis, the court held for the employer.

Most recently, decisions in two circuit courts of appeals have upheld rules by a county employer and by a city police department barring spouses from working in the same department.[19] Each court found that the antinepotism rule did not unduly burden the right to marry because it was merely an unwelcome hurdle to marriage rather than a prohibition. Because the burden on marriage was not a sufficient impediment to trigger strict scrutiny by the court, the rule needed to pass only the

rational basis test. Both courts accepted as rational the same justifications: "avoiding conflicts of interest between work-related and family-
related obligations; reducing favoritism or even the appearance of favoritism; preventing family conflicts from affecting the workplace; and,
by limiting inter-office dating, decreasing the likelihood of sexual harassment in the workplace."[20] In another recent case involving a public
hospital's antinepotism rule, the Court of Appeals for the Sixth Circuit
reached a similar result under both federal and state law.[21]

In *McCabe v. Sharrett*[22] a female plaintiff lost her constitutional challenge to the antinepotism practice of a police department under the
strict scrutiny test. The plaintiff was the confidential personal secretary
to the police chief when she married a male officer in the same department. The chief then transferred her to another department. The move
was unsatisfactory for her because it resulted in a demotion. This court
found it unnecessary to decide whether her right to marry was unduly
encumbered because the rule passed the court's strict scrutiny. The
employer argued that her marital status inhibited the proper functioning of the police chief's office by compromising her loyalty to her boss
and her ability to keep sensitive material confidential. The chief believed
that her marriage to an officer was potentially disruptive of the efficient
and effective functioning and performance of the office. The court
agreed. "It is a matter of common experience," the panel of judges noted, "that spouses tend to possess a higher degree of loyalty to their
marital partners than to their superiors, and often discuss workplace
matters with one another, even matters that a superior has designated
as confidential." The antinepotism practice thus was constitutionally
justified because of the government's compelling interest in the efficient
and effective performance of this governmental function.

Statutory Challenges to the Effects of Antinepotism

There have been a few cases where plaintiffs have claimed that an employer's antinepotism rule disproportionately disadvantages women applicants
and employees. The plaintiffs have been generally unsuccessful.

One unsuccessful plaintiff, for example, could not produce enough
examples of the application of the rule in her company to establish a
pattern showing its adverse effect on women.[23] After she married a co-
worker, the employer informed the couple that they had to choose which
of them would quit. When they both refused to quit, the employer fired
the plaintiff wife because she had less seniority than her husband. There

were only a few other instances of co-worker marriages producing this result, and no record of spouses who would have applied to the company but for the antinepotism rule.

Whereas that plaintiff failed in her proof of disparate impact, another established the disparate impact of the antinepotism rule on women, but still lost. In this case, *Yuhas v. Libby-Owens-Ford,*[24] the court found that the employer's rationale for the rule satisfied the business necessity rule. Ironically, the rationale was morale and efficiency—the same rationale that the Supreme Court upheld in *Kotch* to justify the opposite practice of nepotism. In *Yuhas* the court noted the difficulties inherent in having spouses in the same place of employment. First, the defendant successfully argued, spouses may bring their marital conflicts to work such that the friction would reduce their productivity. Second, co-working spouses would be expected to take the same side in any workplace dispute, thus hampering dispute resolution. Third, if one spouse is in a supervisory position over another spouse, it is difficult to impose discipline or to avoid appearances of favoritism that would cause resentment among other workers. Finally, there would be difficulties in matters such as scheduling vacations at the same time.

It is curious to compare the justification of nepotism in *Kotch* with the justification of antinepotism in *Yuhas*. For the river port pilots, nepotism was found necessary for morale and efficiency, but for the factory workers in *Yuhas* antinepotism was found necessary for morale and efficiency. One difference is the jobs in question. Another is the difference between "relatives" and "spouses." Although neither case makes a point of it, the facts of *Kotch* concerned the hiring of the male relatives—brothers, sons, and nephews—whereas the rule in *Yuhas* concerned the hiring of spouses. The conflicting justifications can be reconciled if one finds that efficiency of nepotism does not apply to spouses but only to other relatives.

In some states antinepotism rules are now prohibited as a matter of state law. Although federal law does not address discrimination on the basis of marital status, a number of states have included this basis in their own civil rights acts.[25] Discrimination on the basis of "marital status" usually refers to differences based upon whether the person is married or single, but some states have extended the protection to address antinepotism practices. For example, an Illinois court recently held that an employer's rule prohibiting one spouse from supervising another is a violation of state law prohibiting discrimination on the basis of marital status.[26]

Programs for Partners

The modern programs for partners now appearing in some universities have no separate legal history. There have not been any recorded challenges to such rules, so any future challenge would be governed by the precedents from the nepotism and antinepotism cases of the past. By definition, such programs are a form of nepotism because an individual receives a benefit in employment by virtue of a familial relationship with another employee. It does not matter whether that benefit is a full academic appointment or something else; any kind of benefit premised upon a familial relationship suffices to make the practice nepotistic.

Disparate Impact Analysis

A claim of race, gender, or national origin discrimination may challenge a partner preference program if the targeted individuals in the program are disproportionately from one group. Plaintiffs have frequently been successful in establishing the racial effect of nepotism when the employer's work force is predominantly white, such as in the old trade unions. It is more difficult to establish disparate impact when there is no practice that is perpetuating past exclusion. For such a case the plaintiff needs proof that the beneficiaries of the program for partners were disproportionately from one group. It does not matter whether the group that benefits is majority or minority, male or female; a disproportionate impact on any group can suffice to establish the plaintiff's initial case. The burden would then shift to the university to establish the business necessity of the practice.

It does not matter if the university has a separate affirmative action plan that targets the group favored by the partner preference program unless the program is a bona fide part of that plan. A university would not be protected, for example, if the numbers reveal that a disproportionate number of the beneficiaries of the partner preference program were women even if the university has an affirmative action plan for women. It would be difficult for a partner preference program to qualify as a bona fide part of a legitimate affirmative action plan because the partner preference program contemplates preference over other qualified individuals of either gender and whatever race or national origin. One cannot declare a "plan" existed after one sees the effect of a practice.

A claim of age discrimination might also be possible if the program has a disparate impact on academics forty and over.[27] Unlike claims for discrimination on the basis of race, national origin, or gender, there is no concept in federal law of "reverse age discrimination," such that a disparate impact on younger individuals is irrelevant. Therefore, if the program benefits only people under forty, the group of disadvantaged older individuals may have an action under the Age Discrimination in Employment Act. Conversely, if the program disproportionately benefits individuals who are over forty to the disadvantage of younger persons, there is no problem with federal law. A few states protect the under forty group, however, as a matter of state employment discrimination law.[28]

The university should maintain records of who benefits from a partner preference program and should monitor whether the practice is benefiting one group disproportionately. There need not be a concern under federal law if the only group disadvantaged by the practice is individuals under forty. For all other categories, however, federal law addresses a disproportionate disadvantage in favor of either group—male/female or majority/minority racial groups. When such impact exists, the university must defend with business necessity.

The numbers of individuals involved in partner preference programs is not likely to be very large, even when the results are amalgamated over several years. Analysis of the data to show disparate impact must take into account, of course, the probability of a pattern appearing by chance alone. Experts should use appropriate statistical analysis.

The Uniform Guidelines on Employee Selection Procedures used to guide the prosecutorial discretion of the Equal Employment Opportunity Commission and other federal enforcers of employment law have chosen a rule of thumb to assess disparate impact. Their rule of thumb is called the "four-fifths rule" or "80 percent rule." The four-fifths rule considers an employment practice to have a disparate impact when one group is benefited at a rate that is less than four-fifths, or 80 percent, of the group with the highest rate. Some cases have followed this rule of thumb, but others have not. In *Clady v. County of Los Angeles*,[29] for example, the court observed that the Uniform Guidelines are not binding and do not have the force of law. The rule has been criticized by courts and commentators, the court noted, as an ill-conceived rule capable of producing anomalous results.

The Supreme Court subsequently confirmed that observation and expressly refused to identify any single method by which the prima facie case for disparate impact can be established. In *Watson v. Fort Worth Bank & Trust*,[30] the opinion notes: "At least at this stage of the law's development, we believe that a case-by-case approach properly reflects our recognition that statistics come in infinite variety and their usefulness depends on all the surrounding facts and circumstances." The Court refused to identify any single measure for assessing disparate impact.

If a plaintiff does establish disparate impact, the university may be able to defend on grounds of business necessity, as previously discussed. The great irony is that whatever justifications the university may have articulated years ago with respect to its antinepotism rule may now work against its ability to show the "necessity" of the opposite rule.

Despite the embarrassment, the argument may nonetheless prevail. It is widely believed in universities that top candidates for academic positions are difficult to attract because such candidates so often have highly qualified spouses who are also seeking employment. In litigation, substantiation of this belief would be necessary. Self-study within the defendant university prior to litigation is helpful. Also useful are more general studies and academic inquiries, such as those contained in this book. If the difficulty of attracting top candidates without partner preference is a modern reality for the defendant university, the program may be a business necessity. The difficulty for the university is that the defensibility of this practice, like any other employment practice, cannot be known in advance of litigation.

Disparate Treatment Analysis

A university might also face another kind of employment discrimination claim with respect to its program for partners—a claim of individual disparate treatment. Whereas disparate impact analysis focuses upon the effect of an employer's practice on groups defined by race, gender, national origin, or age, disparate treatment claims focus upon the individual without regard to any effect upon a group. When one person receives a benefit under a partner preference program, another individual who was qualified for that benefit may sue for its loss.

With respect to partner preference programs, the possibility of this type of suit is present if, for example, a department hires someone's spouse instead of another qualified individual who differs on the basis of race, gender, national origin, or age. Consider the situation, for instance, in which a white male spouse is hired under the program at the expense of a more qualified minority woman. The question is whether the rejected applicant has a claim of race and gender discrimination under federal law.

An individual claim of discrimination on the basis of marital status is possible in some states as well. Although federal law does not prohibit employment discrimination on this basis, a number of state laws provide for this coverage.

Another possibility is claims by existing faculty members rather than by their disappointed partners. The basis for such a claim would be that one faculty member was given a benefit in the form of a job for a spouse whereas another faculty member was not. If the two faculty members differ on the basis of race, gender, national origin, or age forty and over, there may be a claim of disparate treatment. Consider, for example, that two new faculty members receive positions in a department and that one is male and one is female. The wife of the new male employee is also hired by the university under the partner preference program, but no accommodation is made for the woman's professional husband, who therefore remains at his old job in another city. The question is whether the new woman faculty member has a meritorious claim of gender discrimination because she did not receive a benefit—the accommodation of a spouse—that was given to the similarly situated man.

Cases of this type are known as individual disparate treatment claims. It is not necessary to establish the disparate impact of a practice when one is claiming disparate treatment. To succeed, a plaintiff must establish that the defendant employer discriminated "intentionally" on the basis of race, gender, national origin, or age. Notably, an "intention" to discriminate is not limited to an invidious intention. The plaintiff does not need to demonstrate the nature of the defendant's motive; any unjustified difference in treatment suffices if the result is to disadvantage an individual on a prohibited dimension. For example, an employer may not grant favoritism to a less qualified member of an minority group unless the action is pursuant to a bona fide affirmative action plan. The better qualified person can sue for "reverse discrimination." Similarly, an employer may not grant salary benefits to a man simply because he has many dependents at home if his gender plays a role in that decision.

The Supreme Court established in *McDonnell Douglas Corp. v. Green*[31] a three-part approach to disparate treatment claims. First, the plaintiff must establish different treatment on a proscribed dimension. If the plaintiff is successful, the defendant must then articulate a legitimate business purpose for the adverse decision. The defendant's legitimate reason for the decision has the effect of dispelling the inference of improper motivation created by the plaintiff's proof. At the third phase of such trials the plaintiff may introduce evidence to show that the defendant's articulated reason is a pretext to hide the discriminatory animus. The burden remains with the plaintiff at all times to prove that the adverse employment decision was intentionally discriminatory.

McDonnell Douglas itself was a hiring case, but courts use this scheme for any disparate treatment claim. The Court further detailed how the plaintiff can establish the first prong to create the inference of improper motivation. To carry this initial burden, the Court said, the plaintiff may show "(i) that he belongs to a racial minority; (ii) that he applied and was qualified for a job for which the employer was seeking applicants; (iii) that, despite his qualifications, he was rejected; and (iv) that, after his rejection, the position remained open and the employer continued to seek applicants from persons of complainant's qualifications."

Courts have modified this original formulation to make it suitable for claims other than race discrimination and for claims other than hiring. Judges have interpreted the first requirement to mean simply that the plaintiff belongs to a protected group. The Supreme Court has also held that the Civil Rights Act of 1964 protects majority group members in "reverse discrimination" suits.[32]

The requirement that the plaintiff "apply" for a position is meaningful only in cases involving initial hire. The requirement is modified as necessary in other cases, because the act covers all terms and conditions of employment. Moreover, even in a hiring case the plaintiff need not prove "application" if there is evidence that such application would be futile.

After the plaintiff satisfies the first prong, the burden shifts to the employer to articulate some nondiscriminatory reason for its action. In *McDonnell Douglas* the Court referred to this stage as the articulation of a "legitimate business purpose," although the sole purpose of this inquiry is to dispel the inference of discriminatory intent and not to prove the rationality of the employer's practices from a business standpoint.

The third prong of an individual case of disparate treatment gives the plaintiff an opportunity to show that the employer's stated reason was in fact a pretext for discrimination. Relevant evidence includes examples in which similarly situated employees were treated differently. In the case of *McDonnell Douglas,* for example, the employer refused to rehire the African-American plaintiff after a layoff because during that time he had participated in an illegal demonstration against the employer. This reason for refusing to hire an admittedly qualified worker is a nondiscriminatory one, but only if the criterion is applied alike to members of all races. For example, if other employees involved in acts against the employer of comparable seriousness to the plaintiff's act were nevertheless retained or rehired, then the employer's reason for refusing to rehire the plaintiff would be a pretext.

The ultimate question in individual disparate treatment claims is the intent of the employer to treat the plaintiff differently because of race, gender, national origin, or age. The causal connection is crucial. It does not suffice to show that the plaintiff was treated unfairly if the grounds are unrelated to a dimension proscribed by the act. In *Holder v. City of Raleigh*,[33] for example, the employer hired someone solely because he was the son of a crew supervisor. The African-American plaintiff was better qualified. The court held that although the decision was distasteful, it did not violate Title 7 because the decisionmaker was not invidiously motivated. This nepotism was a one-time occurrence, so the plaintiff had no disparate impact claim because there could not be a pattern of exclusion on the basis of race. The individual claim of disparate treatment also failed because the employer's motives were not discriminatory.

Similarly, in *Foster v. Dalton*[34] a more qualified African-American woman lost her case against a naval hospital when a promotion went to a less qualified friend of the supervisor. The white male supervisor formed the intention to give the job to his white male golf buddy before he knew about her application and superior credentials. The court noted that although the episode of cronyism was not the Navy's "finest hour," the conduct did not violate federal law because there was no racial animus.

Reconsidering the hypothetical situations posed at the beginning of this section, the university may well prevail. In the first situation a white male spouse was hired under a partner preference program to the exclusion of a better qualified minority woman. As in *Holder* and *Foster,* the plaintiff cannot succeed without showing that the employer's action was related to race and gender rather than nepotism or cronyism. In the absence of such proof for a disparate treatment claim, and in the absence of a pattern of exclusion showing disparate impact, the university will prevail.

In the second hypothetical case, a female faculty member sues because her spouse did not receive assistance under the partner preference program whereas a male colleague's spouse did receive this benefit. The key question again will be whether gender played a role in the decision.

Recovery under a disparate treatment theory under the Civil Rights Act of 1964 is limited to situations in which gender affected the employer's action.

Most difficult is the question of the university's liability under the Equal Pay Act[35] to this hypothetical new female faculty member. Congress enacted the Equal Pay Act before the Civil Rights Act of 1964 to address specifically the practice of compensating men and women differently solely because of gender, such as school districts paying men more than women to attract more male teachers. It prohibits discrimination on the basis of gender in pay to individuals who are performing the same job unless one of the statutory defenses is present. Our hypothetical new assistant professors would be performing the same job, but the first question is whether the partner preference program is a difference in "pay" to the professors. The question is a close one. On the one hand, the program amounts to a benefit with some monetary value to the professor because of the employment of the spouse. On the other hand, the additional pay is solely for the work performed by a different person and is not paid to the professor personally.

Assuming that a court would find that the partner preference program amounted to a difference in pay to the new male assistant professor, the university may prevail with a statutory defense under the Equal Pay Act. Although an absence of intent is not a defense for this act, it is permissible to make a pay differential "based on any factor other than sex." Such factor must be permissible under other law and cannot be a factor such as race, which would be prohibited by the Civil Rights Act of 1964. The university's argument would be that the difference between the new female assistant professor and the new male was the difficulty in attracting the latter. The preference for the partner was necessary to attract one of them (the man) but not the other (the woman). If this argument is based upon the reality of the negotiations, untainted by gender discrimination and stereotyped assumptions, it should be successful.

Notably, gender bias in the marketplace is not a "factor other than sex" to defend a pay differential. The Supreme Court has held that an employer's general perception that women will work for less is not a "factor other than sex" because it is tainted with the discrimination of the marketplace.[36]

The rule differentiating between wages set by the impermissible basis of bias of the marketplace and by the permissible basis of untainted individual negotiations can be very difficult to apply. For example, in

Horner v. Mary Institute,[37] a school hired two new teachers, one male and one female, at different pay. Originally the same pay was offered to both, and the woman accepted. The man successfully held out for more. The court held that the wage differential was permissible as a "factor other than sex" because the school had attempted to pay them equally and found it necessary to consider the marketplace value of the man only when he held out for more.

The hypothetical assistant professors may be similar to the teachers in *Horner.* The important factual issue is whether the employer is acting under only general assumptions about market value. If the male professor would not come without the partner preference, but the female professor would, then the university may be acting on a "factor other than sex." The problem is that history cannot be recreated to do the necessary "experiment."

Universities would be well advised to monitor the use of partner preference programs. In the hypothetical case with the two new assistant professors, it would be wise to make equal efforts on behalf of both spouses. If monetary or other restraints make such efforts impossible on such a scale, then the university should note carefully the special justifications for accommodating some of its new employees' spouses and not others. Such recorded justifications should note specific problems in trying to accommodate a partner, such as his or her rank or field of expertise.

Conclusion

Both nepotism rules and antinepotism rules have been the subject of litigation, but the resulting cases have not produced clear rules on the legality of their application in particular settings. The nepotism practiced in the white male trade unions is now largely disappearing because of challenges to the racial effect of the practice. The antinepotism rules that often disadvantage women are still present in some employment situations, notably including many governmental employers. It is interesting that, in general, racial challenges to nepotism have been more successful than gender challenges to antinepotism, but there is no guiding principle that would predict this difference.

Among university employers it is noteworthy that the old antinepotism rules that often excluded professional wives from tenure-track positions have now been replaced with partner preference programs.

Even in universities that lack such programs, individual departments may act to hire two spouses in order to attract one in particular. It does not matter whether there is an official program for the practice to be considered nepotism.

There is a great deal of irony that partner preferences, which are especially beneficial to women, who formerly would have been excluded by antinepotism, may be challenged by civil rights laws if their effect is to advantage women disproportionately to men. The most likely challenges to partner preference practices will come from disappointed applicants who lose positions because of the programs. If there is a pattern that shows a disparate impact on the plaintiff's group on the basis of race, gender, national origin, or age over forty, the university must defend with business necessity. This defense may well prevail on the economic necessity of recruitment, but the issue is a close one.

Universities may even be liable in a single case of partner preference if race, gender, national origin, or age played a role in the decision. The presence of an affirmative action plan in the university is not a defense except in the unlikely case that the partner program is a bona fide part of the plan.

Other challenges are also possible from employees who are aggrieved because the university accommodated one person's spouse but not another's. The employment benefit of assisting a spouse affects the employment of both the originally targeted individual and the spouse. Both have legal rights—one concerns a term and condition of employment and the other concerns employment opportunity. A further irony is that a disparate impact on the basis of gender favoring, for example, women spouses, under the preference program may have the opposite impact among employees. Therefore, if a university has a program that benefits only female spouses, then the male employees are receiving more benefits in the form of spouse preference than female employees are receiving for their spouses. Both sets of numbers are relevant, depending upon who sues.

The potential legal problems with partner preference programs are somewhat complicated, but they do not overwhelmingly point in the direction of abandoning such programs. Indeed, it is interesting that there is no recorded challenge to such a program to date. This fact suggests that the legal issues surrounding these programs are not generally oppressive to universities. Moreover, if universities would consider abandoning such programs because of potential legal challenge, then they certainly fail to meet the standard of "business necessity." Universities would be wise instead to monitor the use and general effect of their programs and to keep careful records of the justifications for their use in particular cases.

Notes

1. *Ford v. Nicks*, 866 F.2d 865 (6th Cir. 1989); *McMillan v. Rust College*, 710 F.2d 1112 (5th Cir. 1983); *Weise v. Syracuse University*, 522 F.2d 397 (2d Cir. 1975).

2. 42 U.S.C.A. § 2000e et seq.

3. 330 U.S 552 (1947).

4. 42 U.S.C.A. § 1983.

5. *Washington v. Davis*, 426 U.S. 229 (1976).

6. 42 U.S.C.A. § 631.

7. There is currently a split among federal courts of appeal whether to apply this type of analysis, known as disparate impact analysis, to age cases in the same manner that it applies to cases on the basis of race, gender, and national origin. See *Ellis v. United Airlines*, 73 F.3d 999 (10th Cir. 1996).

8. 401 U.S. 424 (1971).

9. *Wards Cove Packing Co. v. Atonio*, 490 U.S. 642 (1989).

10. 48 F.3d 594 (1st Cir. 1995).

11. *U.S. v. Carpenters, Local 169*, 457 F.2d 210 (7th Cir. 1972).

12. 48 F.3d at 607.

13. 697 F.2d 1297 (9th Cir. 1983).

14. But see note 7.

15. *Montgomery v. Carr*, 848 F. Supp. 770 (S.D. Ohio 1993).

16. See, e.g., *Cutts v. Fowler*, 692 F.2d 138 (D.C. Cir. 1982).

17. *Arizona Public Service Co. v. Aspaas*, 77 F.3d 1128 (9th Cir. 1996).

18. 728 F.2d 1234 (9th Cir. 1984).

19. *Waters v. Gaston County*, 57 F.3d 422 (4th Cir. 1995); *Parks v. City of Warner Robins*, 43 F.3d 609 (11th Cir. 1995).

20. 57 F.3d at 426; F.3d at 615.

21. *Wright v. Metrohealth Medical Center*, 58 F.3d 1130 (6th Cir. 1995).

22. 12 F.3d 1558 (11th Cir. 1994).

23. *Thomas v. Metroflight, Inc.*, 814 F.2d 1506 (10th Cir. 1987).

24. 562 F.2d 496 (7th Cir. 1977).

25. Alaska, California, Connecticut, Florida, Hawaii, Illinois, Iowa, Kansas, Maine (public employees only), Maryland, Massachusetts, Michigan, Minnesota, Montana, Nebraska, New Hampshire, New Jersey, New York, North Dakota, Oregon, Washington, Wisconsin, Puerto Rico, and the District of Columbia.

26. *River Bend Community Unit School District v. Illinois Human Rights Comm.*, 232 Ill. App.3d 838, 597 N.E.2d 842 (1992).

27. But see note 7.

28. Iowa, Kansas, Minnesota, New York, Oregon, Vermont, and the District of Columbia.

29. 770 F.2d 1421 (9th Cir. 1985).

30. 487 U.S. 977 (1988).

31. 411 U.S. 792 (1973).

32. *McDonald v. Santa Fe Trail Transportation Co.*, 427 U.S. 273 (1976).

33. 847 F.2d 823 (4th Cir. 1987). See also *Betkerur v. Aultman Hospital Ass'n,* 78 F.3d 1079 (6th Cir. 1996).

34. 71 F.3d 52 (1st Cir. 1995).

35. 29 U.S.C.A. § 206(d).

36. *Corning Glass Works v. Brennan,* 417 U.S. 188 (1974).

37. 613 F.2d 706 (8th Cir. 1980).

10

· · · · · · · · · ·

Academic Couples:
The View from the Administration

Lilli S. Hornig

ACADEMIC ADMINISTRATORS have dual obligations to fulfill in relation to recruiting and hiring faculty. Their overriding responsibility is
to maintain and enhance the stature and welfare of the institutions they
serve, but they must also deal ethically and humanely with the personnel issues that are part of their charge. Recruiting, hiring, promoting,
and terminating faculty and other staff within their purview are very
high on administrators' lists of priorities in general, and when academic
couples are involved the challenges to administrative wisdom may grow
exponentially. Perhaps the complicated nature of the issues accounts for
the dearth of research on administrative policy regarding the appointment of couples. The questions that may arise in any one instance of
hiring a couple are not only complicated in themselves but are often so
intertwined with specific local or individual problems that almost every case becomes unique. For this reason administrative policies regarding employment of couples are likely to enunciate only general principles, rather than specific guidelines. As a result, policy statements are
likely to be of limited usefulness in examining administrators' views of
couple hirings. Administrative actions and actual decisions yield a more
helpful perspective.

The primary burden of recruiting, hiring, evaluating, promoting, and
terminating faculty rests with department heads in virtually all academic
institutions, although their decisions are generally made in consultation

with others in their departments and, in most cases, must be approved successively by an interdepartmental faculty committee on appointments and promotions, the relevant dean or provost, the president, and, in the case of tenure appointments, also by the board of trustees. In many major institutions, an ad hoc committee of outside experts is also convened to support a departmental decision on tenure before administrative approval is requested. At each of these levels, faculty members and administrators may have separate and distinct concerns about hiring an academic couple, so that such an action may involve extensive negotiations.

Faculty hiring situations are often viewed by aspiring candidates as a buyer's market, especially in times of Ph.D. surpluses, and by administrators as a *selection* rather than a *recruitment* process. Brakeman (1983) points out, however, that finding a new faculty member who precisely fits a given set of requirements is a difficult task even under the best of conditions and that the institution must make itself attractive, especially to women and minority candidates. He maintains that with the growing number of academic couples in the marketplace, colleges and universities must find ways to accommodate professional spouses of job candidates.

For the academic couple, difficult issues are ordinarily limited to two situations: one or both partners are prospective faculty members or one partner holds or is seeking a faculty position and the other an administrative position that might involve supervision of the first. These two general types of cases form the main focus of this chapter. Other types of couple hirings occur frequently in all academic institutions, including at professional levels, but cause little comment or difficulty. For example, faculty wives have long been employed as librarians (where such positions are not of faculty rank), museum aides, secretaries, or research assistants in the universities and colleges where their husbands were faculty members. Wives also commonly held off-ladder and nonvoting faculty jobs as instructors or lecturers; such appointments were generally on an ad hoc basis, for a semester or a year, frequently renewed or renewable but in no sense permanent. In principle the old antinepotism policies prohibited such employment, but de facto they applied only to faculty or equivalent positions. Furthermore, these policies did not necessarily apply to all close relatives.

An interesting illustration of this limited interpretation of nepotism occurred at Princeton University around 1960. For many years, twin brothers who had themselves grown up at the institution as the sons of a geology professor occupied endowed chairs, one in physics and one in chemistry. Concurrently, another senior professor of chemistry was married to a lecturer in a language department who was refused consideration for a regular faculty appointment on the grounds of the existing antinepotism policy. This couple's daughter then married a junior faculty member in her father's department. When her husband came up for tenure, the situation was debated in the department and he was granted tenure.[1] The story illustrates, of course, that the real issue in nepotism regulation had little to do with kinship in general but was specifically intended to preclude faculty positions for wives. Coincidentally, the widespread application of antinepotism policies solely to hiring wives suggests strongly that the presence of wives qualified to be faculty was not rare and that administrators and faculty members were indeed often strongly antifemale. Parenthetically, it should be noted that formal consideration of any partnership other than conventional marriage would have been beyond the bounds of contemporary propriety.

Antinepotism policies generally have now been replaced by statements that seek to avoid conflicts of interest among relatives working for the same institution, as discussed in Shoben (this volume). Possible conflicts of interest are generally defined to include financial interest, as in salary or other compensation decisions, and other material or personal interests that might be affected by one relative having jurisdiction over another. The concerns are therefore quite broad and certainly include situations such as one partner in a couple having a voice in decisions concerning the other's promotion and compensation, access to departmental and institutional resources, and so forth. The degree of detail with which these policies are sometimes defined in public statements indicates how concerned administrators are that their intent not be misinterpreted.[2] These statements are often part of affirmative action plans, an indication of the close connection between sex discrimination and antinepotism rules. While these stated principles have many common features, in practice every administrator is likely to view her or his own campus as having unique needs.

Advantages and Disadvantages of Hiring Academic Couples

As already discussed to some extent in the introduction to this volume, hiring an academic couple has both advantages and disadvantages for institutions. On the favorable side there is the possibility of building the kind of institutional attachment and loyalty every college or university hopes for among its faculty members by hiring two people whose chances for equally good positions elsewhere are uncertain. For example, as Perkins (this volume) mentions, historically black institutions frequently built devoted faculties on this pattern, as did some prominent women's colleges. Such couples are likely to be grateful to the institution and to remain there, lending stability in periods when faculty members may be looking for better offers elsewhere. Satisfied employees add to the campus's general well-being and, especially in a small community, enhance the college's relations with its neighbors. High morale on campus is likely to help create a cooperative and appreciative attitude in the community in which faculty members live and do business, and that community will probably approve such institutional requests as zoning modifications more readily. The institution will also be seen as compassionate and caring about personal needs, and such a view may be helpful in mitigating potential problems between the institution and the community. An astute administrator may thus be able to strike a genuine bargain for the institution by filling two faculty jobs (perhaps at a somewhat reduced cost, because the couple's strong desire for two positions in the same place may outweigh a slight reduction in salary) while at the same time enhancing the institution's standing in the community. The flexibility of the institution in accommodating a couple seems to be an advantage all around.

On the other hand, there are also likely to be circumstances whose ultimate effect is uncertain and which may be deleterious to the institution. High on this list is that any administrator appearing to interfere with the procedures of faculty recruitment and hiring runs the risk of being perceived by faculty members as restricting their right to determine who their own colleagues will be. This power to recruit, hire, promote, and fire is among the most cherished of faculty prerogatives, as the American Association of University Professors states in its basic document on governance: "Faculty status and related matters are primarily a faculty responsibility; this area includes appointments, reappointments, decisions not to reappoint, promotions, the granting of tenure, and dismissal. . . . The governing board and president should, on questions of faculty status, as in other matters where the faculty has primary responsibility, concur with the faculty judgment except in rare instances and for compelling reasons" (1984:109–10). As noted above, ordinarily the recruitment and hiring process for faculty is initiated in the department; a dean or provost who is trying to locate a second position for a partner may be viewed as interfering in the normal process and thus generate opposition.

An additional concern is possible conflict with affirmative action procedures. No matter how careful the language of official policy statements, some problems may still arise. Brakeman (1983) points out that raising questions about a spouse's status is inappropriate in the recruitment process, may be viewed as discriminatory, and may be offensive. Further, even if hiring a couple adds to the institution's desired diversity by adding a woman, it may do so at the expense of other potential candidates in "protected categories"—other female or minority candidates. No institution has unlimited numbers of positions, and this problem has been exacerbated by the recurrent budget crises in academe. If openings are filled by hiring couples, other candidates will ultimately be eliminated. Informal accusations of hiring discrimination resulting from these situations are occasionally heard, although none have resulted in lawsuits (see Shoben, this volume). In an era of frequent litigation as well as severe financial constraints, administrators are always mindful of the danger of being sued and of the expenses to the institution should a suit be filed.

Faculty and staff members may have adverse (as well as favorable) reactions to couple hiring. Will the newcomers constitute a power bloc in a department or division when difficult or divisive issues arise? Will their legitimate collecting of two salaries be viewed as double-dipping by faculty members who were less fortunate, perhaps hired in a period before the college was willing to consider appointing a spouse? What will happen if one member of the couple has tenure and the second does not qualify? Worse than that, what happens to departmental or even campuswide harmony if the couple separates? In this situation, will the more successful partner seek and find another position while the less successful partner stays for want of other opportunities? Is the institution ready to extend the same advantages to unmarried heterosexual and gay and lesbian couples?

Faculty couples are more numerous than pairs of administrators, but these pairs are not at all unusual. A good argument can be made for the view that two administrators, especially at relatively junior levels, represent a more tractable situation in terms of hiring. Administrative slots, except for some of the top positions, are often more fungible, and their requirements less field-related, than faculty positions. While it would be unusual to change administrative areas, for example from student affairs to business, it may be possible to adjust levels or titles within a particular track. Large institutions with a number of different schools may offer multiple opportunities.

Administrators, including department heads, need to deal very tactfully with a couple even if they can offer positions to both. One member of a couple, or sometimes both, may have to give up something in return for being accommodated. For instance, one member may have to accept a lower rank or other reduced status compared with what she or he might expect independently or wait until an appropriate post opens up. In particular, administrators should guard against suggesting that finding a position for a woman in a couple is less important than placing a man or that a less prestigious institution in the area is the right place for her. An example is the case of a senior faculty member in a distinguished department at the University of Michigan at Ann Arbor who was heard to say, "Well, *we* couldn't use her but we could probably find her a place at Michigan State." As the number of women scholars has grown quite rapidly since about 1980 and women's presence as faculty has become less unusual in most universities, however, such attitudes have presented less of a problem.

The Importance of Location

Although the importance of an institution's location with respect to other possible employment sites for spouses is intuitively obvious, it has also been confirmed by empirical studies such as Marwell, Rosenfeld, and Spillerman (1979). Perhaps as a sign of the times, the authors discussed location as a problem for a female member of a couple rather than for both partners. Its main finding, that an institution's location in a major metropolitan area was an important asset for a dual-career couple, is confirmed in an interesting way by Szafran (1984:66–67). In this study of factors affecting equity in recruitment and hiring, it was found that the number of universities in a given area was the single most important factor in securing recruitment equity for women. Such areas attract dual-career couples because of their multiple opportunities; academic women therefore form a higher proportion of candidates in these settings, which makes it more likely that women will find employment in equitable numbers.

Actual Problems and Solutions

The specifics of the couple's situation will vary enough to make an administrator consider all the possible scenarios. Frequently, one partner is being recruited by a college or university and the other is not. If neither is ready for tenure it may be relatively easy to devise a solution because no long-term commitment is necessarily involved and the member not being recruited may be willing to take a less than perfect post. In the past, the person being recruited was almost certainly a male, but since about 1980 that has been changing. Today men are still more likely to be recruited, but the number of women recruits has grown substantially. A subcategory of faculty couples consists of one existing faculty member, again more often male and perhaps also tenured, and one aspiring faculty member just emerging from graduate school or a postdoctoral fellowship. The latter situation commonly arises when a woman completes a late degree after raising children or when a faculty-student romance blossoms.

Unless they married at an early age, both members of an academic couple are quite likely to be in the same department, since graduate students and faculty tend to socialize, like almost everyone else, with those who share both interests and physical space. In the past, when women were scarce or even absent at the graduate and faculty levels in many fields, it was relatively unusual for a man to marry a woman in his field, although the few female students were indeed quite likely to marry their male colleagues. Thus, as Centra (1974) noted, female professionals are much more likely than males to have professional spouses. Among current senior faculty members and recent retirees, same-field marriages are therefore comparatively uncommon, especially in such areas as mathematics and the natural sciences.

As later marriage has become more common and as an increasing number of women have attended graduate school, the number of same-field couples, or those in closely related fields, has risen. Cole and Zuckerman (1987) found, for example, that almost 80 percent of married women scientists were married to other scientists. Such same-field couples usually pose special problems for administrators because it is often difficult to have or create two positions in one department, especially at small colleges or in small departments. The junior member of the couple may initially be eligible or willing to settle for a postdoctoral or similar research training post, which may be an excellent temporary solution, provided the institution offers such possibilities. Most colleges, however, have no graduate programs and hence are unlikely to be able to offer research positions. Among the approximately 3,600 institutions of higher education in the United States, fewer than 300 are universities ("Doctoral Granting Institutions" 1994:42). A few other institutions may offer occasional research positions. In any case, within a year or two the junior partner will be qualified for and requesting a more permanent slot. What then? Has the institution obligated itself to finding such a position or has it discharged whatever it sees its responsibility to have been?

Some situations do exist that defy ready solutions by the institution without recourse to other employers. One of these is a small college with an extremely tight budget. No matter how cooperative administrators are, they simply cannot provide a second position of any kind at any suitable level. At the other extreme is the large, highly selective research university that routinely hires only specifically targeted stars or, at the junior level, individuals with very strong pedigrees and records. Such an institution may be unwilling even to consider their partners. But very marketable individuals are also increasingly likely to have academic partners and some of the partners may also be "hot properties" in their own right.

In a university that can hire virtually anyone it wants, the idea that a department should hire a job candidate's spouse has not generally met with great success. In the past, the partner would have had to put up with the situation or perhaps find a post independently in a lesser institution in the vicinity. But times *have* changed. The star might decide to decline the appointment if another institution can offer a better package. This happened at Cornell in 1992 when a Nobel laureate in physics resigned because Ohio State had made him and his wife a more appealing offer.

By 1989 it became generally recognized that a spouse's or partner's employment or lack thereof might be a critical factor in recruitment and retention of faculty (Mangan 1989:13). At Stanford University, the Provost's Committee on the Recruitment and Retention of Women Faculty (Stanford University 1993) found that of their sample of faculty members who had left Stanford, almost one-third reported a spouse's employment situation as a primary factor in their decision to leave. Similarly, Harvard's John F. Kennedy School of Government had two out of three tenure offers to women turned down in a five-year period because of spousal relocation problems (Kennedy School of Government 1993). In this changing climate, both recruitment and retention of faculty require institutions to be sensitive to the professional needs of spouses.

Field Differences

There are also considerable field differences in the degree of flexibility that both the institution and the couple have. In the natural sciences it is often possible to fund a second position through grants. Although such soft-money positions are considered less desirable by many scientists, they may offer good solutions. In a family with young children, for example, one partner may welcome the opportunity to work productively but under less personal pressure than a tenure-track appointment imposes. If the institution can also relax the common rule of not allowing a non-tenure-track person to be an independent principal investigator, the scientist may then be able to realize at least some of the rewards of a professorial career. On the other hand, in most universities an individual in a soft-money position has few of the rights of regular faculty, such as a voice in governance, a long-term contract or tenure, and independent access to graduate students (who are unlikely to choose to work with someone who may be gone next year). The last is critical to research and publication in experimental sciences unless a researcher can join an existing group working in an appropriate area. A further serious obstacle in these fields is the need for funding (often in very generous amounts) to set up and equip a suitable laboratory. The amounts involved in a field like chemistry range from around $250,000 to perhaps $1 million. Institutions normally provide such start-up money for tenure-track appointees but not for others.

Goldberg and Sakai (1993) have surveyed two hundred institutions for the Ecological Society of America's (ESA) Committee on Women and Minorities to determine current practice in the use of soft-money positions as well as shared positions to accommodate couples. Because it had a response rate of less than 35 percent, this survey gives no conclusive answers but does yield some useful indications. Large research universities predominate among respondents, and the authors caution that their general finding that soft-money positions are readily arranged obviously does not apply to smaller colleges that are not research oriented. They also comment that most cases of couple hirings appear to be solved less by central assistance than by individual arrangements. Only six of their sixty-nine responding institutions have an office or individual specifically charged with giving assistance to spouses of newly recruited faculty in finding professional employment in or near the institution.

The ESA report corroborates the findings of earlier studies, for example Zumeta's (1985) on the uncertain status of grant-supported positions, including their lack of permanency, the failure of policies in many institutions to define their privileges and responsibilities, and their low prestige in the academic hierarchy. Furthermore, it should be noted that continuing reductions in federal funding for research make the provision of soft-money alternatives increasingly problematic.

The shared positions that the ESA survey also addressed refer to single tenure-track positions that are split by members of a couple. Only nineteen of the sixty-nine responding institutions reported ever having used this arrangement, and the ways in which the split was arranged and how the duties were allocated were diverse enough to defy classification. Thus, this solution is highly individualistic and should not be regarded as widely generalizable. However, split appointments apparently can work well, for all twelve persons on such appointments who had advanced to consideration for tenure had achieved it.

Second spouses to be hired who are in the humanities may be even harder to accommodate than those in the sciences. The shortage of regular faculty appointments in these disciplines has been a mounting problem for two decades, easing for a few years in the eighties only to reappear in the nineties. It has had a disparate impact on women because they have been by far the fastest-growing population among recent humanities Ph.D.'s. Between 1975 and 1992 women's share of all humanities doctorates awarded to U.S. citizens grew from 34 percent to 47 percent, with the result that women now constitute 42 percent of that total doctorate pool. In English and foreign languages, 57 percent and 59 percent, respectively, of all doctorates were awarded to women in 1992 (Commission on Professionals in Science and Technology 1994:52, 268).

These and other humanities departments (as well as a number of other fields) have for some years relied on part-time temporary appointments to fill specific teaching needs that may vary from year to year, rather than commit to full-time faculty. In 1991 (the last year for which these data are available), only about 77 percent of academically employed women in the humanities held regular faculty positions compared with about 87 percent of the men, with the difference being made up in adjunct and similar off-ladder appointments (Brown and Mitchell 1994:31).

Such arrangements save money, because per-course salaries are very low and because no benefits need to be provided for people hired on these terms. Thus part-time teaching positions may be available at several colleges in a given area, but this is a high-risk solution for anyone planning on eventually developing a standard academic career. Hornig and Ekstrom (1983:358–62) found that a few couples value the flexibility possible in such an arrangement enough to accept the grave career risks involved. The majority of women in part-time positions, however, had settled for them because no regular career positions were available and regretted the decision because it effectively cut off the careers they had planned.

It is clear from academic employment data that across all fields women are far more likely than men to hold not only part-time positions but also various other non-tenure-track appointments that have few rights and privileges. For example, women doctoral scientists and engineers in academic employment are more than twice as likely as their male counterparts to hold positions as instructors, lecturers, or adjunct faculty (National Research Council Committee on Women in Science and Engineering 1991:25). It is worth noting, however, that the overrepresentation of women doctorates in non-tenure-track positions is declining. In 1991 the excess of women in these ranks was about 30 percent among those who had held a Ph.D. for less than eight years, compared with a 70 percent excess among those with Ph.D.'s for eight or more years (National Science Foundation 1994:377).

In some social sciences and most natural sciences nonacademic employment may be an excellent possibility. Although business or industrial employment may be viewed as less prestigious than an academic appointment, it tends to be better paid. College and university administrators could contribute materially to the solution of dual-career problems by facilitating various nonacademic recruitment efforts.

Potential Pitfalls

Exactly how a particular scenario plays out is highly dependent not only on the obvious factors of institutional size, location, and nonacademic opportunities in the area but also on various preexisting conditions on the particular campus, and these are the details an administrator must consider. Some of these preexisting conditions vary over time and cannot always be foreseen when and if policies are established. For example, if the last couple previously hired had to make do with only a temporary or part-time appointment for the second member, a department head or dean is likely to feel some pressure to equalize the situation, thus compounding the problems of accommodating a new couple. If a faculty couple already in place has just divorced and their various partisans on campus are at odds, no one will be eager to take on another potential set of quarrels right away.

More commonly, difficulties may arise over actually avoiding conflicts of interest regardless of stated policies, especially when both members of a couple are in the same or in neighboring departments or in small institutions. For example, either within or between departments, disputes will often arise over allocation of scarce resources. These may encompass anything from an extra teaching assistant to a library allowance to the use of major scientific instruments to the allocation of space. The higher-ranking member of a couple may be in charge of some or all of these resources and thus may encounter conflicts from which he (usually) cannot readily recuse himself. Turning over such responsibilities to disinterested colleagues might be viewed as an imposition and thus generate discord or opposition to couple hiring. Again, the eventual conflict of interest inherent in the situation could not necessarily have been anticipated.

If both members of the couple work in the same research area they may publish jointly, which often results in the second, usually female, member being viewed as a research assistant. This is not only likely to upset that person and have a negative impact on her career but it also, in a sense, deprives the institution of full credit for having two distinguished faculty members.

A difficult issue that arises occasionally is that the institution interprets "conflict of interest" so broadly that it precludes granting tenure to the second person, though the reasons for such a policy are unclear. Such a rule applies to both sexes and is therefore not necessarily discriminatory, at least not unless a plaintiff could show that it had been applied only to one sex. In 1993 a perceived regulation against tenuring a second member of a couple was tested at Harvard when Maryellen Ruvolo, who is married to tenured professor David Pilbeam, approached the "up or out" stage of her faculty appointment. The issue was resolved, at least temporarily, by granting Ruvolo an associate professorship. Irven DeVore, a senior professor in her department, said: "As far as I know, [her promotion] will make her the one that broke the silly nepotism rule at this university. Over the years, we have had several distinguished husband and wife teams, but only one of them could have tenure" (Montgomery 1994:25). Harvard's assistant dean for affirmative action, however, maintains that no such policy has existed. Nonetheless, this situation remains unclear because Harvard does not normally grant tenure-track appointments; its assistant professors are designated "ladder faculty" and have no expectation of promotion to tenure except insofar as they are free to enter the candidate pool for a *de novo* worldwide search should a tenure position open up. In addition, Harvard has been eliminating the associate professor rank on the grounds that once tenure is granted, the rank distinction is unimportant. In any case, if senior faculty members *believe* that the university will not tenure the second member of a couple, they will be unlikely to recommend one for promotion.

Acceptable Solutions

An institution's location remains perhaps the salient issue once anti-nepotism rules are abolished. In a few large cities or other areas within reach of multiple employment opportunities, academic or nonacademic, no serious problems may arise when an institution wants to hire or retain only one partner. As previously mentioned, the recruiting institution may even assist the couple in locating a second position in the same region. Such a family employment program as devised and implemented at Oregon State University is described by Stafford and Spanier (1990). A similar program exists at Washington State University (Smart and Smart 1990:33). Stafford and Spanier report that although the majority of faculty recruiting at Oregon State University involved dual-career situations, no policy existed for coping with the problem. The family employment program they developed grew out of Spanier's own appointment as provost and his wife's as an English professor and the resulting campuswide discussion of these issues. Many employees of long service had had to cope with dual-career issues on their own, and many were concerned about the impact of assistance to couples on the university's affirmative action goals. The authors ascribe the eventual acceptance and modest success of their program to having developed a broad-based partnership among university, business, and state and local government sectors in the Corvallis area. (A similar program exists at Washington State University [Smart and Smart 1990:33].)

Established in 1986, the program maintains an active information network of existing positions that is administered by a half-time coordinator. Although economic growth was anticipated in that area, not many nonacademic opportunities were initially available. Furthermore, it is not clear what fraction of partners who sought professional employment were qualified for academic positions. This point is important because while having difficulties in a job search is discouraging and may make people resentful, it is not nearly as traumatic as being judged unacceptable for the kind of career one is prepared for and has always wanted. No effort is made to create new positions at Oregon State University beyond granting a spouse a "faculty fellowship" for one year or less, financed primarily through the Office of Academic Affairs with a one-third contribution by the host department or administrative division. The authors report that although the early reception of the program was mixed, much enthusiasm has developed. By 1990 about one-quarter of applying spouses had been aided in finding employment. It is worth noting that the existence of the program has encouraged cooperation among deans and department heads in arranging dual-career placements without recourse to the program. Clearly, the personal interest of the provost in the issues and his willingness to devote time, effort, and resources to the program were instrumental in its success. It is probably reasonable to conclude that without such high-level administrative support and the commitment of adequate resources such a program would be most unlikely to succeed or find acceptance.

In many cases, however, the college or university is the only reasonable employment choice in a given area. Then the type of institution becomes a critical factor because its size and diversity of offerings will determine the kinds of opportunities it can offer. A few additional points should be made. One situation that arises fairly often in major research universities is that of a tenured faculty member (generally male, both because nearly 90 percent of tenured faculty members are male and because more men than women marry younger people) marrying a graduate student, often his own. She then needs to find a position and is hoping for one at the same institution. However, the specialized field is unlikely to have a vacancy if the institution is already awarding graduate degrees in it. Wives of existing faculty members who return to finish advanced degrees after raising their children often find themselves in this position also. The difficulty may be compounded by a policy of not hiring the university's own graduates in order to avoid excessive inbreeding, although a search of such a university's catalog will often turn up a nontrivial fraction of senior faculty who are its own graduates. Resolution of the problem may very well depend on how badly the institution wants to retain the first member of the couple. In fact, it is probably too sweeping to speak of "the institution" in this context. A great deal will certainly depend (as it did at Oregon State) on the individual department, the degree of potential fit, and the personal attitudes of colleagues.

The nonrecruited partner is in an especially difficult situation when the couple considers a move to a major research institution. The failure to be recruited is perceived as a damning judgment of one's competence. Similar problems arise when one member of a couple fails to be retained at the institution where they are both employed. One such case that received wide publicity occurred at the Harvard Law School when Claire Dalton, the wife of then-professor Robert Reich, was denied tenure. A long-drawn-out lawsuit was eventually resolved by a financial settlement, and Dalton now teaches at a neighboring law school.

In contrast to most private research universities, many of the very large public universities, and even large state colleges, have enough different schools or divisions that teach similar subjects so that in theory even a couple in the same field can be accommodated more readily. Examples of such situations are biology departments in both the school of arts and sciences and the school of agriculture, physics departments in both the school of arts and sciences and the engineering college, and statistics departments in both the college of science and the medical school.

The majority of American colleges, however, are not very large institutions and many of them are located in small communities in which few professional opportunities exist outside the campus. Some of the private colleges normally recruit faculty nationally and are reluctant to break that precedent so as not to damage their reputation for being highly selective. Even if an administrator in such a college offers financial inducements or some other benefit to a department to support the hiring of a spouse, the department may feel that its prerogatives are threatened and refuse to cooperate. In contrast to such prestigious colleges, however, many private (often denominational) colleges are even smaller, not wealthy, and somewhat isolated geographically. Many such institutions find hiring couples an advantage, provided a feasible second position exists. While doing the couple a favor, they may simultaneously be able to assemble a better faculty than they could recruit one at a time.

As important as all of these considerations are, the central issue for administrators remains the potential conflict with faculty over the powers of appointment, retention, promotion, and termination. Administrators do retain the purse strings and have a fairly free hand in appointing other administrators. That they can create or deny positions does not necessarily endear them to the faculty. However, if an administrator helps create a position for a job candidate's partner, the department will probably be grateful to the administration and also more tolerant of similar situations.

Thus faculty members become the effective arbiters of dual-career couple issues and will be responsive to many considerations besides a recruit's ability and promise. Inevitably, some faculty members will view couple appointments as double-dipping. For couples who may have settled for one job in other times when spouses were not hired, the presence of a couple with two jobs may be a bitter reminder of missed opportunities. If an unmarried heterosexual, gay, or lesbian couple is hired into a department whose members have traditional ideas about families, considerable social disruption and dislocation may follow. In some states, however, failure to hire a lesbian or gay partner who is otherwise qualified when heterosexual spouses would be hired constitutes grounds for legal action.

Administrative decisions about hiring couples have surely been influenced by the evolving views of faculty colleagues, but they also have been affected by the administrators' own changing perceptions of how best to balance advantages and disadvantages to both the individuals and the institutions. Furthermore, the number of high-level administrators who find *themselves* involved in dual-career issues is growing. As the following examples show, however, the solutions are not necessarily easier or more popular at the top.

Some of the most publicized situations have occurred at the top of the academic ladder, between presidents and deans or presidents and potential faculty members. When Hanna Holborn Gray was appointed president of the University of Chicago and Nannerl Keohane became president first of Wellesley College and then of Duke University, both had husbands with distinguished academic careers but who found their positions in institutions other than those headed by their wives. (The Keohanes had previously both been tenured faculty members at Stanford.) Shortly after her appointment as president of the University of Pennsylvania in 1994, Judith Rodin, the former provost and acting president of Yale, married Paul Verkuil, who had been president of the College of William and Mary but resigned this position to take on an assignment as an arbitrator and be closer to his wife (O'Neill 1994:C1). When men are hired into prestigious administrative positions, as is more common, the situation is more complicated. No research literature seems to exist on this point, but experience suggests that the female partner will almost always be viewed as less competent than her husband, regardless of the facts, and will not be hired at the same institution. Certainly the usual assumption is that if she were good enough, she would not need to be looking so hard for a position.

When they assumed their offices, many male presidents had wives fully qualified to be considered for faculty or other administrative positions in the same university, but if any of the wives was hired it was not publicized. These women have either found positions at nearby universities, as did Sissela Bok when her husband became president of Harvard, or turned their talents to some new enterprise. Many have done what amounts to volunteer work for university or college libraries or museums. Cora Lee Gibbs, for instance, donated her professional services as a curator to the college museum while her husband, Julian, was president of Amherst. Others educated in social work or health-related fields may turn to service positions off campus. In many humanities disciplines, where a large number of women earned their advanced degrees, there are also growing opportunities for independent scholarship (Hornig and Ekstrom 1983:chap. 6).

It is probably true that until quite recently most of the men who were likely to be considered for presidencies or chancellorships were old enough to have generally had very conventional marriages, with wives furthering and sustaining their husbands' careers instead of concentrating on their own. This certainly remains the dominant pattern for top-level administrators. Indeed, it is undoubtedly the arrangement preferred by male administrators, most of whom are well aware of the extent to which they depend on their wives for the smooth running of their households, institutions, and personal lives.

That such a symbiosis is not approved for women administrators, however, became clear in a much-publicized case at the University of Colorado. When the governing board appointed Judith Albino president of the Boulder campus in 1991, it planned to appoint her husband, Sal, as manager of the official residence at a salary of $30,000 per year, the same amount paid to the previous manager. The plan engendered so much opposition in the community that it was abandoned, even though the wives of previous presidents had been paid a "spousal functions allowance" of $25,000 annually. Subsequently President Albino commented, "Yes, there now are women presidents at some of our leading research universities, but you may rest assured that full gender equity remains to be achieved" (*Chronicle of Higher Education* 1991:A25, B4).

In a somewhat similar case at the University of Massachusetts at Amherst, Chancellor David K. Scott in 1993 appointed Marcellette Williams to the newly created position of deputy chancellor at a salary of $110,000 and her husband, Keith, to an associate vice chancellorship for university advancement at $75,000 per year. David Nunez, the Student Government Association president commented: "The whole thing stinks. . . . The rich get richer and the poor get poorer and the students get screwed" (Chant 1993:64). In neither of these cases did the chief opposition come from faculty. It is also worth noting that apparently the nontraditional situation of making accommodations for the husband of an administrator apparently drew more criticism than would have similar accommodations for a wife.

Prospects for the Future

Much of academic planning for the next decade or two has rested heavily on two assumptions: a wave of faculty retirements in the mid-1990s, as the oversupply of faculty members hired during the expansive 1960s reaches traditional retirement age, although mandatory retirement is no longer permissible, and a hoped-for growth in enrollments as the "reflected wave" of the baby boom generation reaches traditional college age. The conventional wisdom was that these two forces would combine to cause a dramatic increase in faculty positions, but a number of factors have begun to cloud this outlook. Even though the relaxation of retirement rules in 1987 produced about equal numbers of early and late retirements during the 1980s, experience through 1994 suggests there will be fewer retirements at or before age seventy than had been hoped for. Further, some of these retirements had to be bought with additional retirement benefits, including allowing the faculty members to stay on to do research. In such cases, the faculty positions are vacated but at the cost, to the university, of giving up space and perhaps other resources.

At some institutions, such as the University of California, these deals are possible because retirement trusts are well funded even though operating budgets have been cut drastically. But increasingly scarce resources for research, both in direct funding and in indirect cost reimbursement, make it less likely that faculty members can continue to support their research after they retire, especially in fields that rely heavily on graduate students and postdoctoral fellows, who must also be supported on outside funds. These circumstances diminish the chances that universities can succeed in encouraging more timely retirements in such fields. Faculty members who reach age seventy in good health (and most do) may not be easily persuaded to give up what they love doing just to make room for younger people, who of course cost the institution much less. However, in fields where research costs are low and outside funding unusual, faculty may indeed welcome a retirement that makes no teaching demands but allows them to continue their research.

On the enrollment side the prognosis is also not clear. Aside from a few static years, enrollments have continued to climb in spite of the decreasing population in the traditional college age group, but have changed in character. Student bodies as a whole are now predominantly female and increasingly diverse in other ways. There are more older, foreign, and minority students and more students going into occupational fields such as health care administration or business than into the old core academic fields. In some fields, notably engineering and mathematics, more than half of the Ph.D.'s are awarded to foreign citizens, who may or may not remain in the U.S. labor force to help populate academic positions. In general, the fields in which faculty are needed are not the ones in which most faculty members are approaching traditional retirement age.

At the same time, the structures of many professions are undergoing changes, and unsuccessful job searches in formerly sure-fire areas such as law and chemistry are discouraging many young people from entering these fields. Such problems, along with the well-publicized dearth of good academic positions, are reflected in stagnant or even declining enrollments in many graduate departments. Although graduate enrollments do not drive faculty needs in the same way as undergraduate enrollments, they do affect the availability of faculty positions to some extent.

All of these factors combine to create what in many fields is a totally unprecedented lack of faculty openings, a situation that may be inherently unfavorable to academic couples because historically women have been excluded from occupations experiencing job shortages. The fact that traditional attitudes about women's careers persist in many quarters also influences the availability of positions for both members of a couple. In many cases not only administrators but also many married couples regard the woman's career as contingent on her husband's and children's needs. Such factors are hard to pinpoint, of course, and are seldom dealt with explicitly. But many discussions in the literature, and certainly many survey and interview data, suggest that in the case of married couples, at least, the woman's career is most often viewed as secondary to the man's. It is still often assumed that the man is the primary breadwinner and that the woman must adapt to whatever situation that places her in. Such attitudes will disappear only when it becomes clear that women have truly equal opportunities and the equal salaries that go with them.

Finally, it must be said that in the matter of teaching about women's status and careers by example as well as precept, most colleges and universities have not set a very high standard. They should be concerned that study after study of undergraduate attitudes indicates a serious discrepancy between men's and women's life expectations. College women expect to have egalitarian marriages and full professional careers while male undergraduates, in contrast, expect that their wives will work only until children arrive and will then devote themselves primarily to home and family for a number of years (Brown Project 1980). Until higher education institutions find ways to demonstrate to all their students that they treat women and men equally, they are not fulfilling all of their educational obligations.

Taken together, these factors make it hazardous to forecast how successful dual-career couples will be in their job searches in academe. It is obvious that any further tightening of academic budgets will make it more difficult for administrators to facilitate satisfactory and appropriate placements for both members of an academic couple. On the other hand, as Fuller pointed out, "it is important that a new awareness of limitations on resources not also serve to limit vision" (1983:99). The new reality is that many potential faculty recruits come in couples, and institutions must seek to adapt to this situation. From the individual's perspective, it is also true that the single lifetime career is no longer the only model; many people find that changing focus or even switching fields can be very rewarding. Finally, couples seeking dual appointments can take heart that a practice decried as unworkable twenty years earli-

er has become fairly common and that institutions are recognizing the
many potential advantages to them in being flexible in their personnel
policies.

Notes

1. Personal acquaintance with all individuals except the twins' father.
2. Appendix C of Harvard University's *Summary Affirmative Action Plan* for
1994, for example, defines "immediate family" as including "husband, wife, son
and daughter (including stepchildren), grandchild, son- and daughter-in-law;
parents (including stepparents), grandparents, father- and mother-in-law;
brother and sister (including stepbrother and stepsister), brother- and sister-
in-law."

References

American Association of University Professors. 1984. *Policy Documents and Reports*. Washington, D.C.: American Association of University Professors.
Brakeman, Louis F. 1983. "Hiring and Keeping the Best Faculty." In *Issues in Faculty Personnel Policies*, ed. Jon W. Fuller, 5–19. San Francisco: Jossey-Bass.
Brown, Prudence, and Susan Mitchell. 1994. *Humanities Doctorates in the United States: 1991 Profile*. Washington, D.C.: National Academy Press.
Brown Project. 1980. *Men and Women Learning Together: A Study of College Students in the Late Seventies*. Providence: Brown University.
Centra, John A. 1974. *Women, Men, and the Doctorate*. Princeton: Educational Testing Service.
Chant, Cate. 1993. "Chancellor's Hiring of Aides Leads to Criticism at U-Mass." *Boston Globe*, Nov. 12.
Chronicle of Higher Education. 1991. Sept. 25.
Cole, Jonathan R., and Harriet Zuckerman. 1987. "Marriage, Motherhood, and Research Performance." *Scientific American* 256 (Feb.): 119–25.
Commission on Professionals in Science and Technology. 1994. *Professional Women and Minorities*. 11th ed. Washington, D.C.: Commission on Professionals in Science and Technology.
"Doctoral Granting Institutions: Selective Liberal Arts Colleges." *Chronicle of Higher Education*. 1994. Almanac Issue, Sept. 1., 42.
Fuller, Jon W. 1983. "Concluding Comments." In *Issues in Faculty Personnel Policies*, ed. Jon W. Fuller, 99–103. San Francisco: Jossey-Bass.
Goldberg, Deborah, and Ann K. Sakai. 1993. "Career Options for Dual-Career Couples: Results of the ESA Survey on Soft Money Research Positions and Shared Positions." *Bulletin of the Ecological Society of America* 74 (June): 146–52.

Harvard University. 1994. *Summary Affirmative Action Plan.* Cambridge, Mass.: Harvard University.

Hornig, Lilli S., and Ruth B. Ekstrom. 1983. "The Status of Women in the Humanities." Unpublished report to the National Endowment for the Humanities.

Kennedy School of Government. 1993. *The 1992–1993 Report on the Status of Women.* Cambridge, Mass.: Harvard University.

Mangan, K. S. 1989. "Colleges Discover That Winning a Top Faculty Recruit Sometimes Depends on Finding Work for a Spouse." *Chronicle of Higher Education,* Sept. 20:A13–14.

Marwell, Gerald, Rachel Rosenfeld, and Seymour Spillerman. 1979. "Geographic Constraints on Women's Careers in Academia." *Science* 205 (Sept. 21): 1225–31.

Montgomery, M. R. 1994. "The Professor's Monkey Wrench." *Boston Globe,* Jan. 4.

National Research Council Committee on Women in Science and Engineering. 1991. *Women in Science and Engineering: Increasing Their Numbers in the 1990s.* Washington, D.C.: National Academy Press.

National Science Foundation. 1995. *Women, Minorities, and Persons with Disabilities in Science and Engineering, 1994.* Washington, D.C.: National Science Foundation.

O'Neill, Molly. 1994. "In an Ivy League of Her Own." *New York Times,* Oct. 20.

Smart, Mollie S., and Russell C. Smart. 1990. "Paired Prospects: Dual-Career Couples on Campus." *Academe* 76 (Jan.–Feb.): 33–37.

Stafford, Susan G., and Graham B. Spanier. 1990. "Recruiting the Dual-Career Couple: The Family Employment Program." *Journal of the National Association of Women Deans, Administrators, and Counselors* 53 (2): 37–44.

Stanford University. 1993. *Report of the Provost's Committee on the Recruitment and Retention of Faculty.* Stanford, Calif.: Stanford University.

Szafran, Robert F. 1984. *Universities and Women Faculty: Why Some Organizations Discriminate More Than Others.* New York: Praeger.

Zumeta, William. 1985. *Extending the Educational Ladder: The Changing Quality and Value of Postdoctoral Study.* Lexington, Mass.: Lexington Books.

11

· · · · · · · · · ·

Programs for Academic Partners: How Well Can They Work?

Jane W. Loeb

As the number of dual-career couples has grown, all sectors of the U.S. economy have responded to some extent by revising employment practices as needed to recruit and retain employees. The 1980 Catalyst survey of Fortune 1300 corporations found that 76 percent of the 374 corporate respondents were concerned about two-career family problems, because such issues could ultimately affect corporate profits. For example, two-thirds said they had already experienced increased resistance to relocation; when provided, assistance to the partner in relocating for the most part consisted simply of informal contacts with other companies or job counseling (*Corporations* 1981).

By 1983, 54 percent of a similar sample offered some spouse employment assistance, largely at the request of the employee (*Human Factors* 1983). This assistance might include payment of spouse job placement fees, job counseling for the spouse, or referrals through company contacts. A few firms participated in consortia of employers to help with spousal relocation, used third-party relocation firms, or tried to place the spouse within their own firms. Various authors have reported a related tendency for companies to relax antinepotism rules to allow employment of couples except in the same department or, perhaps, chain of command (Newgren, Kellogg, and Gardner 1987; Collie 1989).

A review of public sector personnel policies concerning dual-career couples concluded that "except for military (and foreign service) person-

nel, trailing spouses are more or less on their own in finding suitable career opportunities in their new communities" (Bruce and Reed 1991:53).
Even in this setting, however, it appears that informal activities, such as
circulating resumes and finding out about suitable vacancies on behalf of
the spouse are not uncommon. Within higher education, two rather different forms of programs have become commonplace. Some partners of
faculty members seek work that is not academic, either in the community or on campus. Many campuses have employment assistance programs
that attempt to match these job seekers with available positions. A regional,
cooperative community university program at Oregon State University is
one of the best publicized of these (Stafford and Spanier 1990), but many
others exist as well (e.g., see Leff 1992). These programs, and the recruiting and retention problems they seek to address, generally parallel developments in the corporate sector. In addition, however, higher education
institutions are often confronted with two partners who seek academic
positions, often even in the same specialty area, because a relatively large
proportion of candidates for faculty jobs have partners in the same line
of work (Astin and Milem, this volume). In these cases, spousal employment assistance that is ideal from the candidates' point of view requires
two tenure-track positions, preferably at the same higher education institution or at two that are located very near each other. If not unique to
higher education, the challenge of finding or creating a second job in the
same industry and career track, preferably with the same employer, is
probably at least most prevalent there.

It has been aptly stated that "in relatively crude market terms, the
bargaining power of the dual-career couple is increasing while the ability
of the institution to 'buy elsewhere' is declining" (Gee 1991:46). Since
these job seekers are the product of the higher education industry, it is
also the case that the health of the enterprise requires that they be able
to find suitable employment. Thus, shortly after the higher education
community began to embrace open searches, not just as a means to
ensure equal access but also as a good way to find the best possible recruits, these other pressures required that institutions find ways to accommodate well-qualified individuals who become candidates because
of their status as partners rather than as a result of an open search. Initially designed to circumvent the once prevalent preference for white
male faculty, open searches also support the selection of the best-qual-
ified candidates. Therefore, introducing a partner preference raises questions concerning both equity and quality. It is the purpose of this chapter

to review what little is known about the ways institutions are accommodating academic couples, to lay out the concerns that partner employment programs raise, and to provide data from one campus active in partner accommodation in order to begin to address these issues.

Programs for Partners in Higher Education

Raabe (this volume) has documented that at the beginning of the 1990s more than half of a national sample of higher education institutions already had or planned to initiate some form of employment assistance for spouses of faculty members. However, the manner in which these programs assist spouses seeking faculty positions is not reported. A survey conducted by Virginia Polytechnic Institute and State University (VPISU) of provosts at sixteen universities found evidence of a variety of practices (Snyder 1990). At all of these institutions, at least some effort was made to place the spouse of a candidate for a faculty position by circulating information about the person and making inquiries about vacancies. Individual cases were generally handled on an ad hoc basis, and the degree of effort made on behalf of the second spouse depended on the urgency with which the first spouse was being recruited. At each of five institutions it was possible to create or transfer a position for the second spouse. At each of six, a temporary position might be funded or temporary "bridge" funds provided until an expected retirement would make funds available to the employing unit. Shared positions had been offered by four institutions. At five of the campuses, the provost's office was routinely involved in such negotiations, but in seven others this was the case only if funding or other assistance was needed. Respondents reported that in addition to these efforts, they had become aware of a number of arrangements made without prior knowledge of the provost's office, including transfer of resources between colleges.

The VPISU findings appear to reflect the current state of affairs, at least at large university campuses. Contacts with fifteen representatives of the Alliance for Undergraduate Education, a group of major research universities that have joined together to enhance the quality of undergraduate education, revealed a similar pattern at these institutions in 1993. Virtually all of them were dealing with this problem in some fashion. When the campus administration is involved, it may provide permanent or temporary funds to assist the hiring unit. In addition, at these large campuses, as in the VPISU survey, many efforts to place spouses take place without any campus-level involvement, implying that surveys addressed only to the campus level are likely to underestimate the frequency of such arrangements. Most campuses still seem to deal with these issues on an ad hoc basis, though a few have written policies or guidelines. However, there is apparent agreement that standards should not be compromised; the second spouse should be judged to have the credentials required of any serious contender for a position in the hiring unit (Gee 1991), and the final decision rests with that unit.

Issues in Programs for Partners

The literature is consistent in raising a set of concerns that would be expected to be particularly important within a department, or perhaps a small campus, employing couples. These include the difficulties of peer evaluation of faculty performance when some of the peers are married to each other; concern that a couple will tend to act as a unit and thus form a "power bloc" or "clique"; worry that problems between the two will be manifested at work and may adversely affect the department; concern that should the pair leave, two vacancies would occur at once (e.g., see Yanik and Yanik 1992; Pingree, Butler, Paisley, and Hawkins 1978; Barbee and Cunningham 1990).

From a broader institutional perspective, four main concerns are often raised. (1) Hired together, will the partners also stay or go together, or might the stronger of the two leave and the weaker remain? (2) Will preferential hiring of partners undercut affirmative action efforts? This issue has two aspects, the first of which is the possible adverse effect on hiring of minority group members. Less frequently raised is the question of whether partner preference will tend to enhance or detract from affirmative action for women. Hiring of well-qualified women on the tenure track could advance affirmative action, but hiring of these individuals into non-tenure-track jobs could, instead, reinstate the treatment of wives that was typical earlier in the century when antinepotism rules were used to prevent their hiring on the tenure track (e.g., see Stephan and Kassis, this volume; Hornig, this volume). (3) From the standpoint of institutional quality, it is important that individuals continue to be treated not just as well as their merit warrants but also that they be treated no better. Will second spouses receive rank or other perquisites that go beyond what they deserve, possibly as a result of pressure brought to bear by a particularly powerful first spouse? (4) With limited resources, opportunistic hiring of any sort will tend to under-cut the implementation of the priorities an institution's faculty have set for growth and contraction of various disciplinary areas. Thus, there is the concern that partner hiring programs may shift the direction of the institution in an undesirable manner.

These four questions about spousal employment programs are inves-tigated through a case study of one active partner accommodation pro-gram. By examining data concerning spousal hiring at one institution, it is possible to explore the extent to which these concerns may or may not be justified. Further multicampus studies will, of course, be neces-sary to answer a number of other questions, such as which characteris-tics of these programs or the institutions in which they are implement-ed help such programs to work relatively well or seem to cause problems.

Campus-Supported Hiring of Academic Couples at UIUC

The University of Illinois at Urbana-Champaign (UIUC) is a large, mid-western research institution located in a small city surrounded by agri-cultural land. Given this location, partner employment has become a significant issue in faculty recruiting and retention, with the result that the campus has provided some form of assistance for second partner hir-ing since the early 1980s. Throughout most of the 1980s, cases were indi-vidually negotiated, resulting in quite a variety of arrangements. The cam-pus administration would typically fund up to one-third of a position for the partner of a candidate in another college if the units hiring the two individuals would provide the remainder. Frequently the campus contri-bution took the form of "nonrecurring," or bridge, funds, to be replaced by the second spouse's unit within a few years; sometimes a "recurring," i.e., permanent, commitment was given. By the late 1980s, these arrange-ments had become increasingly commonplace, and in approximately 1989, the campus administration began to streamline the process by regularly arranging a three-way split, with funds typically provided on a recurring basis and with no requirement that two colleges be involved. Almost all couples hired under these arrangements have been married.

Couples who were hired in this way were identified through exami-nation of the campus budget records, personnel files, and staff directo-ries for fiscal years (FYs) 1978 through 1994. Cases in which a second spouse was hired or had a job upgraded at the same time the campus committed funds for the support of recruiting or retaining the first spouse were considered to be "spousal hires." For the ninety couples identified, information about each partner's background and position at UIUC was collected from personnel records.

To estimate the rate at which UIUC faculty in general have spouses who are also employed by the campus, a 25 percent sample of the FY 1994 staff directory was constructed. The sex of all individuals with faculty titles, both non-tenure-track and tenure-track, was determined, if possible, from the name. There is a clear Western bias in this procedure; the sample is undoubtedly not representative of faculty with other than Western names. The spouse's name is listed in parentheses after the name of the employee, and these data were used to derive the marital status of individuals. The names of the spouses were then checked for their appearance in the directory as employees. Since individuals have the right to request deletion of the spouse's name, this source yields a low estimate of the number of faculty who are actually married. Despite these limitations, these data offer a context for the spousal hire sample.

Finally, it was also possible to investigate the potential effect of these spousal accommodations on the implementation of priorities for expansion or contraction of units. Two faculty committees had recently recommended priorities for reallocation among major units of the campus and among units within its largest college, Liberal Arts and Sciences (LAS). The campus five-year plan for differential budget cuts to be assigned to the colleges and other major campus units (Committee on Budget Priorities 1991) was combined with budget reductions implied by recommendations for changes in staffing levels over five years for departments in the College of Liberal Arts and Sciences (College of Liberal Arts and Sciences Advisory Committee on Financial Policy 1993). To put these two sets of recommendations on a common scale, the LAS departmental recommendations for staff reductions were adjusted to average the campus-imposed "tax" for the college. The one-year budget cut recommended for the college was used as the unit budget reduction for individuals employed outside of LAS; the adjusted LAS reduction for the person's department was the index used for those employed within LAS.

Description of Sample

Of the 999 faculty members listed in the directory whose sex could be inferred from the name (92 percent of the full directory sample), one-quarter were female and three-quarters were male. Of the women, just over half (56 percent) had a spouse's name listed, but of the men, three-quarters (76 percent) did. These figures compare to marriage rates of 62 percent and 82 percent for women and men, respectively, in Astin and Milem's (this volume) national sample of faculty, suggesting both that UIUC is fairly typical and that the downward bias involved in this particular estimate of marital status may be in the neighborhood of about 6 percent. As shown in table 11-1, 32 percent of faculty women have a spouse employed at UIUC, compared with 18 percent of the men; for those who are married, these percentages are 57 percent for women and 24 percent for men.

The data in table 11-2 indicate the number of married faculty members with tenure-track and non-tenure-track titles and how many of the male and female faculty members have spouses in tenure-track, non-tenure-track, or other positions at UIUC. It should be noted that most but not all faculty members with tenure-stream titles of assistant, associate, or full professor are tenured or on the tenure track; some have

TABLE 11-1. Marriage and Spousal Employment Rates of Faculty

	Total		Spouse Listed		Spouse Employed at UIUC		
	Number	Percent	Number	Percent of Total	Number	Percent of Total	Percent of Married Faculty
Women	249	24.9	140	56.2	80	32.1	57.1
Men	750	75.1	566	75.5	135	18.0	23.9
	999	100.0	706	70.7	215	21.5	30.5

TABLE 11-2. Job Titles of Faculty Spouses

	Spouse						
	Tenure Track		Non-Tenure Track		Other		Total
Faculty Member	Number	Percent	Number	Percent	Number	Percent	Number
Tenure track[a]							
Women	37	72.5	9	17.6	5	9.8	51
Men	26	23.9	17	15.6	66	60.6	109
Non-tenure track							
Women	13	44.8	4	13.8	12	41.4	29
Men	6	23.1	6	23.1	14	53.8	26

a. Chi square = 41.18; $p < .001$.

visiting appointments and others have positions of less than the 51 percent of full time required for the tenure track. For non-tenure-track
faculty, there is no significant difference between men and women in the
types of jobs that their spouses hold on campus, but for those with tenure-stream titles, the sex difference is significant. It seems that women
with tenure-stream titles are more likely than their male colleagues to
have spouses in the same kind of position (73 percent versus 24 percent),
while males with tenure-track titles are more likely than women to have
spouses in non-faculty ("other") positions (61 percent vs. 10 percent).
Taken together, the data in tables 11-1 and 11-2 suggest that quite a few
UIUC faculty spouses are also employed on campus and that married
female faculty members with the rank of at least assistant professor are
quite likely to have husbands in similar positions. While accommodation of the academic spouses of male recruits may be one way to increase
the number of faculty women, accommodation of the academic spouses
of female recruits will very often be necessary to attract and retain them.
In practice, affirmative action (or even equal opportunity) for women
will often involve placing a male spouse as well. Such accommodations
will be especially critical, it would seem, at campuses that, like this one,
are situated in small communities with few other academic institutions
within commuting distance.

Of the ninety first spouses whose partners were accommodated, sixty-nine (77 percent) were men. This represents a somewhat lower rate
of male second spouses, at 23 percent, than in Stafford and Spanier's
(1990) report that about one-third of the clients of the Oregon State
University Family Employment Program were male. However, the proportion of female first spouses has increased somewhat over time; in the
most recent five-year period, the percentage of spousal hires in which
the first spouse is female has been close to one-third, at 29 percent. In
addition, there has been a significant increase in the number of campus-assisted spousal hires over fifteen years. In the first five years of the
program (FY 1980 through FY 1984) only nine couples (10 percent) were
accommodated; twenty-nine (32 percent) were accommodated between
FY 1985 and FY 1989; and more than half of the ninety couples (52, or
58 percent) were accommodated between FY 1990 and FY 1994 (chi
square = 30.86, $p < .01$).

Spousal accommodations have involved retention as well as recruiting. To differentiate between the two types of accommodations, recruitment was considered to be the issue if the first spouse had been em-

ployed no more than three years at UIUC at the time that the spouse was either hired or received some upgrade in status in which campus funds were involved. On the other hand, if the first spouse had been employed at UIUC for more than three years when such action was taken, retention was assumed to be the issue. The three-year "grace period" was arrived at in consultation with Affirmative Action Office staff members, who indicated that it is not uncommon in recruitment cases for the placement of the second spouse to take a year, and that it sometimes takes an additional year or two beyond that.

Table 11-3 presents the number of first spouses recruited or retained and for each of these groups gives the number of second spouses who were hired or whose job was upgraded. Position upgrades involved changes such as movement from a non-tenure-track title to assistant professor, movement from temporary to regular status or an increase in the percentage of time employed. In most cases that involved recruiting the first spouse, the accommodation consisted of the initial hire of the second spouse (84 percent); but in slightly more than half of the cases that involved retention of the first spouse (55 percent), the second spouse's position was upgraded.

Additional analysis indicated that of the 61 recruited couples, 38 (62 percent) of the second spouses were hired the same year as the first. Of the 29 couples in which retention was the issue, most first partners were male (90 percent) and associate or full professors (83 percent). These first partners had been employed at UIUC an average of almost 12 years (11.8) at the time of the hiring or upgrading of the positions of their partners. The second spouse had been employed just under five years (4.6), on the average, at the time of the accommodation; indeed, some of these

TABLE 11-3. Spousal Accommodation Related to Recruitment or Retention of First Spouse

Second Spouse Accommodation	First Spouse				Total	
	Recruit		Retain			
	Number	Percent	Number	Percent	Number	Percent
Hire	51	83.6	13	44.8	64	71.1
Upgrade	10	16.4	16	55.1	26	28.9
	61	100.0	29	99.9	90	100.0

Note: Chi square = 14.39; $p < .001$.

people had coped with part-time, visiting, or otherwise less than ideal status for a number of years.

Table 11-4 provides information concerning the highest degree of each partner at the time of the campus recruitment or retention action. It indicates that, as would be expected, the average educational level of first spouses was significantly higher than that of second spouses. Nine of ten first spouses had or nearly had doctoral degrees at the time of recruitment or retention, while only about three-quarters of the second spouses had achieved this educational level. Thus, it appears that not all of the second spouses possessed the educational credentials required for most faculty positions. Even so, the data in table 11-5 shows that only 62 percent of second spouses had titles of at least assistant professor although 78 percent had a doctorate or had nearly completed one, suggesting the possibility of underemployment of

TABLE 11-4. Highest Degree Earned

	First Spouse		Second Spouse		Total	
	Number	Percent	Number	Percent	Number	Percent
Doctoral (4)	77	85.6	63	70.8	140	78.2
Almost Ph.D. (3)	4	4.5	6	6.7	10	5.6
Master's (2)	6	6.7	15	16.9	21	11.7
Baccalaureate or none (1 or 0)	3	3.4	5	5.6	8	4.5
	90	100.0	89	100.0	179	100.0
Mean	3.72		3.42**			

Note: For one individual, information about the highest degree was not available.
** $p < .01$.

TABLE 11-5. Jobs at Time of Recruitment/Retention

	First Spouse		Second Spouse		Total	
	Number	Percent	Number	Percent	Number	Percent
Full professor	34	37.8	3	3.3	37	20.6
Associate professor	21	23.3	9	10.0	30	16.7
Assistant professor	29	32.2	44	48.9	73	40.6
Non-tenure-track faculty	1	1.1	14	15.6	15	8.3
Nonfaculty academic	5	5.6	20	22.2	25	13.9
	90	100.0	90	100.0	180	100.1

some of these faculty spouses. This question is examined later in the chapter.

The data in table 11-6 indicate that most of these 180 individuals were hired in the Colleges of Liberal Arts and Sciences (LAS), Engineering, Education, and Agriculture, or in administrative units rather than colleges. The table also provides the number of first and second spouses hired by each major unit, the proportion of the total number of spouses employed by a unit who were the first spouse, each unit's percentage of the campus budget base, and the percentage of the ninety first spouses and ninety second spouses hired by each unit. Not shown in the table is the fact that both members of 31 couples (34 percent) were employed

TABLE 11-6. Colleges Employing Spouses

College	Number				Percent of Campus Total		
	First Spouse	Second Spouse	Total	Ratio of First to Total	Budget	First Spouses	Second Spouses
Liberal Arts and Sciences	30	25	55	0.55	20.2	33.3	27.8
Engineering	22	5	27	0.81	14.4	24.4	5.6
Education	7	13	20	0.35	2.7	7.8	14.4
Administrative units	3	12	15	0.20	20.6	3.3	13.3
Agriculture	4	8	12	0.33	12.9	4.4	8.9
Commerce and Business Administration	3	5	8	0.37	4.4	3.3	5.6
Veterinary Medicine	3	3	6	0.50	3.9	3.3	3.3
Law	5	1	6	0.83	1.4	5.6	1.1
Graduate	3	3	6	0.50	0.9	3.3	3.3
Applied Life Studies	2	4	6	0.33	1.6	2.2	4.4
Library and Information Science	1	3	4	0.25	0.3	1.1	3.3
Medicine[a]	1	2	3	0.33	—	1.1	2.2
Fine and Applied Arts	2	1	3	0.67	5.7	2.2	1.1
Aviation	1	2	3	0.33	0.7	1.1	2.2
University Library	1	1	2	0.50	3.7	1.1	1.1
Labor and Industrial Relations	1	1	2	0.50	0.5	1.1	1.1
Social Work	0	1	1	0.00	0.4	0.0	1.1
Communications	1	0	1	1.00	1.1	1.1	0.0

a. The College of Medicine is funded through the University of Illinois at Chicago.

in the same college; however, in only 12 of them (13 percent) were both partners employed in the same department. This is fewer than one might expect (e.g., Hornig, this volume) and may indicate that it is harder to place same-discipline spouses than those in different disciplines. The sample, after all, contains only those couples who were successfully placed; failed efforts to place second spouses are not reflected in it.

Patterns of hiring first and second spouses differ among the units doing the bulk of it, with Engineering hiring mainly first spouses, hires in LAS being split about evenly, Agriculture, Commerce and Business Administration (CBA), and Education employing more second than first spouses, and administrative units hiring primarily second spouses. This pattern is generally consistent with the predominance of men among first spouses, the different distribution of men and women with Ph.D.'s by discipline (e.g., see Stephan and Kassis, this volume), and the number of second spouses without doctorates, who would therefore be more likely candidates for employment in administrative units than for faculty positions. To some extent, the distribution of spouses in the various colleges probably also reflects differences among academic fields in the percentages of male and female faculty members with academic partners, as reported by Astin and Milem (this volume). They found, for example, that the percentages of faculty with academic partners were relatively high in education, at 45 percent for men and 40 percent for women. This could help explain its rather large share of both first and second spouses. That is, the College of Education accounts for only about 3 percent of the campus budget but hired 8 percent of the first and 14 percent of the second spouses. At the same time, fewer of the men in the relatively male dominated fields of agriculture, engineering, and business reported academic partners, at 26 percent, 21 percent, and 27 percent, respectively. This could account for the fact that the College of Agriculture hired only 4 percent of the first spouses compared with its 13 percent of the campus budget. On the other hand, Engineering and CBA are similar in their percentages of faculty expected to have academic spouses and also in both needing to contend with a highly competitive job market, but nonetheless are quite different in their spousal hiring patterns. While the College of Engineering had a large number of the first spouses compared with its share of the campus budget (at 24 percent versus 14 percent), CBA employed slightly fewer first spouses than one might expect based on its budget. It seems that campus units have varied quite a bit in the degree to which they have aggressively pursued job opportunities for the spouses of faculty members they sought to recruit or retain.

The data in table 11-7 shed some additional light on units' hiring practices by revealing that a mere 12 of the more than 85 departments across campus account for more than one-third (37 percent) of the 180 total positions held by those involved in spousal accommodations. Coupled with table 11-6, this again suggests considerable variability in departmental practices. It seems likely that knowledge of the possibilities offered by campus assistance in spousal hiring is not uniform. The fact that a waiver of the search requirement is possible for the second spouse has been written into the campus affirmative action policy, but there have been no written guidelines concerning eligibility for the program. There is some risk that guidelines, once promulgated, can turn what was designed to be a selectively applied opportunity into an entitlement program. Nonetheless, the variable participation of departments in the program suggests that written policy statements or guidelines, which do not seem to exist on most campuses, would be of real value in the fair administration of such programs.

TABLE 11-7. Number of Spouses in Departments Employing Four or More Spouses

College/Disciplinary Area	Number of Departments	First Spouse	Second Spouse	Total Spouses
Liberal Arts and Sciences				
Social/behavioral sciences	2	12	3	15
Humanities	2	4	6	10
Commerce and Business				
Administration	1	1	3	4
Engineering	2	9	2	11
Education	2	4	9	13
Agriculture	1	2	2	4
Professional (Law and				
Veterinary Medicine)	2	7	3	10
	12	39	28	67

Retention

The outcomes of these accommodations cannot be tracked very satisfactorily because too many of the couples involved were hired within the last five years of the study to allow investigation of the long-term success of these individuals. It is possible, however, to assess the extent to which the campus has retained those involved, and of those not retained, the number whose jobs expired or who were terminated as opposed to resigning. Tables 11-8 and 11-9 present these data for the 74 couples hired during or before FY 1993, whose employment status as of FY 1994 would represent at least a one-year outcome.

The data in table 11-8 indicate that 62 (84 percent) of the first spouses were still employed in FY 1994, compared with a significantly lower 54 (73 percent) of the second spouses. In some cases, the second spouse was no longer employed but the first spouse had stayed at the campus nonetheless. In no case had the first spouse left but the second spouse remained. The possibility that the first, and presumably stronger, of the two will leave and the second, presumably weaker, will stay is a frequently raised concern. These data should lay that fear to rest. Such an event will undoubtedly happen someday at UIUC, and has probably already happened somewhere. However, it does not appear to be the sort of high frequency event upon which institutional employment policy might legitimately be based.

TABLE 11-8. Retention, FY 1994

	Second Spouse		
First Spouse	Employed at UIUC	Left UIUC Employ	Total
Employed at UIUC	54	8	62
Left UIUC employ	0	12	12
	54	20	74

Note: Chi square for dependent proportions = 8.00; $p < .01$.

TABLE 11-9. Outcomes after One or More Years, as of FY 1994

	First Spouse		Second Spouse		Total	
	Number	Percent	Number	Percent	Number	Percent
Still employed	62	83.8	54	73.0	116	78.4
Resigned	9	12.2	9	12.2	18	12.2
Job expired	1	1.4	9	12.2	10	6.8
Terminated	2	2.7	2	2.7	4	2.7
	74	100.1	74	100.1	148	100.1

As shown in table 11-9, the same number of first and second spouses resigned (9, or 12 percent) or were terminated (2, or 3 percent), but the number for whom the job expired differs. This partially explains why more first than second spouses were still employed on campus in FY 1994. From the point of view of the eleven second spouses whose jobs expired or who were terminated, these are dismal outcomes. However, it was possible for the campus to retain the first spouse in more than half (55 percent) of these cases. Clearly, these negative outcomes for the second spouse frequently did not cause the first spouse to leave. Put another way, if spouse two is terminated or the job simply expires, spouse one does tend to leave, but the correlation is only a modest .33 and accounts for only 11 percent of the variance. A further look at these data indicated that all of the first spouses who left the campus had been recruited rather than retained; that is, the efforts to retain faculty through spousal accommodation were all successful. Of course, it is not known how many of these individuals who were threatening to leave would actually have done so if an acceptable accommodation had not been offered to their spouses. Ideally, one would compare these retention figures to those for faculty not involved in spousal accommodation, but such data were not available.

As noted earlier, not enough time has elapsed to allow investigation of the long-term retention and success of these individuals. Anecdotal evidence based on couples who have been on campus for a number of years suggests that in some of these cases, the second spouse has turned out to be at least as great an asset as the first. It would be worthwhile to track the relatively large number of couples hired in the last few years at least to the point of the tenure decision in order to gauge their success.

Effects on Affirmative Action

Minority Faculty

The first question to be addressed concerning the effect of spousal hiring on an institution's affirmative action program concerns the effect on hiring members of underrepresented minority groups, especially African Americans and Hispanics. Table 11-10 provides the racial and ethnic backgrounds of the 90 couples as well as the racial and ethnic distribution of FY 1994 tenure-track and non-tenure-track full-time equivalent (FTE) faculty members (Office of Affirmative Action 1993). Of the 180 individuals in the spousal sample, 160 (89 percent) were white or Asian American, while 20 (11 percent) were African American or Hispanic. The differences between the spousal hiring sample and the faculty at large are small, but indicate that the percentage of full-time equivalent faculty who were African American or Hispanic was somewhat lower than the percentage of individuals in the spousal sample. Because of their very small numbers on campus, Native American faculty were not included in this analysis.

The data in table 11-10 allow only a rough comparison given that some members of the spousal sample are not faculty members (as are all members of the comparison group), that only headcounts are available for the spouses and full-time equivalents for the comparison group, and that not all members of the spousal sample were still employed at UIUC during FY 1994. To provide a clean comparison that can directly address the effects of spousal hiring on the hiring of minority faculty members, table 11-11 presents the number of spouses hired into tenured or tenure-track positions during the period from FY 1983 to FY 1994 and the number of all other such hires (Office of

TABLE 11-10. Racial/Ethnic Background

	Fall 1993 Percent FTE Faculty	First Spouse Number	First Spouse Percent	Second Spouse Number	Second Spouse Percent	Total Number	Total Percent
White	84.0	74	82.2	77	85.6	151	83.9
Black	2.3	4	4.4	4	4.4	8	4.4
Hispanic	2.2	8	8.9	4	4.4	12	6.7
Asian	11.1	4	4.4	5	5.6	9	5.0
Native American	0.4	0	0.0	0	0.0	0	0.0
	100.0	90	99.9	90	100.0	180	100.0

TABLE 11-11. Racial/Ethnic Background of Tenured and Tenure-Track Faculty Hires, FY 1983–94

	Nonspousal Hires Number	Nonspousal Hires Percent	First Spouse Number	First Spouse Percent	Second Spouse Number	Second Spouse Percent	Total of Spouses Number	Total of Spouses Percent
White	873	82.4	52	81.3	43	93.5	95	86.4
Black	29	2.7	4	6.3	2	4.3	6	5.5
Hispanic	37	3.5	6	9.4	0	0.0	6	5.5
Asian	121	11.4	2	3.1	1	2.2	3	2.7
	1,060	100.0	64	100.1	46	100.0	110	100.1

Note: Chi square = 8.46; $p < .01$ for proportion of first spouses versus nonspousal hires who are black or Hispanic.

Affirmative Action 1994). As shown there, of the tenure-stream faculty hired in these years without campus-assisted spousal accommodation, 6 percent were African American or Hispanic. Of the first spouses hired with such assistance during these years, however, 16 percent were members of these groups. This difference is statistically significant. While only 4 percent of second spouses hired into tenure-stream positions were Hispanic or African American, 11.0 percent of all the spouses so hired were members of these groups.

It appears that spousal hiring has not decreased opportunities for African-American or Hispanic faculty. On the contrary, that 16 percent of the first spouses were members of these groups suggests that facilitation of spousal hiring is important to the success of efforts to recruit and retain minority faculty members. These findings are consistent with the evidence presented in Perkins's (this volume) historical review of the relatively large number of African-American academic couples and also with Astin and Milem's (this volume) data indicating that African-American, Puerto Rican–American (though not Mexican-American/ Chicano), and Native American male faculty members are somewhat more likely to have academic partners than are white or Asian-American academic men. These data should dispel the common fear that spousal hiring is likely to detract from the recruitment of minority faculty. There is simply no basis for the belief that academic couples are particularly likely to be white or, for that matter, Asian American. On the contrary, there is every reason to believe that recruitment and retention of underrepresented minority faculty members will often involve the suitable placement of their partners.

Female Faculty

The other affirmative action issue that needs to be addressed is the effect of spousal hiring programs on affirmative, or at least equal, treatment of women. As noted earlier, such programs can help recruit women, but the question remains whether the jobs of the second spouses, many of whom are female, are generally consistent with their qualifications. Data concerning the quality of the jobs of first and second spouses are summarized in table 11-12. Assuming that most employees seek full-time work, the extent to which the appointments are less than full time is one measure of job quality. Similarly, the number of units employing first and second spouses are compared on the assumption that a single appointment is generally preferable to joint appointments that involve split responsibilities, espe-

TABLE 11-12. Quality of Job at Time of Recruitment/
Retention

	First Spouse	Second Spouse
Percent of jobs appropriate to degree	98.9	84.3***
Percent of jobs related to prior experience	92.1	77.5**
Mean percentage appointment	100.0	92.2***
Mean number of employing units	1.13	1.14

** $p < .01$.
*** $p < .001$.

cially during the probationary period when clear expectations and consistent mentoring are important to success.

Two additional indices of the appropriateness of the job to the individual's qualifications were created, one based on highest degree and the
other based on the person's work experience prior to the first UIUC job.
For individuals with doctoral degrees or master's degrees in library science, the terminal degree held by many faculty in the university library,
faculty positions with the rank of at least assistant professor were considered appropriate. A few nonfaculty positions, such as clinical coun-
selor or legal counsel, were considered appropriate for those with doctoral or professional degrees if the job involved a form of professional
practice for which the individual's educational program had provided
preparation. For those who had not quite completed doctoral study,
lower-level faculty titles were also considered appropriate, though teaching assistant was not. For people with various other master's and baccalaureate degrees, any job was considered suitable to the degree. For
those with prior experience as a teaching assistant, research assistant, or
faculty member, the UIUC position was considered to be related to that
experience only if it was an academic position of at least the same rank.
For other kinds of positions, the UIUC job was considered related to the
prior job if the titles were similar, e.g., librarian, museum professional.

Table 11-12 provides the average scores on these four indices of the
quality of the UIUC job for both sets of spouses. There were significant
differences between the percentage of first and second spouses with jobs
that were appropriate to their degrees and also related to their prior
experience. The average percentage of the appointments was also lower for second than for first spouses. Only the mean number of units
employing the individuals was equivalent for the two groups.

Table 11-13 displays a cross-tabulation of degree by rank of job held by the pairs of spouses at the time of the spousal accommodation. Both the absolute numbers and the differences between the first and second spouses are small for those holding less than a doctoral level degree. Of those with doctorates, it appears that a sizable majority (78 percent) of second spouses have been accommodated in jobs with the rank of at least assistant professor. However, the remaining 22 percent are evenly split between nonfaculty academic jobs and non-tenure-track faculty positions. In contrast, all but one of the first spouses with doctorates had the rank of at least assistant professor (99 percent).

It is not surprising to discover that individuals the campus has worked to recruit or retain have more desirable jobs, on average, than do those who were seeking work instead of being sought for it. To assess the appropriateness of the ranks of second spouses required a comparison of the ranks at which they and similarly qualified first spouses were hired by UIUC. This comparison was complicated by the fact that first spouses were often hired in an earlier period than second spouses, and standards have shifted over time; in addition, second but not first spouses frequently held nonfaculty positions, for which hiring criteria are often quite different. As a result, the rank of the first job was compared for the sixty-seven first and forty-two second spouses initially hired between FY 1980 and FY 1994 as faculty members with doctorates at least nearly completed. Prior experience and academic degree were used to predict the initial academic rank of these first spouses. As the data in table 11-14 indicate, both prior experience and degree are positively related to the

TABLE 11-13. Degree by Rank of Spouses

Degree	Nonfaculty Number	Nonfaculty Percent	Non-Tenure Track Number	Non-Tenure Track Percent	Tenure Track Number	Tenure Track Percent
Nondoctoral						
First Spouse	4	44.4	0	0.0	5	55.6
Second Spouse	12	60.0	4	20.0	4	20.0
Nearly doctoral						
First Spouse	0	0.0	1	25.0	3	75.0
Second Spouse	0	0.0	3	50.0	3	50.0
Doctoral						
First Spouse	1	1.3	0	0.0	76	98.7
Second Spouse	7	11.1	7	11.1	49	77.8

TABLE 11-14. Prediction of First Spouse Title

	b	Beta
Experience	0.34	0.64***
Degree	0.88	0.16
Constant	−1.32	
R = 0.70		

Note: Data are for faculty hired since FY 1980; $N = 67$.
*** $p < .001$.

level of the job held, and the multiple correlation of 0.70 accounts for about half of the variance. The regression equation for these first spouses was then used to predict the initial academic rank of second spouses with doctorates at least nearly completed who were hired through an accommodation. The results indicate that the actual mean position of these second spouses was assistant professor. Their predicted mean position, based on prior experience and degree, using the relationships among these variables for the first spouse group, was four-tenths of a rank higher. Thus, the second spouses first hired through special accommodations were initially hired at slightly lower ranks than similarly qualified first spouses.

For several reasons, these data do not permit a firm conclusion about whether or not these second spouse jobs are at a reasonable level given the individuals' qualifications: (1) although some information is available, a great deal is not known about the qualifications of the individuals involved, e.g., strength of references, quality of doctoral institutions, productivity levels, and so forth; (2) it is conceivable that some of the second spouses preferred non-tenure-track positions, possibly to permit part-time work or to allow a concentration on teaching without the necessity of developing a productive research program; and (3) the only comparison group available, the first spouses, sets a very high standard in that they are individuals who were especially highly desired by this institution. Two conclusions can, however, be drawn. To date, second spouse accommodations have succeeded in placing most of those with faculty qualifications into positions with at least the rank of assistant professor. It is certainly clear that these positions do not constitute the sort of second or "faculty wives" track that was quite common in the days of antinepotism regulations. At the same time, a minority of these spouses have accepted other types of positions, and the average initial rank of those hired as faculty is lower than that of similarly qualified first spouses. These facts underscore Shoben's (this volume) advice that institutions need to monitor these arrangements closely and document the reasons that particular arrangements are made. It seems advisable that the affirmative action office assume this responsibility to assure that spousal hiring supports and is not at odds with the institution's affirmative action program for female staff.

A related question involves the extent to which male and female second spouses receive similar treatment. Table 11-15 reports the means of male and female second spouses on a host of variables related to their backgrounds and to their employment at UIUC. Background variables again include their highest degrees and experience. Factors associated with their UIUC employment include whether the accommodation related to recruitment or retention of their spouses; whether the accommodation involved hiring them or upgrading their positions; for facul-

TABLE 11-15. Backgrounds and Jobs of Second Spouses by Sex

	Female Mean	Male Mean
Degree	3.46	3.29
4 = doctoral; 3 = ABD;		
2 = master's; 1 = bachelor's		
Recruit (= 1) or retain (= 2)	1.38	1.14*
Hire (= 1) or upgrade (= 2)	1.28	1.33
Rank (faculty only)	2.91	3.35*
5 = full; 4 = associate;		
3 = assistant; 2 = non-tenure track		
Experience	2.97	3.24
7 = full; 6 = associate;		
5 = assistant; 4 = non-tenure track		
3 = postdoctoral; 2 = T.A./R.A.		
1 = other		
Job related to experience	0.735	0.905
1 = yes; 0 = no		
Job appropriate to degree	0.824	0.905
1 = yes; 0 = no		
Number of employing units	1.14	1.14
Percent time	92.41	91.67
Ever appointed "visiting"	0.493	0.667
1 = yes; 0 = no		

* $p < .05$.

ty members only, the rank of their positions; whether their positions were commensurate with their degrees or related to their experience; the number of units employing them and the percentage of their appointments at the time of the accommodations; and whether they were ever on visiting status. For all variables except the rank of the individual, data for the full group of second spouses were examined; nonfaculty were excluded from the analysis of the rank of the position in order to create an ordinal scale. (The ranks of nonfaculty positions vary from very high to very low, e.g., from unit director to staff assistant; as a result they were excluded.)

Significant differences between male and female second spouses were very few. Women more than men were accommodated in order to retain rather than to recruit their spouses, and men tended to hold higher faculty ranks than did women. None of the other differences were significant. While the higher average rank of male faculty members suggests the real possibility that among second spouses faculty women may tend to be underemployed more than men, this is just one of the ways that the second spouse's job might be inappropriate. Rank might be lower than the individual's background warrants; if this were more often true of female than of male second spouses, it would suggest an affirmative action problem. On the other hand, the individual's rank might be higher than his or her characteristics suggest, having perhaps been unduly or spuriously influenced by actions of a particularly powerful first spouse. These two possibilities were investigated in a single analysis in which second spouse's sex and background characteristics, as well as indices likely to be related to the first spouse's power, were all used as potential predictors of the rank of the second spouse's faculty position. The results are described in the next section.

Influence of First Spouse on Treatment of Second Spouse

Factors that might be related to the potential influence of the first spouse on the second spouse's terms of employment would seem to involve the esteem of the first spouse, whether she or he was already established on campus, the relative status on campus of his or her employing unit, and whether or not the two spouses were employed in the same unit. The assumptions here are (1) that beyond the personal status of the first spouse, time on campus is needed to build a power base; (2) that it will be easier for a spouse in a relatively well-regarded unit than one in a relatively low-status unit to exert influence on deans, campus administrators, or on another unit; and (3) that while spouses probably experience both advantages and disadvantages to being in the same unit, it may be harder to turn down the requests of the first spouse regarding the second if they are both in the same unit. Indices of personal status of the first spouse include degree, academic rank, and whether the job was related to prior experience; whether or not he or she was established on campus is indexed by whether the accommodation involved retention or recruitment; the relative status of the unit is indicated by the percentage budget cut assigned to it; an indicator that the spouses were both in the same department was used to investigate the effect of this factor; finally the academic rank of the first spouse times the "same department" indicator allowed for the possibility that seniority and esteem may exert more potent effects on the first spouse's home turf than elsewhere on campus.

Characteristics of the second spouse that could reasonably be related to his or her rank at the time of the accommodation are, again, highest degree, prior experience, and whether the accommodation involved an initial hire or an upgrade. It also seemed worth investigating whether the relative position of the second spouse's unit in the campus priority hierarchy might affect the rank at which she or he was hired; units subjected to higher budget reductions might feel the need to offer lower ranks.

A stepwise multiple regression procedure in which all of the variables listed above were available as predictors revealed that only two variables significantly predicted the academic rank of the second faculty spouse at the time of the accommodation: the individual's prior experience and whether the rank resulted from an upgrade or an initial hire ($R = 0.60$) (see table 11-16). The sex of the second spouse did not predict his or her rank, nor did any of the variables used as potential indicators of spousal influence. Thus, the evidence available supports the belief that the jobs into which second spouses are placed are not related to the sex of either spouse. For those couples for whom an accommodation is provided, it is neither the case that female first spouses are less able to command appropriate treatment for their partners nor that female second spouses tend to be underemployed by the hiring units. In addition, the relative standing of the first spouse in terms of academic rank and whether the person is well enough established to be able to command a retention package does not seem to affect the level at which the sec-

TABLE 11-16. Prediction of Second Spouse
Title

Predictor	b	Beta
Experience	0.25	0.61***
Hire (= 1); upgrade (= 2)	0.46	0.31***
Constant	1.60	
R = 0.60		

Note: Faculty only; $N = 67$.
*** $p < .001$.

ond faculty spouse is placed. Finally, the size of the budget reduction facing the employing unit did not affect the rank of the position offered the second spouse. While this is good news from the point of view of fair employment practices, this last finding also suggests that spousal hiring will work to undercut the implementation of campus priorities for differential growth and contraction of academic units, a possibility that is examined in the next section.

Effect of Spousal Hiring on Implementation of Campus Priorities

Table 11-17 displays the one-year percentage budget cut for units employing spouses in the sample, approximated through review of the priorities for differential budget reductions recommended by UIUC campus-wide and College of LAS faculty committees. The average budget cut of the units in which the first spouses were employed was .58, while the

TABLE 11-17. Percentage Budget Reduction of Units Employing Spouses

Percent Cut	First Spouse		Second Spouse		Total	
	Number	Percent	Number	Percent	Number	Percent
1.60–2.00	2	2.2	11	12.2	13	7.2
1.20–1.59	7	7.8	14	15.6	21	11.7
0.80–1.19	17	18.9	28	31.1	45	25.0
0.40–0.79	44	48.9	24	26.7	68	37.8
0.00–0.39	20	22.2	13	14.4	33	18.3
	90	100.0	90	100.0	180	100.0
Mean	0.58		0.86***			

*** $p < .001$.

units of second spouses averaged .86, compared with a campus average of .83. While the units of second spouses were relatively low in the priority hierarchy compared with those of first spouses, as indicated by a significantly higher average budget reduction, they were about average for the campus. That the departments and colleges employing first spouses were relatively high on the campus priority list for preservation would be expected; units assigned small reductions would be the ones most likely to be in a position to recruit new faculty and also to be able to afford the contribution of one-third of a position to the unit employing the second spouse.

Since priorities should differ from campus to campus in a diversified higher education system such as ours in the United States, the details of these UIUC findings would probably not be replicated in similar studies conducted at other higher educational institutions. However, it seems likely that the general picture would be similar, at least at other large research institutions, because a number of the factors involved on this campus are typical throughout higher education. In the first place, there is a "pecking order" of the disciplines within academe that tends to be rather similar from campus to campus, with the older, more theoretical, and more quantitative disciplines tending to be held in greater esteem than newer, more applied, and less quantitative areas. Beyond that, higher education institutions share a labor market in which practitioners of the various disciplines are in greater or lesser demand. Finally, there are differences among disciplines in the proportion of faculty who have academic partners (Astin and Milem, this volume). These common factors within higher education suggest that the main finding is likely to be generalizable. In short, one would expect that on other campuses as well as at UIUC, the recruited or retained spouses will tend to be in relatively high priority units, while their partners will tend to be accommodated in units of lower priority.

One must conclude, then, that spousal hiring will indeed tend to undermine the implementation of priorities that faculties set for the expansion and contraction of the disciplines at their campuses. At the same time, of course, the job market is such that much of the recruiting and retention needed to implement these very priorities by maintaining or building strength in high priority units will not be possible without adequate accommodation of partners. That second spouses are employed in units that are just about at the average for the campus at least suggests that the potential negative effects of these accommodations need not be severe. However, this is a legitimate concern about spousal hiring programs that needs to be addressed. One way to limit this negative effect would be to return the initial investment of the campus and the first spouse's unit to those units if and when the second spouse leaves.

Summary and Conclusions

These data from a campus with an active spousal hiring program confirm that the faculty couple has become an increasingly common phenomenon at predominantly white institutions in recent years. Among married faculty members, the likelihood that the spouse will be an academic as well is higher for women than it is for men. Thus, the problem of spousal accommodation is likely to be more complicated for female recruits than for males, for whose wives a somewhat broader range of employment options may be appropriate.

While the proportion of female faculty is growing, these data suggest that the spouse initially recruited, or for whom a retention package is developed, is still much more often male. For programs that do not extend to retention, the proportion of female first spouses would be expected to be higher, since women are still better represented among junior faculty than in the senior ranks. Of course, any study of couples actually hired or retained through spousal accommodations relates information about only those efforts that are successful. Anecdotal information suggests that men have been harder to place than women, which may be one reason so many of these second spouses are women. A study comparing both the efforts made to accommodate male and female partners and also the success of those efforts would be useful, since the proportion of women among new Ph.D. recipients suggests that the need for spousal accommodations, including accommodation of men, can only grow.

Academic units differ quite a bit in their involvement in spousal accommodations, and where involved, in their propensity to hire the first, the second, or both spouses. Overall, few of these ninety couples are employed in the same unit, perhaps indicating that it is harder to arrange dual employment within the same unit than in different units. Differences among units in their employment of first and second spouses seem to be related in understandable ways to the differences among the disciplines in the proportion of Ph.D.'s earned by women, the propensity of married academics in the field to have academic partners, and the extent of competition for people in the discipline. Beyond this, however, there are differences that suggest that some departments take more advantage of spousal hiring opportunities than do others. Relatively few higher education institutions have developed guidelines or policy statements for these programs, but these seem to be needed to help assure fair administration of efforts to assist in spousal accommodations.

The long-term success of spousal employment accommodations could not be fully investigated with the current sample because too many of these couples had been hired quite recently. There is a real need for further investigation. It would be particularly desirable to follow a group of spousal hires at least to the point of tenure to evaluate how well these accommodations worked out, both from the point of view of the institution and of the individuals.

A major finding of this study is that the most common concerns about the campuswide effects of spousal hiring are generally unwarranted. First, of the ninety couples accommodated over fifteen years, in no case did the first partner leave and the second remain. The fear that the campus might be left with only the second partner is apparently not based on the frequent occurrence of this phenomenon. In addition, first partners involved in these accommodations were more often members of underrepresented minority groups than were faculty at large who were hired during the same time period. It seems that accommodations of spouses need not undermine affirmative hiring programs. In fact, these data confirm that the ability to accommodate a spouse is at least as important, and probably even more so, in recruiting members of these minority groups as in recruiting other faculty members.

A third, less frequently voiced fear is that these programs might develop a second, lower, mostly "wives" track, as in the days of antinepotism rules. Evidence from this sample does not support this concern either. However, for second spouses who are faculty members the average level of their jobs is lower than that of first spouses, even when differences in credentials are accounted for to the extent possible. Therefore, it is important that institutions monitor these arrangements both, as Shoben (this volume) suggests, to defend against potential legal action and also to assure that they support affirmative action programs.

Finally, sex of the second partner does not seem to affect the level of the placement, nor apparently does the academic rank of the first partner. In this program, at least, the second partner's credentials appear to be the primary consideration in the details of the accommodation, and there seems to be neither discrimination against a first or second spouse on the basis of sex, nor a tendency to elevate the second spouse based on the "clout" of the first.

While these findings may not accurately describe the situation on small campuses, it is likely that they correctly reflect the status quo on large campuses, where several different units are involved in the hiring or retention of the two individuals.

There is, however, one commonly expressed fear about spousal accommodations that is confirmed as valid by this study: the units into which the second spouses were hired tend to be of lower standing in the campus priority list for preservation than are the units employing the first spouses, which is a matter of concern in an era of major, repetitive budget cuts. This difference seems likely to exist at other campuses as well, given similarities in the academic "pecking order" and the common reliance on a labor market that varies by discipline in competitive level, the percentage of women, and the prevalence of academic spouses. This is a serious problem with which higher education institutions will need to contend. Even though faculty members from widely different disciplines are rarely in full agreement concerning the priorities that should be set at a particular campus, it is nonetheless generally believed that maintaining excellence in an era of declining resources requires planned, rather than across-the-board, contraction and expansion. Recovery of the funds supplied to the unit employing the second spouse when that spouse leaves could at least prevent the campus priorities from becoming permanently distorted by spousal hiring. At the same time it must be recognized that for the second spouse's job to be a real one, worthy of recruiting or retaining the couple on campus, the unit employing the second spouse needs to integrate him or her, as they would any other faculty member, in the regular operations of the department. That means, however, that the unit will become dependent on his or her services. As a result, pulling the funds out would present real problems to the unit.

As long as a number of the scholars institutions seek to recruit or retain find employment of their partners a major concern, some form of employment accommodations for partners will be necessary to preserve the quality of academic units. Without such hiring the recruiting and retention of faculty needed to preserve quality in high priority units would be undermined. Consequently, it seems that the tension between institutional priorities and the need for spousal hiring should be resolved by softening institutional priorities somewhat to accommodate the need for partner hiring.

References

Barbee, Anita P., and Michael R. Cunningham. 1990. "Departmental Issues in Dual-Academic Marriages." Paper presented at the annual meeting of the American Psychological Association, Boston, Aug.

Bruce, Willa M., and Christine M. Reed. 1991. *Dual-Career Couples in the Public Sector.* Westport: Quorum Books.

College of Liberal Arts and Sciences Advisory Committee on Financial Policy. 1993. "LAS Resources 1993–2000." University of Illinois at Urbana-Champaign.

Collie, H. Chris. 1989. "Two Salaries, One Relocation: What's a Company to Do?" *Personnel Administrator* 34 (Sept.): 54–57.

Committee on Budget Priorities. 1991. "Campus Planning for the 1990s." University of Illinois at Urbana-Champaign.

Corporations and Two-Career Families: Directions for the Future. 1981. New York: Catalyst.

Gee, E. Gordon. 1991. "The Dual-Career Couple: A Growing Challenge." *Educational Record* 72 (Winter): 45–47.

Human Factors in Relocation: Corporate and Employee Points of View. 1983. New York: Catalyst.

Leff, Lisa. 1992. "Picking Professors in Pairs." *Washington Post.* Sept. 27:B1, B6.

Newgren, Kenneth E., C. E. Kellogg, and William Gardner. 1987. "Corporate Policies Affecting Dual-Career Couples." *SAM Advanced Management Journal* 52 (4): 4–9.

Office of Affirmative Action. 1993. "Minority Faculty Representation by Rank: FTE." University of Illinois at Urbana-Champaign.

———. 1994. "Affirmative Action Departmental Status Report: Fall 1993." University of Illinois at Urbana-Champaign.

Pingree, Suzanne, Matilda Butler, William Paisley, and Robert Hawkins. 1978. "Anti-Nepotism's Ghost: Attitudes of Administrators toward Hiring Professional Couples." *Psychology of Women Quarterly* 3 (1): 22–29.

Snyder, Julie K. 1990. "Comparison of University Practices on Dual Career Couple Issues." *Virginia Polytechnic Institute and State University Institutional Research and Planning Analysis* 89–90 (53a).

Stafford, Susan G., and Graham B. Spanier. 1990. "Recruiting the Dual-Career Couple: The Family Employment Program." *Journal of the National Association of Women Deans, Administrators, and Counselors* 53 (2): 37–44.

Yanik, Elizabeth, and Joe Yanik. 1992. "A Dual Career Couple in the Same Mathematics Department." Paper presented at the National Conference on Dual Career Couples in Higher Education, University of Kentucky, Oct.

Findings and Conclusions

Jane W. Loeb and Marianne A. Ferber

TAKEN TOGETHER, the studies presented here paint a reasonably full and detailed picture of the history and current status of academic couples in the United States, including common institutional accommodations to them. In this chapter, we will summarize their findings, pointing out both the consistent themes that emerge from these investigations and also the gaps in the picture that might usefully be filled in by further research.

It is resoundingly clear that academic couples are a major phenomenon. Their numbers are large and growing, and all types of higher education institutions are affected. Thus, for example, Astin and Milem found that among married faculty members in their national sample of full-time faculty, 35 percent of men and 40 percent of women had academic spouses. Similarly, Bellas found that in the Illinois sample she and Ferber collected, 55 percent of the respondents had a partner employed at an academic institution at some time during their careers. Since most faculty in Astin and Milem's national sample were married (82 percent of men and 62 percent of women), these figures indicate that a substantial subset of the candidates for any faculty position are likely to be members of academic pairs. As shown by Stephan and Kassis, the contributing factors to this development include a dramatic increase in the proportion of doctorates awarded to women, which reached more than one-third by the late 1980s. Both the Astin and Milem study, using a national sample, and the Bellas study document the employment of members of academic couples within all types of higher education institutions, both public and private and ranging from two-year colleges through doctorate-granting universities.

As the proportions of academic couples and of women in the faculty candidate pool have grown, so have pressures on higher educational institutions to accommodate their needs in order to recruit and retain faculty. Raabe's national survey of chief academic officers concerning institutional accommodations to couples and, more broadly, families, indicates that close to half (44 percent) offer some form of job assistance for spouses, and about a third (36 percent) provide accommodative scheduling to meet family needs. It also reveals that a wide range of family-supportive arrangements is offered by many colleges, both large and small, public and private. In addition, Hornig discusses the many considerations that may make the hiring of an academic couple relatively attractive or unattractive to a particular institution, and Loeb describes an active program of spousal hiring at a major research university.

Just as couples are employed throughout higher education, across all institutional types, they are also found within all racial/ethnic groups and all disciplines, albeit in different proportions. Concerning racial/ethnic groups, Astin and Milem found that African-American (48 percent), Native American (42 percent), and Puerto Rican–American men (41 percent) were somewhat more likely than white men (35 percent) to have academic partners, while Asian-American (28 percent) and Mexican-American/Chicano men (29 percent) were somewhat less likely to have them. Among women, Native Americans (50 percent), Asian Americans (44 percent), and African Americans (41 percent) were more likely than Caucasians (39 percent) to have academic partners; Puerto Rican Americans (22 percent) and Mexican Americans/Chicanas (37 percent) were less likely to have academic partners. Consistent with these data, Loeb found that tenured and tenure-track faculty members whose hiring involved an employment accommodation of the spouse were more likely to be African American or Hispanic than were faculty members hired without this kind of spousal assistance. Thus, the need for spousal employment assistance is certainly not limited to white candidates. On the contrary, since a relatively high proportion of African Americans, Native Americans, Puerto Rican–American men, and Asian-American women have academic partners, their hiring is especially likely to require spousal employment assistance.

The likelihood of a faculty member having an academic partner varies by discipline, and these disciplinary differences in likelihood that a faculty member has an academic partner also affect institutions. Astin and Milem's national survey results indicate that the differences are sizable. The percentage of faculty men with academic partners ranges from 21 percent in engineering to 45 percent in education to the fine arts. For women the range is from 22 percent for health-related fields to 55 percent in agriculture. For some fields, the proportion with an academic partner is relatively high for both sexes. In five areas—biological sciences, education, English, other humanities, and fine arts—the percentage of faculty members with academic partners is at least average for one sex and above average for the other, yielding a mean for the two sexes of more than 40 percent. As a result, dual hiring issues will tend to be concentrated in certain fields, putting especially heavy pressure on some departments. Indeed, Loeb found particularly heavy use of the campus program of employment accommodation for the spouses of faculty in education, where the proportion of academic couples is high. If a department with many such requests is to cooperate in the interests of the recruiting and retention needs of other departments, the costs will need to be underwritten at least in part by other units, the college, or the campus administration. Just as important, however, a degree of over-staffing will probably need to be tolerated so that the department can chart its own direction through occasional planned hiring.

These current-day accommodations by individuals and institutions are not new in kind but rather in their widespread nature. Some institutions have hired couples from their founding, and some couples have accepted the need for commuting relationships in order to meet the educational and professional needs of both spouses ever since women began to earn advanced degrees. Thus, Stephan and Kassis found evidence of couples on the faculty during the nineteenth century, primarily at private coeducational schools rather than public or single-sex institutions. For example, Grinnell College appears to have hired couples almost from its founding in 1846, and the University of Chicago actively recruited couples as early as the late nineteenth century. Grinnell consistently had couples on the staff throughout the twentieth century, even at the time when antinepotism regulations barred the hiring of wives at most colleges and universities, though the Grinnell women were typically not on the tenure track.

Similarly, Perkins has documented that the nineteenth-century and early twentieth-century norm that middle-class married women should not work for pay did not apply to well-educated African-American women. On the contrary, these women were expected to put their hard-won education to use in the service of their race. These women pursued careers in their own right, using their own names, and their husbands took pride in their accomplishments. As the historically black colleges and universities (HBCUs) developed throughout the second half of the nineteenth century and in the early part of the twentieth and those with black presidents sought black faculty members, women were hired onto faculties regardless of their marital status. Indeed, a large number of couples were employed by these institutions at the same time that Grinnell College was unusual in this regard among white institutions.

Although there were faculty job opportunities for African-American women and couples at HBCUs, Perkins nevertheless found that many couples needed to live separately, at least temporarily, to pursue higher degrees or to continue their professional careers until they could arrange suitable employment in the same city if not on the same campus. In fact, commuting marriages were relatively common among professional African Americans as early as the late nineteenth century. Thus, the recent changes in the status of academic couples involve a large increase in their numbers at predominantly white institutions, a new willingness of these institutions to hire both partners on the tenure track, and, because of the great increase in the numbers of career-oriented white women, an increase in the number of white couples who live separately when necessary to pursue their careers.

Miller and Skeen, writing about unmarried couples, and Perkins in her study of African-American couples have detailed the difficulties specific pairs have had finding good career opportunities for both individuals. Frequently, they were unable to get acceptable jobs at the same or at nearby institutions that would have enabled them to avoid a commuting relationship. Further, this is often true even when there are no arbitrary barriers to hiring, such as the antinepotism rules common during the earlier part of the twentieth century or prejudices against particular groups. At the same time, as Miller and Skeen show, unmarried couples, particularly those in which the partners are of the same sex, are still likely to encounter hostility.

As Hornig has shown, anti-nepotism regulations were largely enforced against wives who sought tenure-track employment. Other relatives were not generally barred, nor were wives necessarily barred from non-tenure-track positions. Shoben has made it clear that employers' difficulty in recruiting argues for the hiring of relatives, while fuzzy, subjective performance evaluation argues against such practices; higher education tends to experience both of these conditions, but recruiting difficulties vary in degree as market conditions change. Earlier in the century, when most members of the doctoral pool were male, refusal of institutions to hire wives on the tenure track would not have created or added to recruiting difficulties to any great extent for most institutions. On the other hand, Perkins has shown that the antinepotism regulations were very often ignored by administrators at the HBCUs when they were building up their institutions and needed to recruit well-qualified faculty very actively from a limited pool of candidates. Indeed, Shoben has noted that with increased difficulty in recruiting faculty, higher education institutions in general have shifted from the imposition of antinepotism regulations to the initiation of partner preference, or spousal hiring, programs. Should conditions change at some future date and recruiting and retention of faculty become markedly less competitive, it will be important that in adjusting to changed conditions institutions go no farther than becoming neutral to the hiring of partners. Certainly, reinstating antinepotism rules would have a devastating effect on couples.

Current conditions in higher education appear to be reasonably favorable for academic couples. Institutions are increasingly hiring both members of a pair, and, frequently, both are given the opportunity to achieve normal progression through the academic ranks. The effects of having an academic partner on productivity and career success seem to be small, where found, and generally positive for women, but often negative for men. Bellas found no difference between the number of lifetime publications produced by faculty members who had at some time had academic partners and those who had not. This held true for both men and women. Astin and Milem, on the other hand, found there were differences in publications between faculty with academic partners and those with nonacademic partners. Men with academic partners published slightly less than men with nonacademic partners, while women with academic partners published somewhat more than those with nonacademic partners. Concerning academic rank, Astin and Milem found that an academic partner is a positive indicator for both men and women. After accounting for other factors associated with rank, such as age, highest degree, and publications, men and women with academic partners held slightly higher rank, on the average, than faculty with nonacademic partners. Ferber and Hoffman, on the other hand, found that the number of years a person spent with a partner who was a member of the same faculty was not useful in predicting the achievement of the rank of full professor.

In Astin and Milem's national sample, salaries of men with academic partners were lower than salaries of those with nonacademic partners after various indicators of longevity and productivity had been accounted for. In contrast, women with academic partners earned somewhat more than women with nonacademic partners. As with rank, Ferber and Hoffman found that the number of years a person's partner was a member of the same faculty was not useful in predicting salary. Both studies used employment at a research or doctoral university as their final indicator of career success. Astin and Milem found an academic partner to be an impediment to this achievement for both men and women, after accounting for longevity and productivity indicators, although the magnitude of the difference between those with and without academic partners was not great. Once again, Ferber and Hoffman were unable to demonstrate a relationship between this form of employment and the number of years a faculty member had a partner on the same faculty.

From these data it appears that having an academic as opposed to a nonacademic partner is likely to have small positive effects on productivity and career success for women and small negative effects for men, though for men the effect is positive for rank and for women the effect on employment at a research or doctoral university is negative. On the other hand, having an academic spouse at the same institution as opposed to having no partner, a nonacademic partner, or an academic partner at another institution does not seem to be a factor in scholarly productivity or other forms of career success.

Astin and Milem conclude from their survey results that academic partners tend to have more egalitarian arrangements than do those couples in which only one is an academic. They found, for example, that men with nonacademic partners report slightly less stress from family concerns such as household responsibilities and child care. Women with academic partners, on the other hand, report less stress stemming from these sources. It is also interesting to note that the studies reviewed by Miller and Skeen indicate that unmarried couples tend to be more egalitarian than married ones, and that with egalitarian personal arrangements comes a degree of "career leveling." For heterosexual couples in more egalitarian relationships this translates into somewhat greater career success for women but somewhat less success for men when compared with partners involved in less egalitarian relationships, as was the experience of the academic couples in Astin and Milem's study. It should be noted that Perkins has described much more egalitarian arrangements between members of African-American couples than often pertain to white couples, and Miller and Skeen have pointed out that gay and lesbian couples tend to be more egalitarian than heterosexual couples. Thus, it seems likely that "career leveling" among academic partners is a phenomenon primarily affecting those white heterosexual married couples who are relatively egalitarian.

Both Ferber and Hoffman and Bellas found results consistent with the view that academic couples tend to be somewhat more egalitarian than others, so that women's productivity and success may be enhanced but men's somewhat hampered. Ferber and Hoffman found that the salaries of young men were negatively associated with the number of children they had, although for middle-aged men the effect of children was positive, probably because the household and child-care arrangements of the younger couples are more egalitarian than those of the older couples. Bellas found that for both men and women, the number of years a partner was not employed was positively associated with a faculty member's scholarly productivity. In addition, the number of miles the faculty member lived away from the partner was a positive factor for women and a negative factor for men. A nonemployed partner of either sex would presumably take responsibility for a significant share of the household tasks, thus freeing time of the employed partner for scholarship. In heterosexual couples, living separately from the partner probably requires the male to do more household work, thereby interfering with scholarship, while permitting the female to simplify her household routine and turn more time and attention to scholarship.

These findings concerning academic couples have many implications for higher educational institutions. Raabe has shown that like other employers, colleges and universities are changing their practices to become more accommodating toward the family responsibilities of their employees. Both she and Miller-Loessi and Henderson have pointed out the need for further developments, such as more flexible career paths and more readily available child care. To the extent that a growing proportion of faculty are members of two-career couples likely to experience a degree of career leveling, institutions have a vested interest in providing arrangements that help faculty members meet their dual responsibilities while minimizing the sacrifice of time and energy that could be spent on professionally productive pursuits. Egalitarian arrangements within families may allow married women to succeed to a greater extent than was possible when they bore essentially the whole burden of house and child care. At the same time, however, the net productivity of a faculty that includes fewer individuals free to pursue their scholarship single-mindedly will tend to be lower. Thus, more than equity is involved in calls for family-friendly employer practices. Just as the abolition of antinepotism rules not only helped couples but also made a larger talent pool available to schools, whatever institutional supports higher education can provide to ease the difficulties of juggling family responsibilities and professional commitments will also help to increase faculty productivity.

A related question we need to face is what kinds of benefits to extend to unmarried couples. Miller and Skeen's report of the literature on this subject suggests that U.S. colleges and universities are moving slowly to provide benefits for domestic partners but that the tremendously important benefit of health insurance has remained a major stumbling block for many, especially public institutions. Their review suggests that fear of astronomic costs, such as those arising from inclusion of some additional individuals at greater risk of being HIV positive in an extended health coverage pool has been a problem. The evidence from employers who have extended health coverage indicates such fear is unwarranted.

One requirement for extending benefits to unmarried partners is that the term "domestic partner" must first be defined. This is no easy matter and for some benefits at some public institutions, could even require action by state government. Miller and Skeen's review indicates that institutions that extend benefits to domestic partners typically require that a number of conditions be met, such as cohabitation for a minimum time period, mingled finances, and naming of the partner as beneficiary in insurance and pension plans. They found that many schools that extend benefits to domestic partners do so only for same-sex partners, based on the rationale that opposite-sex couples have the choice to marry or not. Certainly, there are serious equity issues involved in the failure to extend spousal benefits to same-sex partners, who are legally barred from marriage and thus from becoming eligible for benefits that require it. The situation is exacerbated by partner preference in hiring if it applies only to heterosexual married couples. Colleges and universities which have not yet grappled with this issue will surely need to do so in the future, and the issue is likely to be especially difficult for publicly controlled institutions.

Partner preference in hiring will be needed as long as current market conditions last. While Loeb's study of individuals hired through a spousal hiring program shows that such programs can work reasonably well and that the most common fears about them are largely unfounded, further study is needed. A longer term follow-up of the success of the individuals so hired would be useful. In addition, it would be helpful to study efforts to recruit or retain faculty members that were unsuccessful because the partner's job needs could not be met. It seems likely, for example, that couples in the same discipline are harder to accommodate than couples in different fields. The chapters by Hornig, Loeb, and Miller-Loessi and Henderson have suggested that "trailing" male partners may face special problems. Looking at unsuccessful efforts to accommodate partners would provide additional understanding of the issues involved.

Indeed, a study of the problems faced by these male partners would be useful in itself. Many possible factors could account for difficulties in accommodating them. It seems likely that willingness to move is related to the career stage, with a new graduate being more willing to compromise than a very well-established scholar. To the extent that males are typically farther along in their careers than are their female partners, this could account for differences that may exist in the difficulty of accommodating them. However, is it possible that regardless of the stage of their career men may be less willing than women to compromise on the kinds of positions they will take? Alternatively, are employers less willing to run the risk of offending a male than a female by making a less than ideal offer to him? Or, are men who are willing to compromise, or perhaps even to move to accommodate the professional needs of their wives seen as suspect or as "not serious" about their careers by potential employers and selection committees?

Other avenues for further research include the question of just how egalitarian academic partnerships have become. How much of the house- and child-care responsibilities are currently accepted by the two partners? If, on the average, men in academic partnerships tend to fare less well than those with nonacademic partners while women tend to benefit from being part of an academic pair, can the productivity and rewards of individuals be related to the degree to which they personally undertake house- and child-care responsibilities?

Similarly, it would be useful to investigate whose career takes precedence in decisions about location (Miller-Loessi and Henderson). How willing are male and female academics to move to accompany a partner who has an offer elsewhere, and how important is mobility to academic success and rewards? How does this vary for same- and opposite-sex partners? How do men's attitudes toward moving with their partners compare to selection committees' attitudes toward "trailing" males? Is there a mismatch? The experiences of couples who have undertaken commuting relationships might be useful in studying these phenomena, assuming that failure of institutional efforts to accommodate one partner or the other is often involved in the decision to commute.

Finally, Raabe has suggested the need for longitudinal study of the effects of family-supportive environments on both individuals and institutions. It would be very useful to know the extent to which the various institutional accommodations actually have the intended effects. In like vein, it would be helpful to study productivity of same-sex partners as it relates to the degree of supportiveness and hostility such couples find in their institutional environments.

Miller-Loessi and Henderson have reminded us that women's participation in the labor force steadily increased from the late 1800s through World War II. A very brief drop after that was reversed in the early 1950s and was followed by a dramatic increase beginning in the late 1950s. The recent sharp increase in the number of academic couples is part of this very long-term trend. There may be short-term vacillations in the future, but it is hard to picture a significant and lasting decrease in the prevalence of two-career families. Thus, colleges and universities will undoubtedly need to continue their efforts to attract, accommodate, and retain faculty members with academic partners. We believe that the information presented in this book will help them to shape and refine policies that will work well for the institutions and the individuals involved.

Contributors

HELEN S. ASTIN, a psychologist, is a professor of higher education and associate director of the Higher Education Research Institute at UCLA. She has served as a member of the board of the National Council for Research on Women and as a member of the Committee on Women's Employment and Related Social Issues of the National Research Council. She has been president of the Division of the Psychology of Women of the American Psychological Association. From 1983 to 1987, she served as associate provost of UCLA's College of Letters and Science. She has published numerous articles and eleven books, including *Women of Influence, Women of Vision: A Cross-Generational Study of Leaders and Social Change* (1991), *The Woman Doctorate in America* (1969), *Some Action of Her Own: The Adult Woman and Higher Education* (1976), and *Higher Education and the Disadvantaged Student* (1972).

MARCIA L. BELLAS is an assistant professor of sociology at the University of Cincinnati. Her research focuses primarily on gender stratification in academia. Her recent work examining sources of bias in faculty salaries appears in *Gender and Society, Social Science Quarterly,* and the *American Sociological Review.*

MARIANNE A. FERBER is a professor of economics and women's studies emerita at the University of Illinois at Urbana-Champaign and was the Homer Distinguished Visiting Professor at Radcliffe College from 1993 to 1995. Within the broad field of the economic status of women, she has concentrated on the standing of women in academia, the family as an economic unit, international comparisons in the position of women, and recently on feminist theory and economics. She is the co-author (with Francine D. Blau) of *The Economics of Women, Men, and Work* (1986), coeditor with Brigid O'Farrell of *Work and Family Policies for a Changing Work Force* (1991), and the coeditor (with Julie A. Nelson) of *Beyond Economic Man: Feminist Theory and Economics* (1993).

DEBORAH HENDERSON is a doctoral student in sociology at Arizona State University. Previously, she worked in the Northeast as a program evaluator and coauthored several articles on epistemological and methodological issues involved in evaluation research. Her more recent work, however, informed by her own personal history, focuses on skilled blue-collar workers who have made the transition from work to the university—a qualitative study in the social construction of "class" and the negotiation of meaning, power, and knowledge.

EMILY P. HOFFMAN is a professor of economics at Western Michigan University. She received her Ph.D. in economics from the University of Massachusetts at Amherst in 1975. Her dissertation provided conclusive evidence of the underpayment of female faculty members there, which sparked a lawsuit, the settlement of which resulted in substantial equity adjustments. Since then her research has concentrated on the empirical analysis of large data sets in the areas of labor market discrimination, unemployment, and poverty.

LILLI S. HORNIG, who received her Ph.D. in chemistry from Harvard, served as a staff scientist at Los Alamos during World War II and taught chemistry at Brown University and at Trinity College (Washington, D.C), where she was department chair. She has served on various national research and policy panels, including a number of White House science missions, and on equal-opportunity advisory committees of the National Science Foundation, the National Cancer Institute, and the American Association for the Advancement of Science. She chaired the National Academy of Sciences' first Committee on the Education and Employment of Women in Science and Engineering (CEEWISE), which issued a series of four reports on the status of women scientists and engineers that remain landmark documents. She currently is a visiting research scholar at the Wellesley College Center for Research on Women and a senior consultant to Higher Education Resource Services at Wellesley, having served as its founding director from 1972 until her retirement.

MARY MATHEWES KASSIS received her B.A. from Agnes Scott College and is currently a doctoral student at Georgia State University. Her research interests include issues related to family labor supply and the incidence of the social security payroll tax. She has been an intern at the Federal Research Bank of Atlanta and has worked for three years as a research assistant in the Economic Forecasting Center at Georgia State University.

JANE W. LOEB is a professor of educational psychology at the University of Illinois at Urbana-Champaign, where she also served for many years in administrative capacities, including associate vice chancellor for undergraduate education and director of admissions and records. Her research focuses on equity issues in higher education, including equitable admission practices, access and success of minority students, and the role and status of women on the faculty, and reflects a concern for policy implications. Her monograph *Academic Standards in Higher Education* (1992) examines the interplay of student preparation for postsecondary education with curriculum, standards, and outcomes of college.

JEFFREY F. MILEM is an assistant professor in the Department of Educational Leadership at Peabody College of Vanderbilt University. Before joining the faculty there, Milem served as a research and policy analyst in the Office of Dean of the Graduate School of Education at UCLA. Prior to that he worked for four years as a research analyst at the Higher Education Research Institute at UCLA. He received his Ph.D. in Higher Education at UCLA. Milem's most recent research focuses on issues relating to diversity in higher education. In addition, he is interested in how differences in departmental affiliation affect how faculty approach their work, including differences in the types of pedagogical practices faculty use.

DOROTHY C. MILLER is an associate professor in the Center for Women's Studies at Wichita State University. She received her Ph.D. in social welfare at Columbia University and has written *Women and Social Welfare: A Feminist Analysis* (1990). She teaches, speaks, and writes about women's social issues and economic well-being. Her most recent project, a study of welfare and poverty in Kansas, will be published shortly. She is currently working on a book about altruism, family ties, and public policy.

KAREN MILLER-LOESSI is an associate professor of sociology at Arizona State University. One of her major research interests has been the representation of women in the professions. She has authored or co-authored numerous papers on this topic and edited a special issue of the journal *Sociological Perspectives* on women in the workplace. She has also authored or co-authored research on the social-psychological aspects of education, work, and aging. Her current research is a study of men and women workers who return to school at different points in the life course.

LINDA M. PERKINS is an associate professor of educational foundations and women's studies at Hunter College of the City University of New York. She has published and lectured extensively on the history of African-American and women's higher education. Perkins is the author of *Fanny Jackson Coppin and the Institute for Colored Youth, 1837–1902* (1987) and is currently completing a manuscript on the history of African-American women's higher education entitled "The Black Female Talented Tenth: A History of African-American Women's Higher Education, 1850–1963."

PHYLLIS HUTTON RAABE received a doctorate in sociology from Pennsylvania State University and is an assistant professor in the sociology department of the University of New Orleans. She teaches courses in and does research on work-family trends and policies and is particularly interested in viable, alternative work arrangements and career paths. Her current research includes a study of part-time managers in the federal government, a study of family-friendly policies and Women's Employment in the Czech Republic and Slovakia, and a study of pluralistic work and career arrangements that are family—and work—friendly.

ELAINE W. SHOBEN is the Edward W. Clearly Professor at the University of Illinois College of Law. She received an A.B. from Barnard College and a J.D. from Hastings College of the Law, where she served as the first woman editor-in-chief of the law journal. She has written numerous articles and books on employment discrimination law, including *Employment Discrimination Cases and Materials* (casebook with Mack A. Player and Risa L. Lieberwitz, first edition 1990, second edition 1995), *Employment Law* (with Mark A. Rothstein, Charles B. Craver, Elinor P. Schroeder, and Lea S. VanderVelde, 1994), and *Cases and Problems on Remedies* (with Wm. Murray Tabb, first edition 1989, second edition 1995).

ANITA SKEEN is a professor of English at Michigan State University, where she teaches creative writing, women's studies, and Canadian literature. She is the author of two collections of poetry, *Each Hand a Map* (1986) and *Portraits* (1992), and has published poetry, fiction, and essays in numerous journals and literary magazines. She was co-chair of Michigan State's University-Wide Task Force on Lesbian and Gay Issues from 1991 to 1993, and while she was on the faculty at Wichita State University was the recipient of the Regents Award for Excellence in Teaching. She has recently completed another manuscript of poetry and is currently at work on a collection of short stories.

PAULA E. STEPHAN is a professor of economics in the department of economics and a senior associate at the Policy Research Center at Georgia State University. A labor economist by training, she has authored numerous works on the economics of science, including (with Sharon G. Levin) *Striking the Mother Lode in Science: The Importance of Age, Place, and Time* (1992). Stephan has served as a consultant to such groups as the National Research Council and the Office of Technology Assessment of the U.S. Congress. Other research interests include the labor supply of women. She is a frequent visiting scholar at the Wissenschaftszentrum Berlin für Sozialforschung.

Index

Academic couples: acceptance of, 1, 6, 11, 17; accommodative scheduling for, 214, 217, 221, 300; administrative policy toward, 248–69 passim; African-American, 15, 25, 80–105 passim, 286, 300, 302; background characteristics of, 131; career advancement of, 16, 96–100, 110, 134–35, 171, 182–207 passim, 303–4; child care for, 29, 34–35, 124, 210, 214, 217, 219, 220, 305; children of, 197, 198; commuting (long-distance) by, 38, 80, 118–19, 164–65, 176, 200n. 13, 301, 302, 305; competing career demands of, 13, 158; current status of, 7–12, 128–55; differential accommodation by academic field, 256–58, 294; distribution of household labor in, 16, 30–32, 35–36, 109, 141, 193, 304–5; employment patterns of, 132, 139–40; history of, 4–7, 14–15, 25, 301; in Illinois, 7–12, 187–98; institutional advantages and disadvantages of hiring, 12–13, 17, 250–53, 273–74, 283, 294–95, 296–97; job assistance programs for, 214, 216, 219, 260–61, 270–71, 300; legal issues concerning, 226–47 passim; mobility (geographic relocation) of, 36–38, 114–19, 122, 123, 186, 189, 191, 253, 260–61, 262, 270, 308; numbers of, 2, 4, 6, 25, 28, 299; personal advantages and disadvantages of being in, 28–29, 182–207 passim; preferential programs for, 17, 227, 228, 232–33, 234, 237–46, 271, 272–98 passim, 303, 307; productivity of, 128–55 passim; research interests of, 133–34; salaries of, 186, 193–98, 304; stress in, 13, 134–35, 141, 221; systematic study of, 14; work-family policies for, 208–25 passim

Academic fields: differential accommodation of academic couples in, 256–58, 294; gender differences in, 7, 34, 52, 55, 132, 184, 281, 301; salary differences in, 194–95, 196–97

Academic labor market: acceptance of couples in, 1, 6, 11, 17; compared to large U.S. companies, 217–21; constraints on faculty replacement, 3–4; employee benefits in, 110–14, 306; history of women in, 45–52; job availability in, 2–3, 46, 48, 114–19, 265–67; as less gendered work environment, 33–39; part-time employment in, 193–94, 209, 210, 221, 257–58; percentage of women in, 5, 6, 7, 9, 14–15, 34, 46–52, 74–75, 208

Career advancement: of academic couples,
16, 96–100, 110, 134–35, 171, 182–207
passim, 303–4; and cohabitation, 110, 114;
gender differences in, 16, 96–100, 128,
134–35, 183
Career leveling, 110, 114, 304–5
Carnegie Foundation of the Advancement
of Teaching, 18n. 6, 157
Carter, Lawrence, 100–101
Cartter, Alan M., 184
Carver, Marva Griffin, 100–101
Centra, John A., 254
Child-care programs, 29, 30–32, 34–35, 124,
210, 214, 217, 219, 220, 305
Children: of academic couples, 197, 198;
custody of, 11; effect on men's salary, 197,
240, 305; of same-sex couples, 124
Children of Gays (organization), 124
City University of New York: domestic
partner benefits at, 112
Civil Rights Act of 1964, 227, 228, 230, 241,
243
Clady v. County of Los Angeles, 238
Claremont College, School of Theology
(STC): academic couples at, 101
Clark, Kenneth, 90, 100
Clark, Mamie Phipps, 90, 100
Clark, Shirley M., 129
Clarke, Edward, 82
Clement, Rufus, 93, 97
Co-authorships, 8, 19n. 13. *See also* Publica-
tions
Cohabitation (unmarried couples): of aca-
demic couples, 6, 15, 106–27 passim; and
career advancement, 110, 114; and distri-
bution of household labor, 35, 109, 304–
5; duration of, 106–7; egalitarianism in,
109–10; and employee benefits, 110–14,
306; and geographic relocations, 37, 122,
123; rates of, 106; secrecy about, 108
Cole, Jonathan R., 184, 254
Columbia University: African-American
students at, 90, 91, 92, 96
Committee on the Status of Women in the
Economics Profession, 185
Commuting (long-distance) couples, 38,

80, 118–19, 164–65, 176, 200n. 13, 301, 302,
305
Conrad, Laetitia Moon, 67
Coppin, Fanny Jackson, 83–84, 85–86
Coppin, Bsp. Levi, 83–84, 85
Corcoran, Mary, 129
Cornell University: academic couples at,
255
Coverman, Shelley, 35
Cronyism. *See* Antinepotism rules; Nepo-
tism rules
Crow, Martha, 65, 67

Dalton, Claire, 262
Dartmouth College: domestic partner
benefits at, 112
Davis, Diane E., 128
Decker, Wayne H., 185
Department of Education, U.S.: National
Center for Education Statistics, 18n. 10,
130
DeVore, Irving, 259
Diggs, Mary Huff, 102
Discrimination: against African Americans
and Hispanics, 5, 231, 284–86; by age,
237–38; against homosexuals, 107, 119–25;
legal issues concerning, 226–47 passim;
by marital status, 226, 236, 240; measurement of, 183; and occupational segregation by gender, 29; against women, 5, 34,
44, 183–87, 273, 286–91, 302–3
Divorce rates, 13, 27
Doctoral programs: African Americans in,
87–88; gender differences in hiring from,
49, 184; gender differences in participation in, 2, 4, 6, 48, 49, 52–57, 257, 295,
299; gender differences of graduates
from, 8, 11, 15, 53–57, 131–32; median age
of graduates from, 58; numbers of graduates from, 2–3, 53, 266
Doctorate Records File, 48, 53
Dual-career couples: acceptance of, 1, 6, 11;
child care for, 29, 30–32, 34–35, 219, 220;
distribution of household labor in, 16,
29, 30–31; economic advantages of, 27,
28; gender differences in salary of, 29;

Oaxaca, Ronald, 197
Oberlin College: African-American gradu-
ates of, 83, 84
Ohio State University: academic couples at,
255
O'Neill, June, 184
Oregon State University: job assistance
program at, 260–61, 271, 277

Palmer, Edward N., 90
Palmer, George Herbert, 57
Palmer, Margaretta, 62
Palmer, Viola Goins, 90
Palmieri, Patricia, 87
Parental leave, 212–13, 218–19
Parker, Candace, 67
Parsons v. County of Dell Norte, 234
Part-time employment, 193–94, 209, 210,
221, 257–58
Paternity leave and benefits, 31, 212–13, 214,
218–19
Pearce, Diana, 30
Perkins, Linda M., 101, 251, 286, 301–2, 303, 305
Ph.D. programs. *See* Doctoral programs
Pieper, Paul J., 184
Pilbeam, David, 259
POSSLQs (persons of the opposite sex
sharing living quarters). *See* Cohabita-
tion (unmarried couples)
Preferential programs (for hiring spouses),
17, 227, 228, 232–33, 234, 237–46, 271, 272–
98 passim, 303, 307. *See also* Job assis-
tance programs (for spouses)
Pregnancy Discrimination Act of 1978, 212
Princeton University: antinepotism rules
at, 249–50
Productivity, 128–55 passim. *See also* Career
advancement; Publications
Professional degree programs: participation of women in, 4, 6
Programs for partners. *See* Job assistance
programs (for spouses); Preferential
programs (for hiring spouses)
PSSSLQs (persons of the same sex sharing
living quarters). *See* Cohabitation (unmarried couples); Homosexuality

Publications: gender differences in, 8–9, 16,
133, 138–39, 156–81 passim, 191, 303; salary
differences related to, 195

Quarles, Benjamin, 96

Raabe, Phyllis Hutton, 37, 272, 300, 305, 308
Radcliffe College: African-American gradu-
ates of, 88; establishment of, 46; marital
status of women on faculty at, 58
Radcliffe Oral History Project, 91
Ransom, Michael R., 185
Reedy, Hilda Lawson, 95
Reedy, Sidney, 95
Reich, Robert, 262
Reilly, Anne H., 37
Reskin, Barbara F., 29
Retirement: of current faculty members, 2–
3, 4, 265–66; end of mandatory, 3, 265
Richter, Margaret Rose, 70
Robinson, John P., 35
Rockefeller Foundation, General Education
Board (GEB), 89, 92, 95
Rodin, Judith, 263
Rosenfeld, Rachel, 253
Rosenwald Foundation. *See* Julius Rosen-
wald Foundation
Rossiter, Margaret, 87
Rubenson, George C., 185
Ruhter, Wayne E., 184
Russell, Susan H., 2
Ruvolo, Maryellen, 259

Sakai, Ann K., 256
Sakano, Ryoichi, 184
Salaries, academic: of academic couples,
186, 193–98, 304; differences by academic
field, 194–95, 196–97; differences by academic rank, 195; differences by numbers
of publications, 195; effect of number of
children on, 197, 240, 305; gender differences in, 9–11, 29, 34, 136–37, 183, 184, 185,
197–98, 304; mean, 28, 197
Same-sex couples. *See* Homosexuality
Scheduling, accommodative, 214, 217, 221,
300

University of Pennsylvania: African-American graduates of, 88
University of Vermont: domestic partner benefits at, 112
University of Virginia: undergraduate enrollment at, 46
University of Wisconsin: African-Americans students at, 90; antinepotism rules at, 59
Unmarried couples. *See* Cohabitation (unmarried couples); Homosexuality

Vacancies. *See* Academic labor market; Jobs, availability of; Retirement
Valien, Bonita, 89, 99–100
Valien, Preston, 89, 99–100
Verkuil, Paul, 264
Vermont: professional salaries in, 184
Virginia Polytechnic Institute and State University (VPISU), 272
Visiting faculty positions, 4

Wages. *See* Salaries, academic
Walker, Kathryn E., 35
Washington, Booker T., 93
Washington, Margaret Murray, 93
Washington State University: job assistance program at, 260
Watson v. Fort Worth Bank & Trust, 238–39
Wellesley College: woman president of, 46, 57; women on faculty at, 87; work and marriage of graduates of, 82
West Virginia State College: antinepotism rules at, 95
Wilberforce College: faculty composition at, 86

Williams, Keith, 265
Williams, Marcellette, 265
Willis, Rachel A., 184
Wimbush, Vincent L., 101
Women: age as factor in employment of, 191; changing social status of, 14; current status of, 7–12; discrimination against, 5, 34, 44, 183–87, 273, 286–91, 302–3; education viewed as damaging to, 82; in graduate degree programs, 2, 4, 6, 48, 49, 52–57, 257, 295, 299; history on college faculties, 45–52; mentors for, 9; percentage in labor force, 1, 4, 6, 26–28, 46–48, 52, 109, 308; percentage on college faculties, 5, 6, 7, 9, 14–15, 34, 46–52, 74–75, 208; poverty of, 30; salary of, 9–11. *See also* Gender differences
Women of color: percentage in labor force, 27; poverty of, 30. *See also* African Americans
Women's colleges: discrimination against women on faculty at, 184; establishment of, 46; women on faculty at, 48
Woods, Margaret E., 35
Work-family policies, 208–25 passim

Yale University: academic couples at, 64; faculty composition at, 53, 59, 62–64, 74; faculty wives at, 58–59; history of, 61; undergraduate enrollment at, 45–46, 61
Young, Claire, 114–16
Yuhas v. Libby-Owens-Ford, 236

Zimbler, Linda J., 2
Zuckerman, Harriet, 254
Zumeta, William, 257